the Outlaw's story

the Outlaw's Story

HE ROBBED 30 BANKS. NO JAIL CAN HOLD HIM. THIS IS THE TRUE STORY OF THE WORLD'S MOST NOTORIOUS ROBBER. YOU'LL LIKE HIM!

DEREK PEDLEY

JOHN BLAKE

Published by John Blake Publishing Ltd,
3 Bramber Court, 2 Bramber Road,
London W14 9PB, England

www.blake.co.uk

First published in paperback in 2007

ISBN: 978 1 84454 418 9

British Library Cataloguing-in-Publication Data:

A catalogue record for this book is available from the British Library.

Design by www.envydesign.co.uk

Printed in Great Britain by William Clowes Ltd, Beccles, Suffolk

1 3 5 7 9 10 8 6 4 2

Papers used by John Blake Publishing are natural, recyclable products
made from wood grown in sustainable forests. The manufacturing processes
conform to the environmental regulations of the country of origin.

Author's Note

This is an authorised biography. Brenden Abbott co-operated with this book and provided access to two extensive autobiographical documents. In exchange, the author agreed to give him final veto over the manuscript. Abbott played no role in how the book was written and requested only minor changes.

As required by state and federal Australian law, no criminal received any payment for their co-operation. Some characters' names were changed or surnames withheld to protect their identities.

Acknowledgements

Brenden Abbott's sister, Diane Abbott, made a significant contribution to the research and writing of this book over a six-year period, motivated only by her desire to see her brother – and his story – given a fair hearing.

Police officers across Australia gave generously of their time and knowledge of the case, as did Brenden Abbott's family, friends and criminal associates.

Special thanks to: John Silvester and Andrew Rule, the Godfathers of Australian true-crime writing, for giving me a second shot at this story; Andrew and Doreen Burge, for their incisive editing; Advertiser Newspapers colleague and friend Bernard Humphreys, for editing the first draft of the manuscript; Carmel Galati in Perth, for providing valuable legal advice; Doug and George; and two gentlemen of Australian journalism, Norman Aisbett and John Whistler, whose work has been an inspiration.

To my wife, Belinda, for her eternal patience and support – no more bank jobs, sweetheart, I promise.

Bibliography

Tell 'Em I Died Game – The Legend of Ned Kelly
  Dr. Graham Seal (Hyland House Publishing, 2002)
Ned Kelly – A Short Life
  Ian Jones (Lothian Books, 2003)
Dirty Dozen – 12 True Crime Stories That Shocked Australia
  Paul Anderson (Hardie Grant Books, 2003)
Justice in the Deep North
  McCartney, Lincoln & Wilson (Bond University Press, 2004)
Bombs, Guns and Knives – Violent Crime in Australia
  Edited by Malcolm Brown (New Holland Publishers, 2000)
Writing on Gravestones
  Gary Tippet and Ian Munro (HarperCollins, 2001)
Fremantle Prison – A Brief History
  Cyril Ayris (1995)
No Fixed Address – The Hunt for Brenden James Abbott
  Derek Pedley (HarperCollins, 1999)

The book also draws on information from hundreds of articles published in Australian metropolitan daily newspapers. Individual media organisations and journalists are credited throughout.

For John Pedley
1938–2005

Dear Sir,
I wish to acquaint you
with some of the occurrences
of the present past and future.

Ned Kelly
The Jerilderie Letter

Prologue

1986–1987

The burglary suspect sitting in the corner had a winged serpent tattooed on one shoulder and a chip on the other. His name was Brenden Abbott, he was 24 and he looked like trouble.

The young detective who had been told to watch Abbott was betting there'd be some action when they took him back into the interview room. But that particular treat was on hold for a while: his bosses were busy grilling Abbott's girlfriend while they waited for a lawyer to arrive. It could be a while before they got around to the main event. Meanwhile, it made sense to keep the surly suspect on side.

'You want a cuppa?' the detective asked Abbott, who was slouched in the corner on a chair, arms crossed.

'Sure, thanks.'

It was early on the morning of 16 December 1986. They were in a small room at the rear of an old double-brick house that was headquarters for the detectives of Nollamara CIB, in Perth's northern suburbs. On the way in, Abbott had noted its security didn't extend much beyond flywire screen doors at the front and back. He was young but he was a thinker. When Detectives Mick Bourke and Jeff Beaman tried to extract information from him about an electrical store burglary, he wouldn't play ball.

BOURKE: 'Brenden, all your clothes and papers are in the flat, so it's obvious that you live there.'

ABBOTT: 'So? I live there now and again.'
BOURKE: 'Before we speak to Rhonda ['Rhonda Green', the alias used by Abbott's girlfriend, Jackie Lord], do you want to help us? All the gear that we have at your flat appears to have come from a breaking and entering at Homecraft at Whitfords two nights ago.'
ABBOTT: 'Rhonda is big enough to look after herself. I'm not saying anything until my lawyer's here.'
BOURKE: 'That will be arranged.'

When the young detective guarding him wandered out and pulled the door closed, Abbott's brain kicked into top gear. A few seconds later, charged with adrenalin, he stood up and strode to the door.

Turning the knob gently, he peered out. There were voices to his left, probably Jackie giving the jacks the shits in the interview room. To his right, only a few metres away, was the unlocked back door. Footsteps to his left forced him to dart back into the room, but the door did not close properly. Seconds later, the young detective pushed it open and walked in with a cup. He glanced back, suspicious.

'Why'd you open the door?'

Abbott's head pounded after the near-discovery – 'I was like a cat on a hot tin roof' – but he feigned boredom. 'I didn't touch the door; you didn't close it properly.' He sipped the tea. 'Just the way I like it, thanks.'

The detective looked unconvinced. On the way out, he made a point of shutting the door with a firm click. Abbott waited a few seconds and then crept back to the doorway. He didn't need to think about this. He had learned the hard way it didn't matter what he said in police interview rooms, the situation always ended up worse – he was going to be locked up today, regardless of what he did or didn't say. And the criminal record he had compiled so diligently in recent years meant that any more charges would automatically lead to another long stretch in that shit-hole Fremantle Prison. Fuck that.

Abbott turned the handle again. Bet the sneaky bastard's waiting for me, he thought. But there was no one in the corridor. He instantly strode to the unlocked back door, opened it and pushed the screen door, which creaked loudly.

The young detective, meanwhile, wandered up to Jeff Beaman. 'How's it going?'

Beaman ignored the question. 'Where's Abbott?' he asked. The slam of the back door provided an instant reply.

The four detectives in the building rushed to the back of the house and into the backyard, but Abbott had vanished.

Brenden Abbott had been heading for trouble most of his life. But if there was a turning point, one at which he stepped up from the petty crimes that many young men commit before they grow out of adolescent escapades, it had been earlier that year. In the months leading up to his escape from custody at Nollamara, Abbott's burglary crew had grown increasingly confident and started causing serious headaches for Perth police. In fact, by November 1986, they were cleaning out electrical stores to order. Demand had skyrocketed to the point where it was a full-blown commercial operation.

There never seemed to be a shortage of buyers for hot stuff. Most of the gear I'd knock off was brand new. When I started out, the items in most demand were the stereo TVs and convection microwaves, which were the latest gadgets. As demand grew, so did orders. Power tools, car fridges, gas cooker tops, lounge suites, alcohol, cigarettes, tyres and clothing were just some of the things. People I least expected were buying gear from me, knowing it was hot.

It got to the point where I couldn't keep pace with the demand and was getting harassed by buyers. All the stuff I sold was at a third of its value new, if not less. One person I was offloading gear to had his own customer base and was making a profit.

Initially, those involved with me were my brother Glenn and 'Stabbie', who I met in Canning Vale Prison during my last sentence. Later, the numbers grew, and then they were also off doing jobs that I saw no real value in. For Glenn, it wasn't just for the money, he enjoyed the rush, the thrill of it all, and that I can relate to. He and Stabbie were also doing their own jobs and some of the items they'd keep for themselves. Items that easily arouse suspicion, for example, two fucking jet skis.

I was making good money and would do a job about once every month. I was still on the dole and was also getting cash in hand working part-time as a mechanic at a service station. I was also still doing the occasional backyard car repairs. I wasn't making tens of thousands a month, but at the time I was comfortable with what I had coming in. I was on the dole, but it was just a front – I was still on parole and I thought a form of income was a necessity.

The gang's next big target was a Homecraft store in Whitfords, a northern coastal suburb of Perth, on 14 December. They got in through the roof, then backed a stolen truck up to the rear roller door. Radio scanners tuned to police frequencies remained silent, meaning no alarms had gone off; it was a simple matter of filling the truck with electrical goods and driving away.

But a single phone call brought their profitable suburban business unstuck. One of the gang had upset someone in his life, and that someone tipped off the Nollamara detectives, who raided his home within 24 hours of the burglary.

The gang member wasn't involved in the Homecraft job, but his place was brimming with goods from many others over the past six months – exactly the kind of situation Abbott had been careful to avoid. A quick check with the break squad established that the scuba-diving equipment, chainsaws, sheepskin seat covers, car stereos, microwaves, coffee table, washing machine and TV were all stolen. The gang member told police most of it came from two brothers he feared: Brenden and Glenn Abbott.

On 15 December, at 141 Surrey Road, Rivervale – the home of Abbott's mother, Thelma Salmon – Abbott dropped off a new Hoover washing machine, unaware that detectives were watching the home. Thelma later vowed to never again accept a 'present' from Brenden without an accompanying receipt.

The other detectives then followed Abbott's Torana – towing a trailer filled with white goods and electrical items – to gang member David Knapp's Sorrento home, where it made the second of several deliveries across the metropolitan area. Now Brenden Abbott was in police sights.

That evening, he returned to the unit in Ozone Parade, Scarborough, where his girlfriend Jackie lived, to unload the rest. He says, 'That evening at Jackie's, I still recall clearly how I sensed something wasn't right that night and even mentioned it to her.'

At 6am the next day, 16 December 1986, Detectives Jeff Beaman and Mick Bourke were banging on their door, armed with a search warrant.

I got out of bed and stuck my head into the laundry area. Through the window I could see someone I figured was a jack. He didn't see me as I spotted him moving off to the glass sliding door further along the walkway. There was knocking at that door as well and it was obvious this was no social call. I raced

*back into the bedroom and told Jackie we had visitors and she
was quickly out of bed getting dressed.*

Jackie:

> *The day that they came to bust us, [Brenden] had a wallet full of
> money. It was the only thing he was concerned about. He said,
> 'Stick it down your pants because, if they get it, they'll bloody
> keep it. They've thieved off me before.' [Police in general, not
> these specific officers.] This Mick Bourke's standing at the
> bedroom door. Brenden says, 'Do you mind? We're getting
> dressed. Can we have a little privacy?'*
> *I said, 'What if they want to search me?'*

The detectives seized a freezer, hairdryer, food mixer, frying pan and
iron. Rattled and angry, Abbott demanded his lawyer and urged
Jackie to get a tape recorder so they wouldn't 'verbal' him (make a
false statement or confession): 'I even tried to have a drink of bourbon
while they were there – can't figure out why. I was, however, trying to
figure a way out of the place, to do a runner.'

Bourke assured him the tape recorders were in good working order
at Nollamara CIB, where their conversation about the Homecraft
break would continue. Jackie also had a boarder at her flat who was
asleep in the other room on the morning of the raid. He'd recently
split up with his wife and hadn't long been staying at Jackie's. He,
too, found himself at Nollamara CIB.

> *The poor bastard had no idea of what I was up to. He just
> thought I worked as a mechanic at a service station in Como for
> a living. He worked for a TV rental company and there were TVs
> and VCRs in his delivery van, which was parked at the flat. The
> jacks thought they were on to something, but the poor bastard
> had nothing to do with anything I was involved in.*

Since Abbott's back-door exit brought the investigation to an abrupt
halt, Beaman and Bourke went back in to question Jackie Lord:
'Jackie was only charged because I did the runner that day. She
couldn't help but grin when she heard I'd split out the back door. She
later told me that Bourke gave her a shove into the chair. I guess he
wasn't too impressed with my exit.'

After bolting through the back door of the detectives' office, Abbott hoisted himself over the side fence into the backyard of the home next door. He sprinted to the back fence and leaped over, and, around the same time his feet hit the ground, the potential threat of guard dogs crossed his mind. 'There wasn't one dog, but two. They shit at first when seeing me come over, but, before they got their wits about them, I was already over the next fence.'

Minutes later, Abbott was running down a lane when he spotted a thick shrub next to a bedroom window of a home adjacent to the end of the lane. He crawled under it, just as a police car pulled up at the front of the house. Abbott heard a voice say he'd been seen running in a particular direction; the tyres squealed and footsteps pounded down the lane.

The search moved on momentarily, but police lingered in the area and it was another hour before an impatient Abbott felt safe enough to begin walking cautiously through the streets to a phone box at some nearby shops. He needed to warn his brother and the others about the police operation. While in the police car en route to Nollamara CIB, he'd picked up on the fact that most of his mates were under surveillance.

But Jackie had his wallet and he had no change, so, when he called his mother, the phone call was cut off. He rang the operator and complained that he'd lost his 30 cents. He was connected to Thelma Salmon, who wearily agreed to pick up her son from the Belair Tavern in half an hour and to have some cash to cover a cab.

She knew something bad was afoot. The police had earlier taken custody of Glenn, in addition to the washing machine that Brenden delivered the day before.

On arriving at the pub, Abbott began making calls on the public phone and discovered everyone was in custody.

I rang Perth CIB's break and enter squad and posed as Glenn's solicitor, Bill Harris, a name I'd use as an alias in the future. I demanded that I be allowed to speak to my client and, you wouldn't believe it, they put Glenn on the phone. Glenn was obviously shocked; I told him not to sign anything and tried to find out what had happened. My advice to him came too late – Glenn had already owned up and made a signed confession. Like most, he also had to learn the hard way. I tried to ring him again later using the lawyer tactic, but I think they were on to me and

I hung up. I did the same thing years later (when I was on the run) while Glenn was at Albany Prison and I managed to have a chat with him.

David Knapp, Mark Reynolds, Glenn Abbott and 'Coops', a close mate of Abbott's, got bail later in the day after being charged with multiple break and enters. And, as well as Jackie, another ten people were charged for receiving stolen property. It was soon noticed that Abbott was the only one not yet facing charges.

I made a trip over to Coops's house to get the latest after his release and sensed something not right among those in the house. They suspected the story that I did the runner from the Nollamara CIB was just a blowie [false story], and thought I'd given everyone up. It wasn't until some time later that they let me off the hook and found out about who the so-called friends were that sold them out. Jackie was the last to get bail that day and I soon caught up with her and retrieved my much-needed cash.

Days later, police botched a surveillance operation to catch Abbott at the Scarborough unit. Glenn – the spitting image of Brenden – had dropped in, looking for his brother. As he drove off and approached a roundabout, police cars screeched to a halt from all directions, blocking him in.

They were just in the process of handcuffing him and [Detective] Bourke walked up to the car and realised they'd got the wrong Abbott and blew his top. [He said] 'You fucking idiots, that's his brother.'

One of the cops said, 'We'll pinch him for driving without a licence.'

Bourke turned around and said, 'Nah, fuck him, let him go.'

Glenn couldn't believe it. He'd just been surrounded and was being handcuffed and, the next thing, he's back driving down the road without a licence.

Jackie:

We had a lot of laughs over that one. But I had to pay ten grand up front on that [Homecraft] stealing and receiving matter. They pinned it on me because he took off ... they said, 'We won't go as hard on her.' But [the court] gave me a ten-grand on-the-spot fine or six months' prison. My mum paid and I had to pay her back.

(The other members of the burglary gang faced a string of charges. In August 1987, three of them would plead guilty to 25 charges over stolen goods valued at $242,000. They each received four years' jail, except for Coops, who received three years. The judge described their technique of driving vehicles through walls and breaking doors and windows as 'no less than looting, pillage and plunder'.)

Jackie and Brenden met up again about four days later at the Flag Inn on Great Eastern Highway, Belmont. Jackie faced serious charges and Abbott was now a criminal fugitive who couldn't hold down a legitimate job. Yet in recent times, he'd given every indication to her of wanting to go straight, even holding down good jobs for extended periods. They'd had many ups and downs, but Jackie always believed their relationship, their love, could survive Brenden's thieving. But, now, settling down was out of the question. Abbott needed to keep moving; after a last night with Jackie in the Belmont motel, he left.

I figured some days later it may be best if I left the state for a while until the heat died down. I was still in touch with Lou [Miraudo, his former employer at a Port Hedland hotel, who was also a close friend] at this stage. Lou had also moved on from Port Hedland and was now living in Brisbane. After a chat with him, he was more than happy to let me stay at his place. He had bought a house in the northern suburb of Kallangur and was living there with his girlfriend Paulette and two mates, one of whom I knew from the hotel in Hedland.

Abbott sold his car to his brother Glenn and says he 'scraped together' enough cash to move to Queensland. He hitched a ride on a truck to the South Australian border and says he then caught a bus to Brisbane. Brenden Abbott was now an interstate fugitive.

A month or two after my arrival, Lou decided to sell the house and move to Wollongong, where he had a job lined up at the North Beach International Hotel as a bar manager. The job included accommodation in a house directly behind the hotel. I moved down with him, Paulette and one of his mates. Lou soon scored me a job at the hotel, working on the door in the nightclub a few nights a week. I was using the name Brenden Simmons. The only thing I enjoyed about that job was the women I met. One I was seeing had recently separated from her husband and he approached me at another nightclub that the staff from the North Beach would move on to after knocking off. He came up to me and said, 'How are you going, Brenden?' I didn't have a clue who he was and asked how he knew my name. 'From your name tag at work,' he replied.

He said he knew about me fucking his ex-wife and left it at that. Being in jail and meeting blokes who had killed those who rooted their wives, I soon gave her a miss. This type of drama I could do without.

About four months after I left Nollamara CIB, I decided to head back to Perth. The plan was to make some big money and return to Wollongong and invest in a restaurant or the like with Lou, who would get a bank loan. I was to be the silent partner and put up the majority of the deposit.

With a plan for the future in mind, Brenden Abbott's new life as a fugitive now had purpose. He set out for Perth, intent on arranging his own bank finance with a large withdrawal.

Chapter One

1962–1974

The kid shat himself. The jolt of adrenalin and shock of discovery briefly distracted him from the warm feeling spreading across the seat of his pants and down his legs.

Soon enough, they'd laugh at the stench, but, in that split second of terror, it seemed the least of his worries. This was the worst thing he'd done in his life. They had finally caught him. And, for the first time in his short life, Brenden James Abbott was bound for an interview room in a police station.

He was all of seven, a slight kid with a tousled mop of brown hair, piercing hazel eyes and a mischievous grin that worried his mum and infuriated his dad. Their next-door neighbour, old man Spargo, was a serious pigeon fancier, the Bill Lawry of Boort Street, Broadmeadows, a misunderstood suburb north of Melbourne. He bred and raced homing pigeons and also kept pure white fantails for show. It was the fantail pigeons that fascinated young Brenden. Eventually, temptation won and the boy planned his first robbery. He built a makeshift cage beneath his own home, nailing timber slats to the house stumps as the back of the cage and bits and pieces of junk from under the house for the other sides.

Brenden jumped the side fence late one night, walked into the pigeon coop and gently scooped up one of the still white bundles. He crept home, slipped under the house, secured his new pet and went to bed satisfied. So did another neighbour's cat after it found the cage.

Bloodied white feathers greeted the boy the next morning. He was undeterred, determined to hang on to one of the lovely creatures long enough to show his mates. He twice repeated the night-time visit to Spargo's. Again, he got the birds without any trouble, but each morning there was the same messy result.

Clearly, a change in tactics was needed before the coop emptied. The kid planned to eliminate the competition with a rabbit trap. He placed it where he'd found the feathers, but prising the jaws apart and setting it seemed beyond the strength of a seven-year-old. Brenden bounced up and down on the trap's spring with his foot, while trying to set the trigger in place. When it finally locked into place, he smiled to himself in anticipation. Sweet revenge.

Brenden's father Brian Abbott didn't much like cats; they ate the baby rabbits he kept for the kids. So he'd lean on the bathroom window with an air rifle, picking off strays unwise enough to enter his backyard.

But Brian's next encounter with a mortally wounded cat was not as precise and clinical. Woken by a cat thrashing around under the house at 3am one night, he crawled beneath and silence returned abruptly. After getting rid of the evidence, Brian checked the trap. Surely, a seven-year-old couldn't have set it? He guessed that David, his eldest, must have done it. Brenden kept quiet while his older brother took the heat. With the cat eliminated, he was free to be a pigeon fancier again.

He kept one in the cage for a few days and then released it while the neighbouring birds were out, in the vain hope that it preferred his cage over the coop. He raided the thinning flock several times until the Spargo family put a lock on the coop. But it was no match for a determined seven-year-old pigeon thief. Brenden decided he could crawl through the small entry hatch, grab another bird and then fly the coop.

There was one hitch: someone peering through the Spargos' kitchen window spotted him crawling through. Old man Spargo confronted Brian Abbott, who in turn put it to his son, who denied all. Brian simply warned him, 'They're on to you, boy. Look out if they catch you at it again.'

They did. Old man Spargo grabbed him while he was halfway through the hatch. The old bloke had been hiding in a nearby shed with his son. They put him in their car and drove down to the local police station. Brenden sat in an interview room, but, after a bemused cop heard what had happened, he ordered the Spargos to sort it out with Brian Abbott.

By this time, young Brenden was rancid. The cop wrinkled his face and laughed, and soon they all joined in. The shame burned up his neck and cheeks. Back in the Spargos' car, he didn't feel any better. He was worried about the reaction at home. But his father saw the funny side and he was spared a clip around the ear.

Brenden Abbott's interest in fantail pigeons ended that day. And it was the last time he shat his pants in the commission of a robbery.

As Michelle Griffin reported in *The Sunday Age* in September 2003, Broadmeadows, 16 kilometres northwest of Melbourne's inner city, is a suburb famous for both its social stigma and its many local-boy-made-good exceptions: 'For the past 50 years, Broady has been a source of endless fascination for policy wonks and social theorists. It was invented overnight in 1952 by the Housing Commission, as a ready source of labour for all the factories Victoria wanted to attract to town. The first homes were built in 1953 and, in the 1950s and 1960s, more than 12,000 moved in each year to the suburb's spartan pastel concrete prefabs.'

Among them were Brian and Thelma Abbott, who moved into their new home in Boort Street in June 1962, with six-week-old Brenden and their two older children, Janet, five, and David, three. Brian, 24, and Thelma, 22, had lived at Brian's parents' place for the best part of five years – so long that they ended up building a bungalow in the backyard of Norman and Jean Abbott's home. Thelma says she never really knew what her husband did for a living, only that he was working for a 'gas cylinder mob' when they moved in. Brenden's birth certificate lists his father's occupation as 'storeman'. Decades later, Thelma has little to say about a relationship that soured and ended long ago. However, she does recall her former husband's temper:
'[While I was pregnant with Janet] he came home one day and the people across the road were yelling out and calling him names. He went inside and got the gun and went out and shot it over their heads. They took him to court. He reckons they were only rat pellets in the gun. I know better.'

Brenden's mother Thelma was born in Melbourne to Robert Peters, a cabinet-maker, and his wife Matilda. She was one of a family that grew to five girls and two boys. Thelma remembers, 'My childhood was all right. I was very quiet and shy. Didn't go out much. Then I fell pregnant at 15 (May 1956) and I married him at 16 [September 1956].'

Thelma left Flemington Girls School behind for her new life with Brian at his parents' Essendon home. When they finally moved into their own Broadmeadows home, life seemed on track. Diane Abbott, who arrived just over a year after Brenden, says,

> We had a pretty good life when Dad was there. We didn't want for anything. It wasn't until the last ten years that I've realised how well off Dad was. Back in those days, to be able to support a wife and five children and have everything we had. I think the only thing he paid off was the house, but he owned his car outright. He owned every piece of furniture. He's never in his whole life ever had hire purchase. He always paid cash. We had clothes, shoes, everything.

Abbott:

> It's alleged I was born on 8 May 1962, in Melbourne, Victoria. From what my mother has told me – and the documentation I've seen – I guess I'm good for it. I'm the third eldest of five children, the eldest being Janet, then David, myself, Diane and Glenn. In my earliest years, up until 1971, we lived on Boort Street in Broadmeadows, an outer suburb of Melbourne. In my first years of schooling, from 1968 to 1971, I attended Dallas State Primary School, also in Broadmeadows.

It might not have been the most desirable address, but the Abbott household in Boort Street seemed relatively stable and content. Then something happened in 1971 that set the family on a course that eventually tore it apart. No one's saying why, least of all Brian Abbott, the man responsible for the decision to leave. He sold the house, bought a caravan and, a few months later, the family hit the road with the intention of moving to Darwin. But they didn't make it that far. Brenden says,

> [In 1970 and 1971] we spent a few months living at my grandfather's house on Holmes Road in Moonee Ponds, another suburb of Melbourne. For those few months, I attended the primary school nearby. We made our way to Alice Springs in May 1971 by car, towing a caravan. The first few months after arriving in Alice Springs, we lived at the Heavytree Gap Caravan

Park. Some months later, we moved to a property east of the caravan park that belonged to someone my father knew. We were still living in the caravan there and remained on that property for months, before moving into a house in town. I attended two schools in Alice Springs – Alice Springs Primary and then Gillen Primary. I recall my [paternal] grandfather died while we were living in Alice Springs, in 1972. My father went back to Melbourne for the funeral. In the early part of 1973, my parents separated. Janet and David had left home and my mother was left supporting the remaining three kids.

Thelma:

We had a house in Alice Springs after the caravan. Brian was working ... I know he used to drive the grader out at the tip. That's when we were in the caravan park. I had a scooter accident and I did me back, me shoulder, but it was mainly me knee.

[Months later] I was in the bathroom and was just about to wash my hands and [Brian] came in ... He just said, 'I'm leaving.'

And I wasn't game to turn around. And I said, 'What do you mean?'

And he said, 'I'm going.'

I said, 'Yeah, all right.' Then I heard the door go. And that was it. He left.

Brian Abbott says he wanted Thelma to leave. He says she refused his offer of money for a train ticket to go back to Melbourne, so he left instead. Thelma continues, 'I stayed in Alice Springs for three months. I just sold up everything and went to Mount Isa. And then I came across here [to Western Australia]. People don't know what fear is until they've been there.'

Brian Abbott's departure was also a big financial blow. Thelma, on her own with three kids, was still getting over the scooter accident. Diane says, 'I think that really had an impact. To go from having everything to going to ... there's not always food in the cupboard and your parents aren't always home. And when you need new shoes and clothes, but you can't get them. I think that was really a shock to all of us.'

Abbott:

I don't recall missing the presence of my father when he left, but years later I wanted to catch up with him. I've got no ill feelings towards him whatsoever, unlike some who in later years hung shit on him through the media and painted him up as some type of animal. One of a number of nasty things that were claimed was that he used to beat me up as if I was a grown man. That is absolute rubbish and these types of comments are obviously from someone [Abbott's sister, Janet] who still feels some bitterness over his departure in 1973. He used to dish out discipline that in this day and age may seem a little harsh in some people's eyes, but then it was generally accepted.

Later that year, my mother moved to Mount Isa, taking myself, Diane and Glenn. By then, Janet and David had already left home and remained living in Alice Springs. In the time we lived in Mount Isa, I recall my mother having a few relationships that didn't go too far, until she met a bloke by the name of Ted Springall.

I attended the Mount Isa Primary School for the time we lived there, which was a number of months. Mount Isa was the first place I'd ever had a paying job during the school holidays. It was in a watchmaker's shop in town, owned by a bloke by the name of Steve Hogan. My main job was dismantling clocks and washing them in a tub of solution. The relationship my mother had with Ted appeared to be going well and in 1974 [the year Brenden turned 12] we all moved to the iron-ore mining town of Tom Price in northwest Western Australia, where Ted had gained employment. He had claimed to the company that he was married and had three kids. So the mining company supplied a house. We made our way from Mount Isa to Tom Price in a new HQ Holden station wagon that Ted recently bought.

The trip was a long one, because we travelled down the east coast, firstly to Brisbane, where Ted's mother lived, then to Melbourne, where Mum caught up with her relatives, then it was across to Perth and eventually to Tom Price. The school I attended was the local junior high school. I recall it was solely for grade six and seven. By now, this would've been the sixth school I'd enrolled in. It was drummed into us kids that Mum and Ted were married and our surname was Springall, the name I also took on at school. By then I was beginning to hate school.

It was unsettling for me having to try to fit in again. (That analysis wasn't what I'd come up with at the time.) I wasn't at the school long before I was in trouble for being a disruptive student. One time, I was kept back for detention – what for, I can't recall – but no doubt for being a shit of a kid. I wasn't impressed with the teacher for keeping me back and, come time to go home, I left the classroom telling her she was a fucking bitch, or words to that effect. I made the comment at the door of the classroom. I could see she was totally shocked. She started to scream at me to get back into the classroom, but I thought it best I hightail it out of there.

When I fronted school the next day, she obviously hadn't got over it and didn't they carry on about it? My punishment was two weeks' suspension. For a kid who hated school, you can imagine I was devastated! At that age, I was a bit of a loner and not being able to play with any other kids over those two weeks didn't have me missing school at all. As I had done while living in Alice Springs and Mount Isa, I used to wander off into the bush around the town with my dog. The dog I had prior to moving to Tom Price was given away, regardless of my objections. I wasn't happy about it at all. Not long after arriving in Tom Price, Mum got herself a Labrador pup, but she soon became my dog and my best friend and went with me everywhere. Even when I went to school, she tried following and needed to be locked inside until after I'd left.

In 1974, while I was at Tom Price Junior High School, I was involved in an incident that was a major turning point in my life. I was charged with aggravated assault for hitting a girl at school with a bike pump. I can't even recall how it all came about; it was nothing more than the everyday tiff kids have at school. There were no injuries inflicted on the girl whatsoever. It was by no means a savage attack, she was only hit once. All I recall after the incident was the girl's mother attending the school while I was in the headmaster's office and hissing something at me. I became aware that her parents were well respected and had some pull in the town. At this time in my life, I'd never been in any trouble with the law, other than the pigeon-stealing incident, and no action was brought against me then anyway.

I was charged and brought before the Tom Price Children's Court and was sentenced to be a ward of the state until the age of 16. It may have been a day or two, then I was picked up by someone employed by the Child Welfare Department and taken to Perth. Just prior to leaving, I recall Ted's mother was also in Tom Price and staying with us for a short time. She was reassuring me that I'd be fine and I recall her telling me stories about a place in Brisbane for boys, and painting it up as some sort of holiday camp. I guess she was easing the fear of the unknown for me.

When the chap from the Child Welfare Department picked me up from home, I was placed into the back of the vehicle. I think it was a utility which had a canopy. As we drove off, I recall I started crying; not because I was taken away from home, more so for being taken away from my dog.

Diane:

And then that was when Brenden went into a home. I've talked to David about this as well, and he said something about a bike pump.

I remember Mum telling her boyfriend that she couldn't deal with him anyway [because] he was uncontrollable. I didn't think he was. He was just being a kid. I didn't think he was bad … I was walking down the street with Brenden one day when he ran up a mound of sand that was on someone's front lawn. This old lady came out and told us off. Brenden told her to get fucked. I was like … Oooooh. Because we just didn't swear. And he stuck his finger in the air. And I said, 'Brenden, you can't do that to people.' He was like: 'Oh, it's all right.' So he went into a home for behaviour like that, which, now, would be nothing – but back then …

He had a fight with somebody at school … When he went into the home, there was no warning about it. He was just gone. [Mum said,] 'Brenden's gone to a home, he's living in Perth now.'

Decades later, asked to recall what led to her son being taken away, Thelma frowns and shakes her head. It's all too long ago. 'He hit a girl. I don't know. I can't remember.'

Chapter Two

1974–1977

The smell of the place hit him first. Brenden got used to it in the years to come, but never liked it. Walking through the doors at Mount Lawley Reception Home in Walcott Street, Mount Lawley, the pungent institutional odour drifted up his nose and imprinted itself on his mind. A disinfected home for disaffected youth.

One of the child-welfare people told him his home was now a dormitory with another dozen or so boys; he looked and felt like the youngest there. On the first morning, he endured the embarrassment of his first communal shower and then being dressed in the uniform. For the first few weeks, Brenden was shell-shocked. Shit, he'd only whacked the girl with a bike pump – but now he was banished from his home, the property of the state until age 16. His nose gradually grew accustomed to the smell and his mind to the institutional routines. He even started looking forward to the weekly ice-rink outing.

They had plenty of activities, but, no matter what they put on, I couldn't help but miss being home and being with my dog. My mother telephoned me a number of times. On one occasion, when I asked about my dog, as I often did, she told me how she'd wander off for the day and sometimes returned smelling of sewage. This went on for some time after I'd left Tom Price.

After a few months in the reception home, Brenden moved to Hilston, a boys' home in the hills west of Perth. There were usually 35 to 50 boys in residence, most aged around 15, and Brenden, barely 12, found himself locked in a cell for the night. The official view of the institution and the majority of its inmates was summed up in a Hilston annual report that said, 'Most boys admitted to Hilston are educationally retarded and display behavioural problems associated with poor adjustment at home, at school or in employment. Therefore, emphasis is placed on remedial education and the modification of behaviour.'

Staff decided that Brenden was not a hardcore troublemaker. Within days, he was moved from the main building to a cottage on the road into Hilston, where a married couple acted as foster parents to about six less troublesome boys. Brenden welcomed the change to a friendlier atmosphere, although the cottage kids copped plenty of flak from the tough guys down the road.

Late in 1974, he moved to another new cottage, in Darlington, also a hills suburb. Six other boys lived under the guardianship of an older married couple, Ted and Peggy Tasker. They insisted the boys call them Mum and Pop. With Hilston still fresh in his memory, Brenden couldn't believe his luck.

> *I knew straight away that I was going to like it there. It was quite a large house and not that old. It had a large in-ground swimming pool, new pushbikes, I was fitted out with all new clothing. I'd never had it this good at home. It was the living that was equivalent to most upper-middle-class families. I quickly got to enjoy this type of lifestyle as a kid.*

Ted Tasker – a strict but fair old bloke, Abbott remembers – knew how to keep the boys in line. He encouraged them to play Aussie Rules, cricket and basketball, but, if they did the wrong thing, 'he'd give you a fair clipping, and then some'.

At the start of 1975, Abbott began high school, and caught a bus each day with the other boys to Eastern Hills High School. There, he became good mates with two other wards, Peter Lievense and Ian S, who would later figure prominently in his life, but there was no sign of the trouble ahead.

Ted Tasker was the first steady father figure since Brian Abbott had left. With strict boundaries again in place, Brenden seemed to change. He got on well with the other Darlington boys and their shared circumstances made them a tight-knit group. Even at school, the other kids and the teachers accepted them.

Life was good, and election to the student council confirmed the Year-8 student's popularity with his peers. But this one shining year was the exception in Brenden Abbott's short-lived academic career. Thelma:

> Glenn perforated his ear drums when he was little. Brenden had trouble with his ears while at Darlington requiring surgery, which cleared it up. His younger brother, Glenn, suffered similar ear problems, only worse. And he had concussion a couple of times when he was little. He fell off a wooden bench [in primary school] and we took him into the hospital. And I think he was nine when he got hit by that [utility vehicle]. He was hit at 9am on the Friday and he didn't come out of it until 7am on Saturday. And that's when they were able to operate. Thirteen stitches on one side and more on the other. I mean, I've always thought there could have been pressure there that made him go off. It's got something to do with the base of the neck. When the air doesn't go through the ear channel, it builds up pressure that can't be released, as the doctor explained. Glenn used to wake up screaming and he would scream through the night.

Brenden's response to the stable environment of Darlington Cottages did not go unnoticed. Thelma and Ted had moved to Perth with Diane and Glenn to be closer to Brenden. Thelma came to visit, delivering the news that she had got rid of his dog. He was devastated by the loss of another loyal pet. During the summer school holidays at the end of 1975, the authorities allowed him to spend time at home. When those visits passed without incident – and after much debate – he returned to Thelma's care. Not everyone was happy, Thelma included:

> I didn't want them to send him home. I said to keep him there another 12 months. I thought it would have done him good. I knew that he wasn't ready to come home. He came home at Christmas and he was before the courts again in February. But they just didn't want to listen. Mum and Pop [at Darlington Cottages] wanted him to stay.

Brenden put up the emotional defences. He acted as if he didn't much care where he went. As an adult in a maximum-security prison, he thinks differently.

> *In hindsight, it was a bad move. I should have at least spent another two years at Darlington. It was a far more stable environment there than living at home with my mother. I was doing well at Eastern Hills High School; my grades were good and I had settled in with my surroundings.*

After arriving in Perth from Tom Price, the family briefly lived with Thelma's two sisters in Inglewood. But the inevitable arguments that arose – with too many cousins and aunts in a confined space – soon prompted her to move to nearby Bayswater. Her relationship with Ted Springall ended badly that year and she was in Maylands when Brenden finally came home in December 1975. But the hills were a long way from the inner Perth suburb and he was forced to attend another school, John Forrest Senior High. He'd made some good mates among the boys at Darlington – and also at Eastern Hills High School – and tried to keep in touch with them. He kept travelling up there to play cricket, but the time, cost and distance soon put an end to that. Brenden felt angry with his mother for not helping him maintain the friendships.

> *My mother wasn't too supportive when it came to me playing in sports. I never did join any of the local teams when living back home with my mother, nor did I participate much in school sports after Darlington. My mother played ten pin bowling and I did join a league at the same venue, but that didn't last too long, it wasn't my cup of tea. I recall fishing as a pastime around then. Many a night, I'd head up behind the Sandringham Hotel on Great Eastern Highway. K-mart, at the Belmont shopping centre, was my supplier of tackle equipment, courtesy of my parka with a slit on the inside lining. Some of the very few times I'd shoplift.*

The family moved to a State Housing Commission home at 13 Dudley Street, Belmont, a working-class inner suburb of Perth beginning an era of rapid development. The Belmont City Council area – which takes in Ascot, Redcliffe, Rivervale, Belmont, Cloverdale and Kewdale – is bisected by the Great Eastern Highway. It carried traffic from nearby Perth Airport, and tourists flowed in from the east. Belmont's slice of the highway became the Gateway to Perth, and motels and hotels sprang up along it. They offered cheap rates, pools, air conditioning and colour TV. The move meant yet another school for Brenden – Belmont Senior High School. But, this time, student councillorships seemed unlikely.

I was involved in a number of breaking and enterings, mostly of businesses and of some schools. Breaking into houses was an area that I never wanted to get into. The majority of my juvenile offences I did in the company of those who were a number of years older than I was. When we were all pinched, their parents had a habit of pointing the finger at me for their sons committing the crimes. There was a stigma attached to me for being in a boys' home in their eyes, as well as many others who knew of my past. They made this quite obvious when in my presence. Adults tend to think kids are blind and deaf.

One of Brenden's best mates was Coops. They first met when Coops's father began a long relationship with one of Thelma's sisters. Thelma and the kids lived in Maylands at the time. Coops and Brenden's cousin, Wayne, effectively became stepbrothers, and, when Thelma moved to Dudley Street, the boys regularly rode their bikes over there to see Brenden. After school, the trio made a beeline for the pinball parlour, Leisure Machine, at Belmont Forum. One afternoon, after discovering the owner kept cash on the premises, they hatched a plan to break in. The boys met up and rode to the back of the parlour late that night, and, after smashing a window, Brenden kept watch while Wayne and Coops climbed in. A minute later, they were back, groaning under the weight of a small safe. It was a bold heist with only two glaring faults: bikes and safes didn't work well together and they couldn't get to the loot. To finish the job properly, they needed to think on their feet.

Wayne, an apprentice welder, claimed to be competent with oxyacetylene gear, which happened to be part of the equipment in the pre-vocational centre, about 500 metres away at Belmont Senior High School.

After hauling the safe through the window and into a shopping trolley, they wheeled it to the school via back lanes. They broke into the administration area first and settled on the principal's office as a good place to try their hand at safe cracking.

The trio crept down to the centre and wheeled the oxy gear back to the office. Wayne went to work on the safe door's hinges, but got nowhere. Brenden and Coops stayed busy putting out spot fires, giving the smouldering carpet a warm spray of piss whenever necessary. By the time Wayne had cut through the steel plate, exposing the concrete inside the door, the gas bottle had run out. They resorted to using a couple of hammers, belting the concrete until it began to crumble. Finally, hours after they set out in search of a king's ransom of 20-cent pieces, they plucked the money out.

Before they left the scene, Brenden broke all the principal's canes. It was the signature act of the crime spree, and showed Brenden's growing hate for school and authority. Coops remembers their triumphant departure: 'After we broke into the pre-voc centre, we've broken into where the cadets were, and we had all these air rifles. This was the same night as the safe. So we rode away with all the cash from the safe and all these air rifles. And we fucking almost burned down the principal's office!'

It was too good to be true. Thelma burst in to find the boys sprawled across Brenden's bed counting the takings. She confiscated the money and sent the other two home.

Thelma:

There were air rifles as well. They'd shoved them in a green garbage bag under my bed. I pulled the bag out and said, 'What the hell are these?' One of the bloody things went off and I just crashed. Margaret [her sister] turned around and said, 'You bloody little bastards. See what you've done to your mother?'

Thelma didn't know what to do with the money, so she hid it while considering the situation. Brenden spent days searching the house. Finally, he tried his mother's car, and discovered that, by putting his hand through a hole in the ledge behind the rear seats, he could reach down and liberate some of the cash from the boot. Coops helped in the search and shared the spoils. For the next couple of days, they lived like kings, going to the movies and hitting every pinball parlour in sight – except Leisure Machine. Wayne, who'd worked so hard to help get the safe open, lived on the other side of the river and was busy doing what apprentices have to do, and so he missed out. But it didn't take long for word to get around. The boys were arrested and charged within a few days. Thelma handed what was left of the hidden money to the police. The police questioned Brenden and informed him a lot was still missing – a lot more than Coops and Brenden believed they took.

The jacks said, if I didn't own up to taking the amount that was short, they would charge my mother. I owned up to the amount missing. Years later, when I started to wake up and got my head out of my arse, I began to realise that many that represent the law are worse than many of the crooks they pinch.

He later put it to his mother that she took the money. She told him she most certainly did not. 'My mother is as honest as they come when it comes to obeying the law. It used to shame her that I was a criminal in my early days. She would blame my criminal behaviour on my father's side of the family.'

While living in Dudley Street, Thelma formed her next serious relationship. Her divorce from Brian was finalised on 3 May 1976.

Thelma took up darts and occasionally visited her local, the Belair Tavern. She took a shine to one of her darts opponents, John Salmon, a laconic carpenter with a sharp sense of humour. He needed it. She was staying at his home one night when he received a call about a burglary at his father's sports store. He drove straight there and sat in the place until morning when the glaziers arrived. That morning, two new bikes and an assortment of bike parts appeared in the Abbott backyard. A livid Thelma ordered Brenden to confess.

Diane:

Mum came home and said, 'You little bastard. I've never been so embarrassed in all my life. You're going to tell John that you did that so he can tell his father.' I don't think charges were ever laid, but John's father came back and said, if he got the parts back, they could keep the bikes. And then, of course, Mum ended up marrying John.

Brenden felt terrible. He hadn't known about John's link to the bike shop. But John didn't hold it against him and Brenden got on well with the man who became his stepfather. John Salmon soon handed out new nicknames for the family. Thelma, to her chagrin, became Bucket Arse, Diane was Sally and Brenden was Bren-gun, then just Gun.

'He was a gun at whatever he done,' Salmon would say later.

Thelma remembers it differently: 'He was always gunna do this and gunna do that. But John and him were close.'

John says, 'He was a bit rebellious, but I wouldn't say out of control. Brenden was easy to get along with. He won't give you a hard time unless you give him a hard time.'

John moved in with Thelma and the kids at Dudley Street. Like Brenden, John was a hands-on man, and they both loved working on cars. But domestic harmony lasted only a few short months. On 3 December 1976, the charges arising from the pinball parlour, school and cadet storeroom break-ins went before the Children's Court. The state ward knew what came next: 'But this time it wasn't the luxury of the Darlington Cottage. I'd do time – I was sent to Hilston. All those pinched with me received probation, if that. In their parents' eyes, it was my fault their sons broke the law. Gets back to the fact I'd been in that boys' home for that incident in Tom Price.'

After a month back in Hilston, Brenden was in no mood for an education when he returned to Belmont High at the start of 1977. 'It was the first day in starting Year 10 and I didn't last the first hour at that school. I was expelled. I guess the headmaster was still dirty about his carpet being burned. Or maybe it was over the canes?'

Kewdale High School warily accepted him for Year 10, although he travelled back to Belmont High to use the facilities. Working in the pre-vocational centre, where they'd stolen the hammers and oxy gear, he appreciated the irony. Otherwise, though, he was stuck in a classroom at Kewdale until his time was served. Sitting in a maths class one day, bored, Brenden leaned over and asked the kid in front if he could borrow his rubber. The kid told him to get stuffed. Brenden whacked him in the back of the head with a ruler. That was how Brenden and Robert Allen, the kid they called Rabbit, struck up a friendship. Rabbit remembers, 'He really felt like he got screwed over the bike-pump incident. When I first met him in high school in Year 10, it was still on his mind. He wasn't very good when it came to discipline at school. There was a male maths teacher who was a right bastard. He was rotten to the kids and Brenden went eye to eye with him and told him exactly where he could stick that cane. The teacher never pursued that any further.'

Abbott: 'That maths teacher was authorised to give the cane. He tried it with me. I told him to stick it up his arse. The end of term one couldn't come soon enough. I absolutely despised school and, when I look back, I understand why that was.'

As much as Abbott hated school and in spite of his record, he found a job. He lasted barely a month at Moore Power engine reconditioning, and then began working for a transport company, Brambles Manford, in Kewdale with his cousin Neil Doherty. Brenden wrapped furniture and helped with deliveries; it wasn't brain surgery, but the money seemed reasonable enough. He began boarding at his aunt's place in Maylands, where Neil lived, making transport to work easy. He made another new mate, Ron, while working for Brambles. Ron was based in the company's Fremantle depot, where Brenden did pick-ups and drop-offs. Ron was old enough to drive, so Brenden sometimes cruised the city with him. He seemed like a good bloke.

One of the boys from Eastern Hills High invited him up to a party in the Chidlow–Mundaring area, so Brenden invited Ron and 'Hood', another mate he made through Kewdale Senior High classmates. Ron's car played up on the night of the party, so Janet, back staying with Thelma to help out with the younger kids, let them borrow her 1972 four-cylinder Torana, equipped with a CB radio.

The trio stayed at the party several hours and enjoyed a few drinks. Brenden doesn't recall drinking, but Hood had a few and Ron knocked back plenty. During the evening, the CB radio was shown off and, before the night ended, it disappeared.

After much finger-pointing, Ron was ordered to leave before punches were thrown. Driving back down towards Perth on Great Eastern Highway, with Ron at the wheel, they saw a person hitchhiking towards the city. They slowed as they drove past and recognised the young man as one of the partygoers. Someone suggested him as a suspect for the CB theft. 'I'll go back and sort him out,' Ron told the boys, full of bravado.

At this point, Brenden wasn't sure what he meant. Ron did a U-turn, and then another, before approaching the hitchhiker from behind. As they got close, Ron steered the car directly at him and the man jumped clear in time. Initially, Brenden didn't believe it was deliberate. But then Ron said, 'I'll get him next time,' and did another U-turn, heading back again. Brenden froze.

This time, Ron was travelling a bit faster as he got near him and then he suddenly steered the car off the road, directly at him. The poor bastard didn't stand a chance. There was an almighty bang, the guy's come over the bonnet and hits the left side of the windscreen. The force of the impact shatters the windscreen, showering me with glass. I couldn't believe what had just happened. I screamed for Ron to stop the car, but he proceeded to drive towards Perth at a speed well over the limit.

Brenden looked sideways at Ron. A muscle below his jaw twitched and he glared intensely off into the distance. 'He just totally dipped out. I was sitting next to a complete fucking madman. I didn't think I was getting home alive.'

They drove in silence. The closer they got to Belmont, the better Brenden felt. But, as the Torana continued down Great Eastern Highway and approached the lights at Belmont Avenue, a car turned across them into Belmont Avenue. Ron accelerated, clipping the rear of the car as it crossed the intersection, and kept driving. Five minutes later, they were at Hood's house. 'By the sound of Hood's voice, it was obvious he was as shaken up about the whole ordeal as I was, but I still had to get back into the car with this maniac to go home.'

Ron came back to earth. He parked the Torana on the Abbotts' front lawn and left immediately, the thousand-yard stare finally fading. Brenden ran to the nearest phone box and rang the police.

A police van arrived at my house within about five minutes. At first, they didn't seem to take me seriously, but, as I was talking to them, something came over their police radio about a hit and run victim. They quickly changed their tune and, the next thing I know, I'm put into the back of the van and taken to the Victoria Park police station.

They arrested Hood and Ron the same night, with Ron facing the serious charge of attempted unlawful killing. Residents heard the injured hitchhiker's screams of agony, and found him before shock set in. His injuries included two broken legs and a broken arm and he hobbled into court on crutches when Brenden testified at Ron's trial. The night of the crime brought Brenden a year of nightmares, sitting frozen in the speeding car, Ron's crazed stare and the terror on the face of the hitchhiker. The Crown called Brenden and Hood as witnesses, and Ron got seven years' jail for causing grievous bodily harm. After the trial, Brenden never saw him again. But Brenden Abbott's honesty did him no good.

Within the criminal world, those who testify against another, especially to aid the Crown, aren't looked upon lightly. Because of my actions on that night and at Ron's trial, I've copped some flak over it, regardless of the fact that I was 15 at the time. At that point in my life, I did what I thought was the right thing to do.

His mere involvement in the incident, combined with his growing criminal history, didn't look good. The truth only emerged in court many months later. The consequences left the boy bitter. 'As a result of that incident, I was fired from my job at Brambles Manford, which I wasn't too happy about. Talk about guilty by association.'

Chapter Three

1977–1979

Brenden Abbott grew up to be a fugitive and bank robber who some people saw as a latter-day bushranger. But his first 'escape' from custody – and subsequent chase – was more Benny Hill than Ben Hall.

At the time, though, the angry young man saw little to laugh about in the fallout from his clash with an officer at the Belmont police station. To him, it seemed like more evidence in his case against a system he felt was out to get him.

In mid-1977, Abbott was 15 and still living with his aunt Margaret, but had already lost his job at Brambles Manford.

On this particular day, he and Peter Lievense were out driving around with Peter's father, running errands. Abbott asked to drop by his mother's place in Dudley Street, where he found a calling card from Belmont police wedged in the front door, requesting that he contact them. His conscience was unusually clear, so he asked his mate's father to drive him to the police station and find out what he was supposed to have done this time. They parked in the Hungry Jack's car park and Abbott crossed Hardy Road to the police station. He stood at the front counter and handed the card to the lone officer, who informed him of a warrant for his arrest over an unpaid fine. It was a case of pay up or be locked up.

'I suddenly realised what a goose I was, going there. I didn't have the cash required and had better things to do for the day.'

Abbott told him, 'I've got some friends waiting outside. Can I just tell them I won't be coming with them?'

The copper didn't buy it. 'That's all right, son. I'll let them know. You can just wait in here.'

The officer thought they were in the station's car park and went to the back door. Abbott bolted for the front door. But the cop was already at the corner of the building and only three metres away by the time Abbott stepped outside. Abbott shot past the bemused Peter and his father, around two fast-food stores and then up to the corner of Great Eastern Highway and down another road. The cop stayed with him, a few metres behind most of the way, but the teenager finally lost him.

A few streets away, Peter and his dad pissed themselves with laughter when they picked up the gasping fugitive. But, as Abbott recalls, the cop had been embarrassed, and that meant trouble. 'He claimed I took off out the front door and he followed, and I slammed the front door into him. I was wanted for escaping legal custody and assault. I eventually surrendered to them and fronted the Children's Court.'

Abbott went to court with his aunt Margaret, his jaw set and mind focused on his defence to the assault charge. But when police heard from his aunt that Abbott planned to call witnesses – Peter and his father – the assault charge suddenly evaporated. 'I still recall being upset with my aunty for telling the cop at the court that day about the witnesses. I was looking forward to bringing this prick undone.'

The small fine he received over the 'escape' mattered little to Abbott, but his bitterness over the conviction resonated down the decades, all the way to a punishment cell in a high-security prison on the other side of the country.

Abbott's next brush with the law earned his first known media headlines and, predictably, it involved cars. Specifically, an XW V8 Ford Fairmont belonging to Coops. Abbott's older cousin, Wayne, was behind the wheel while Coops and Abbott scanned for targets as they cruised the streets of Dianella and Morley.

The gleaming chrome wheels on a Holden HT panel van caught their eye. The driver's side was closest to the street, parked on the verge at the front of a house. They parked a few houses back and hatched their plan: Coops and Brenden would steal the van and meet up with Wayne to strip the wheels and anything else they could get.

As he got out of the car, Abbott saw that the rear passenger window was down in the Ford – but, crucially, he didn't see Wayne reach back and wind it up.

Abbott and Coops crept up to the van and found the driver's side door unlocked and that the ignition lock wasn't on. Coops decided they should just get in and take off. Abbott slid across to the passenger seat and Coops got behind the wheel. The engine turned over, but didn't start. He kept trying and soon faces peered out the lounge window.

Two older teenagers rushed from the house. Abbott covered his face with his hand. 'Hurry up and get the fucking thing started,' he yelled at Coops.

One of the teenagers ran to the driver's side, opened the door – the lock was broken – and dragged Coops out. The other teenager, by now at Abbott's door, raced around to help his mate.

Abbott leaped from the van and ran towards Coops's car. The other teenager gave chase. Abbott dived for the back window of the Fairmont, assuming it was open. After hitting his head on the glass like a short-sighted bird, he opened the door and dived in. The pursuer grabbed for his legs, and Abbott kicked back, trying to shake him off. He gave up on Abbott and headed back to Coops. Wayne drove up to Coops as Abbott climbed over to the front seat. They weren't sure what to do, and hoped Coops could make a break for it.

But Coops wasn't doing so well. His windcheater was pushed up over his face and he couldn't see a thing as the pair pounded into him. Inspiration struck. Abbott reached down and picked up a large screwdriver off the floor of the car. He pointed it out the window and yelled, 'Let go, or I'll shoot.'

The pair sought cover on the other side of the van, dragging Coops with them. Wayne reversed, smoking the tyres, until they were in view again.

When Abbott could see them, he repeated his threat. This time, they both let go of Coops and put their hands up. Coops struggled to pull his windcheater back down and took a moment to get his bearings. Then he suddenly bolted to the Fairmont and dived into the back seat, screaming, 'Go, go, go!' The tyres screeched and they left the shaken but victorious van defenders behind in a cloud of smoking rubber.

Abbott looked at Coops. Welts criss-crossed his face, he'd lost his glasses, his hair was a mess and the bruises were gaining colour. Coops broke the silence. 'Jesus, that was fucking lucky.'

Suddenly, hysterical laughter filled the car and tears filled their eyes. They were exhilarated by the narrow escape.

'Well, that wasn't the end of that night's event. It was major news the following day, because a firearm may have been involved.'

Someone got the Fairmont's registration and the trio was quickly rounded up and taken to Dianella CIB for questioning. Coops remembers, 'The cops have got us within 24 hours, and we're all like "get fucked, no way". The cops have said to me, "Well, here's your glasses."'

Abbott:

I wasn't really saying anything and one of the jacks was dirtying up. While he was questioning me, I was sitting in a chair next to a desk. This jack was standing beside me, leaning over with his face just inches from mine and pulling faces. Meanwhile, his right hand was on the table in front of me and his other hand hanging on to a leg of my chair. It was obvious what he was going to do and I braced myself for it. He's then pulled the chair out from under me, expecting me to go arse up on the floor; instead, I've remained in the same spot, as if sitting on an invisible chair. Well, fuck me, didn't this goose play up about that!

An open hand struck his face hard, knocking him from his balanced position to the floor.

As I've got to my feet, there was more to come from this prick. He then tried to kick me in the stones, but I managed just in time to bring my legs together enough to take the blow before his foot connected with them. I made out he scored a direct hit and dropped to the floor, faking I was in trouble, as one does when your stones are getting a work-out. If I didn't do that, I was sure I was in for some drama over the chair incident. It seemed to have worked, because he backed off and it appeared to help restore some of his lost pride. He left the interview room and was soon replaced by a 'nice cop'.

Abbott knew enough about the system now to keep his mouth shut and head down while the cops went through their routine.

I was worried about being placed into a boys' home again, so I wasn't going to own up for trying to knock off someone's car. I had no understanding other than the thought that trying to steal a car was a serious enough crime to see me getting locked up for some time again.

Wayne, meanwhile, was being drilled in another room. As a result, an officer came in to Abbott with the story that they only wanted to steal cassettes from the van.

I thought, Yeah, I'll go with that one, so I put my hand up for it. In hindsight, after gaining some knowledge about the law, I realised why they were more than happy to charge us with attempted stealing. They were aware that we had attempted to start the car. Because none of us owned up to our real intentions that night, the best they could have charged us with would've been attempted unauthorised use of a motor vehicle. Compared with the attempted stealing, it's nothing, really. Should've shut my mouth and got a lawyer, but, like I said, I didn't know any better. It then took some convincing that there was no firearm involved.

All three boys were charged with attempted stealing, with Abbott facing the additional charge of threatening words over the screwdriver. Back to Hilston for sure, he thought. But, when he faced Perth Children's Court on 2 August 1978, he was fined $10 on each charge.

As Brenden says, 'One of the few occasions I didn't get locked up when I fronted the Children's Court.'

With no job, Brenden moved back in with his mother and John Salmon, in Dudley Street. The unpleasantness at Belmont police station and the attempted car theft demonstrated yet again to his mother that he was a trouble magnet. It was only a matter of time before he attracted more – and his young brother Glenn idolised Brenden, regularly getting caught up in his schemes. Thelma was at her wits end. 'You boys'll be the death of me,' she'd scold them.

John Salmon arrived home on a break from a contract installing drains, roofs and steel frames up in the state's north. After sizing up the situation, he decided the cure for Brenden's criminal malaise was hard work. He talked to his business partner, Mal, and they agreed to ask Brenden to join their team as a labourer and return with them to Tom Price, of all places.

John Salmon:

I talked to my partner at the time and said, 'We'll get him away from the city, make a quid, get him away from trouble.' I'd been working up there 20-odd years, so, for me, it wasn't hard yakka. There were probably easier options for Brenden at the time, but he stuck it. I'll give him that.

Abbott went with them, happy to get away from the city. He liked John and still felt as though he owed him over the stolen bikes. John, Mal and Abbott were among 1,400 men living in a construction camp some distance from the town, where John says a 'good bar and good tucker' kept them happy. On his visits into town, Abbott saw many of the same faces from when he had last lived there, just over three years previously; some even addressed him as Brenden Springall, the surname he'd taken temporarily from his mother's former partner Ted. Abbott impressed John and Mal with his willingness to work. The steady exercise built a ferocious appetite, and the generous mess hall diet took effect: 'I was still growing at that time, and, with the heavy lifting of the steel frames all day and eating as much food as I wanted, I filled out and was in good shape.'

Abbott liked the work-hard, play-hard philosophy in the camp and the money was good. He met a girl in town – Linda – and on weekends he went into town and took her to the drive-in. Some nights, she'd slip into the construction camp with him. John and Mal loved it. They gave the young bloke endless rubbishing about his escapades and were full of bedroom tips.

When the contract ended after several months, they returned to Perth for a break. John didn't want to go back to Tom Price, so Abbott hooked up with Mal and they returned to work six-day weeks. After a few months, they completed the contract and went back to Perth, where Abbott moved in with his younger sister, Diane, at a duplex in Oats Street, Kewdale. He kept working with Mal for a couple of months, erecting patios. But, when Abbott asked for more money, they parted company.

The months of physical labour put money in the 16-year-old's pockets and meat on his bones. Linda from Tom Price had been good for his education but she was soon to be a distant memory.

It was Allison who caught Brenden's eye first, down at the Belmont pool. But it wasn't long before her 15-year-old friend, Jackie, distracted him with her oceans of blonde hair, the sweetest of shy smiles and sensational set of legs. Jackie would recall later:

> *I'd never met this guy in my life. I'd heard about this safe thing. In the school newsletter, they called him a cocky little so-and-so. He walked up to me, picked me up off the side of the pool and threw me in the water. I thought, Who the hell do you think you are? I was gonna floor him. My sister was with me and she went up and kicked him up the backside and he fell in the pool. And that's when I got to know him.*

About a week later, Brenden charmed her again. His endless innuendos, delivered with that sly hungry grin, were irresistible. 'She came home with me and eventually spent the night. She had never spent a night away from home without her mother's permission before. Her mother was none the wiser to where her daughter was this night and, understandably, was doing backflips over it.'

Next morning, Jackie's mother had a hot lead. Brenden answered the phone to angry demands about her daughter's whereabouts, and threats of police involvement. Brenden feigned ignorance, but sent Jackie home, walking her most of the way. 'Be fucked if I was taking her to the front door, though.'

Jackie:

> 'My mother wouldn't let me have anything to do with Brenden after that. I assumed that Brenden had 'used me up'. I was pretty ashamed of myself and everything that had happened. Put it down to: "You'll know better next time a man tries to sweet-talk you."'

Abbott:

> *Jackie gave me my marching orders not more than a few days after that, but it wouldn't be the last I'd see of her ... from then on, we had an interesting sort of relationship.*

Unemployed and at a dangerous loose end again, Abbott suggested to Peter Lievense that they go back to Tom Price, spurred by his memories of good women and good money. Hopefully, he could hook up with Linda. It all went to plan. Abbott picked up work with an electrical company, working on the wiring at a new crushing plant. Abbott doesn't explain how he managed to talk his way into a job that required years of training and a licence. But it clearly indicated his mind operated at a level significantly higher than that of the average Year-10 high-school drop-out with a criminal record. His sister, Janet, later told police,

> *I know Brenden to be quite intelligent. He was gifted in a way that if he put his mind to something, he could achieve it. I recall that he loved fast cars. He spent a lot of time working on cars. I recall that he built and designed a motor for a car. He was very mechanically minded ...*
>
> *Brenden was also excellent with electrical items. He often repaired radios and televisions. I recall seeing him with a few broken radios and pulling them apart and making a radio that worked correctly. He did this without any instructions or training. He also played around with taking televisions apart and rewiring them.*

Abbott's new job came with one other hitch: he had no steel-capped boots, a safety requirement on all mine sites. The company didn't supply them and Abbott couldn't afford them. He was living in the construction camp he'd stayed at with John and Mal and considered swiping a pair there. But the risk of getting stomped by a workmate who saw him in his boots wasn't worth it. The night before he started work, he and Lievense went for a wander through Tom Price, managing to find a pair the right size on a front porch. The foreman smirked at Abbott when he arrived the next day. 'I see you managed to get yourself some boots,' he said.

But, good job or not, Brenden Abbott didn't belong in Tom Price. He and Peter started knocking around with some other teenagers in town. One joyride later and Abbott's criminal record grew longer – he was convicted of stealing in January 1979. The others with him, including Peter, got bail because they were aged over 18. But there was a sting in the tail for Abbott.

> *Being only 16 at the time and having no guardians in Tom Price, I was kept in the lock-up. Come court day, I pleaded guilty and,*

*as was the case three to four years ago in the same fucking town,
I was made a ward of the state, but this time until the age of 18.
The others copped a fine and were told to fuck off out of town.*

A child-welfare officer escorted him on a flight to Perth. The deja vu
only made him angrier. His journey ended at Longmore Training
Centre, in inner suburban Perth, the place West Australian parents
threaten to send their kids when they misbehave.

*Longmore was a real fucking shit-hole. Nothing like the cottages
of the past, even Hilston was a luxury compared to this place. It
was a prison and I can't say I enjoyed the place for a moment.
At first, if the opportunity arose, I would've jumped the walls
without a doubt.*

After a month at Longmore, Abbott moved to a work-release centre
in North Perth. It was a lot more relaxed and the boys could sneak
off for a bit of fun without dramas.

Not long after arriving, Abbott found work at a panel beaters in
Belmont near where John and Thelma lived in St Kilda Road,
Kewdale. The authorities were satisfied and he was released into
Thelma's custody again. But he threw in the job a few months later
because 'the money was shit' and he could see no future in it.

There are two offences on Abbott's criminal record from mid-1979 –
disorderly conduct and unlawful possession – which he cannot explain.

But an incident not long after his 17th birthday – involving one of
his mate's girlfriends, Lisa – perfectly fits the offence descriptions.
One afternoon, on a couch in her mother's lounge, the busy couple
failed to notice Lisa's prison-officer mother standing agape in the
front doorway. She let loose with a string of profanities as the
mortified teenager scrambled for his pants and bolted out the door.
When he got home, still red with embarrassment, John Salmon asked,
'What's wrong with you?'

When Abbott confided the truth, his stepfather roared with laughter.

*I still had contact with that girl for many years after. It took
years before I faced her mother again. When I did, I had the exits
mapped out in my head. I don't recall seeing the couch again. I
guess watching TV on it was never the same for her.*

Chapter Four

1979–1982

Women and cars were two great passions of youth that Brenden Abbott never really left behind. He was a horny teenager with firm ideas on what he wanted in a woman: blonde hair and a big chest. He liked chasing fast cars, too. In mid-1979, aged 17, Abbott somehow convinced the state of Western Australia that he was a competent, responsible person who could be trusted behind the wheel of a motor vehicle. The state erred. Other than his blonde fantasies, Brenden Abbott was consumed by one simple overwhelming desire – to travel the quarter-mile in the shortest possible time in the fastest possible car. Brenden says, 'This obsession led me to obtaining many traffic offences and criminal convictions, which eventually got me time in jail. What a waste.'

He briefly held a job as a delivery driver for Major Motors, managing to write off a company vehicle. Then, through Coops, he got a job south of Perth at Pinjarra, building mudlakes for waste water at the Alcoa plant, and he bought an LC Torana for $300 from a workmate, which was 'a piece of shit'. Abbott and Coops lived with Coops's mum, Val, in Armadale, and they drove to work together. Coops says,

When we were working at Pinjarra mudlakes, that's when Brenden really got interested in his Torana. We worked there for about four to six months. He was always getting something done

to it. I guess he was obsessed. Why else would you work so hard? That was his dream. See, Rab had an XU-1. Mine was just a GTR.

Rabbit:

Nah, mine was an LJ. All you guys had LCs. His car went through a few versions. He kept it for a long time. He [later] dropped a 253 in it. He had problems getting the gearbox in, it was a turbo 350. It was a beautiful car. To get it licensed like that, he had to whack a tow bar on the back and tell them he was dragging a boat around.

The Torana became the centre of Abbott's universe. It was not an automatic choice for a 1970s Holden muscle car fanatic, a breed usually obsessed with Monaros. Lack of money forced him to settle for the smaller car, but he grew to love the manoeuvrability of the smaller, less famous Holden. And its power-to-weight ratio was insane – especially once he had finished working on it.

Years later, a mechanic who examined the Torana said whoever had worked on it had no formal mechanical training – but clearly knew exactly what they were doing.

Abbott says that hanging around with his cousin Wayne and Coops contributed to his passion for all things mechanical. His reputation grew among friends, and eventually he started making a dollar out of it.

I charged far less than any mechanic and they knew I'd do a good job – I took pride in my work. With this ability, making the Torana into the type of car I wanted I could do mostly myself, with the help of a few dollars. My main goal was to get it to go as quickly as possible down the quarter-mile. I'd blown up numerous engines, gearboxes and differentials in my quest for speed. I was a complete maniac on the road and at times was lucky not to kill myself, or others. Often, I'd take part in illegal drag racing on the streets; I wasn't the only maniac with the same obsession.

Rabbit:

We were lined up in the city one night in Murray Street [Perth] at the lights. Brenden sees a copper up the road. The guy next to us is revving his car and giving Brenden the shits. So Brenden's

revving his car, the light turns green and this guy just dumps it.
Brenden casually drives off in first and the cops bust this guy.
Brenden's done a couple more laps to get the satisfaction out of it.

By mid-1980, Abbott was unemployed and back on the dole. His job
at Pinjarra had come to an end months earlier when the contractors
completed the mudlakes. Abbott and his mates would cruise the
streets in pursuit of gleaming silver wheels, grilles, lights, panels,
motors – anything that could be bolted down and everything that
wasn't. And then police caught them in the act again.

I was pinched with three others over the stealing and stripping of
some poor bastard's pride and joy and received two years probation
and 240 hours community service order. The community service
was a killer, working for nothing really hit a nerve. But I completed
it. Turned out to be a waste of time in more ways than one.

Abbott turned up for the community work with one of his mates. The
man in charge asked him what skills he had. 'I'm a house painter,' the
mate replied.

Stripping back the paint on an old weatherboard house, Abbott
resolved to go it alone next time.

A far more appealing task was working for the YMCA setting up a
fun run on Rottnest Island, a holiday destination for generations of
Perth people. He soon cut out the required hours, but fulfilling his
probation conditions proved more difficult.

Abbott was walking down Murray Street in Perth city when she
walked straight past. He turned and followed, acting on instinct that
he knew her. She was walking quickly and suddenly changed
direction, into the famed Perth restaurant Miss Maud's and darted
behind the counter. Abbott sat at a table and she came and took his
order, and then he finally placed her: it was Jackie. She didn't pick
him straight away. Moments later, his hazel eyes, easy smile and
messy mop of hair brought the guilty memory flooding back:

I was pouring someone a coffee when I felt this tap on the
shoulder. I turned around to see Brenden standing there. Talk
about shocked, nervous and excited all in one hit. I was really
pleased to see him, even though I really didn't know him that well.

'How about a drink after work?' he asked, casual as can be.

'Sure,' she said.

Jackie had moved out of home and into a flat in McMaster Street, Victoria Park. Mum wouldn't be waiting up this time. Abbott liked the sound of that. He bought her a snowball cocktail at a city tavern, where she told him she was sharing her flat with a boyfriend. Abbott was undeterred. In a picture of them taken at the flat soon after they met up again, the chemistry is clear. Perched on Abbott's lap, Jackie is flushed with excitement.

> *I continued to try to woo her from then on. Whenever I could, I'd call into her work to do my stuff and it soon paid off. It was obvious from the beginning that she wasn't really happy with her current relationship; before long, he was out the door. From then on, I was on and off with Jackie for many years to come. Jackie has always been the special one in regards to the women I've had relationships with. Of all the women in my life, I haven't been able to love another woman as much as I did Jackie. On the other hand, she has also caused me the most grief. It must be chemistry; I can't explain any other reason for it. I had numerous girlfriends before Jackie and after, but never has there been that connection as I seemed to have with her.*

Jackie:

> *I remember we talked and laughed a lot. He's the sort who will make sexual innuendos during conversation. He offered me a lift home and then he knew my address. Then, of course, things went wrong because the other guy turned up, and I thought, What am I doing?*

Abbott became a regular at the McMaster Street flat and their relationship blossomed. One morning, he went to the shop for some smokes and came back to find Jackie sitting in the lounge room with her mother, whose lips were thinner than a razor. 'Who's this?' she asked Jackie.

> *Soon as Jackie mentioned my name, well, didn't her mother play up? Ordered me out of the place. She told me that, while she was there with her daughter, she didn't want me there. I immediately*

*left, telling Jackie that I'd come back later. I didn't say a word to
her mother. I figured the old girl was still a little bitter about
what took place a few years earlier.*

In August 1980, Abbott was belting around the suburbs in the
Torana, months before he could afford to begin serious work on it. In
fact, on this particular night, he couldn't even afford $5 petrol money
for a city cruise. Instead, he and another mate, Ray S, dropped by the
home of a mutual friend, Craig W, in northeast suburban Bassendean.

Abbott says one of them told him they could get a few gallons from
one of the cars in the backyard that was being worked on. But it
turned out that he got it from a car in someone else's front yard.
When the petrol thief went back another time to steal more, and was
caught by the owner, Abbott ended up being charged with receiving
because some of the fuel went into his car. Abbott says he approached
Ray before they went into court and asked him to tell the truth about
the night's events. Ray went into court and told the magistrate that
Abbott wasn't aware the petrol put into his car had been stolen.
Abbott was duly found not guilty and emerged triumphant from the
court. In his view, he had finally beaten the bastards.

*Some months later, I was pinched for the stealing and stripping
of another motor vehicle. A few mates from the earlier incident
were pinched over it, too.*

*The second car theft I was pinched for was to be dealt with in
the District Court, due to the vehicle's value. I prolonged the
sentencing date as long as I possibly could, as did Hood.*

Because Abbott was now 18, he knew that he would probably go to
jail. With this in mind, and on the advice of his lawyer, he returned to
full-time employment. When a detective approached him at his new
work site – at Wagerup, a short distance further south from Pinjarra
– in April 1981, he assumed it must be something to do with his
driving or his car. But Detective Brian Brennan instead took him to
nearby Waroona police station, where he told him that Ray S and
Craig W, both involved in the petrol-stealing case, were facing charges
of conspiracy to pervert the course of justice. And now, so was
Abbott, based on threats he was supposed to have made against Ray S:

I don't know what it was with Detective Brennan, but he had it in for me. At the time, I was on remand for the stealing of the car and that matter was brought up while at the cop shop. I was filthy on the fact that they could've got me somewhere else other than at work. I told him that things were going well for me on this job and I was hoping to move on to other machinery. With the other matter before the court, I was hoping to show the judge that I was getting somewhere with my life. Now that they've come to work to pinch me, it could fuck it all up. Guess what? It did. I was soon fired from that job.

Abbott's third legal problem also related to his car. He'd taken it to the Carlisle Transport Inspection Centre, after being given a yellow sticker by a traffic cop. Abbott can't remember what the specific defect was, but considered it unjustified. He copped a 'right prick' for the inspection, who not only failed it on the original fault, but added more to the list. Enraged, Abbott left a strip of rubber on the inspection centre's driveway on his way out.

He says, 'Yeah, all right, I know I'm a dickhead.'

He drove home and was sitting out the front of the house with another mate, 'Che', when the police car pulled up ten minutes later. When the cop asked who was responsible for the incident at the inspection centre, Che, who often lived up to his revolutionary nickname, put his hand up for it. Abbott told him that, when it came time for him to face court later in the year, he would appear as a witness to sort it out.

Abbott had met him through his cousin Wayne, who worked with him in the mining town of Goldsworthy, near Port Hedland in Western Australia.

Che became a good friend and started to mix in the same circle of friends and he was well liked. He was very sharp minded and had an odd but funny sense of humour. He was a member of a socialist party and often preached politics. At that age, that type of chatter went in one ear and out the other. Later down the track, I had a falling out with him, mainly due to my ignorance and bigotry. Che and I remain friends. I class him as one of the few very loyal ones. He has helped me out in situations that very few would.

Brenden Abbott's criminal record around this time read like this: 23 July 1980, resist police, stealing, two years probation, 240 hours community service; 5 November 1980, speeding conviction, licence suspended; 11 December 1980, driving while suspended, licence suspended; 22 December 1980, dangerous driving, licence disqualified; and 9 January 1981, speeding, licence disqualified.

He found himself in an increasingly familiar position: unemployed, in trouble with the law, and facing the prospect of being locked up for a long time. Twice, he'd gone north in search of better times. Now his attention turned east and somewhere even more remote – the Madura Roadhouse on the Nullarbor in Western Australia, where Jackie worked in the dining room and reception, and Debbie, Coops's girlfriend, worked behind the bar. Rabbit and Abbott decided to head out in the Torana in search of adventure.

Jackie:

We were all looking for a change and some fun. The bonus was we made some money as well. We had a great time out there, went down some of the tracks to the ocean, up to Border Village for discos. They were paying good money to work out there in '81–82. We got to know a lot of the truckies that stopped to have a beer, so there was always someone to have a yak with.

Abbott arrived with the simple ambition of 'pumping petrol and pumping Jackie', before facing the music in a few months' time. But repairing vehicles became a lucrative sideline. People stuck on the Nullarbor couldn't call a 24-hour breakdown service then, so their options were limited and their desperation genuine. The roadhouse manager saw this kid doing well and he wanted a piece of the action, using his knack of sizing up travellers and deciding who could afford big dollars and who couldn't. Abbott's conscience – clearly ruled by an unusual set of morals – was pricked by this, but it didn't stop him raking in the dollars.

Rabbit:

There was a truck that broke down, and its wiring had been burned out. Brenden took a look at it and said, 'I can fix it.' And he sent the bill to the trucking company. It needed an auto electrician, but he just gets in there and tries everything until he gets it right. He won't give up. He got a nice big fat cheque for that.

They met many truck drivers going backwards and forwards across the Nullarbor, and one day asked one to bring back a 'good smoke' from Queensland.

Rabbit:

> *I don't know what this stuff was, but it was dynamite. We were on the midnight-to-dawn shift and Brenden's rolled up a joint and said, 'We'll smoke this and then have a sleep.' We smoked one and nothing happened so we smoked another one. Then the first one hit and we're crawling around on the floor, laughing our heads off. Then a Greyhound bus pulls up for some diesel. I remember this bloke knocking on the door and we've told him, 'You'll have to do it yourself.' Brenden took off around the back and hid and I had to do it. We were so paranoid we were going to get done. We were supposed to fill in the account card, and neither of us could utter a word. We were annihilated.*

Abbott made a new mate at Madura. Paul was an Aboriginal youth employed to work at the roadhouse. He was a Norseman boy, used to living on the western edge of nowhere. Now he was right in the middle, on a big adventure.

Rabbit:

> *Brenden really liked him. He figured out how to make matchbox bombs. They didn't hurt anyone but they made a hell of a bang. One day he's made about half a dozen of these things and thrown them in Paul's door. He was asleep. They scared him, but he's come out laughing. He's seen the funny side straight away. I think Brenden liked that.*

When it came time to go back to Perth, Paul tagged along, after Abbott promised to show him around the city. But a reception committee stopped them when they arrived in Norseman.

Rabbit says,

> *I remember when we were coming back to Perth – I don't remember what happened to the Torana – Brenden, myself and Paul came back in a truck. Paul's dad had done some checking up on Brenden. When we came through Norseman, they had a roadblock set up to grab Paul, because his dad didn't want him going to the city with Brenden. I think that had a bad effect on*

Brenden. I don't think Brenden would have got him into any trouble. He just wanted to show Paul the city, because he'd never been there.

The first legal matter Abbott faced on his return to Perth was Che's dangerous driving charge. But Abbott says 'vehicle problems' caused him to be half an hour late for court.

He [Che] was found guilty and lost his licence over it. He was totally innocent and wasn't the one behind the wheel, it was me. It was a complete act of stupidity on my behalf. The maggot that inspected the car gave evidence and even pointed Che out as being the driver.

Che took it on the chin. He was that kind of bloke. Jackie also returned to Perth shortly after and found herself in the office of Ross Lonnie, Abbott's lawyer. He explained the situation to her. They didn't stuff around in adult court. There was every chance that a guilty verdict for car theft in the District Court would mean jail.

Jackie says, 'He wanted me to go as a character witness for Brenden. He said it would look good that Brenden had found a sensible young lady, as he called me.'

Jackie developed into what she herself describes as 'a kleptomaniac', and Abbott often worried that she would get herself – or him – into trouble. As it turned out, he was already in plenty of trouble on his own account.

On 7 August 1981, Brenden Abbott and Hood, who was also Diane Abbott's boyfriend, faced the Perth District Court and pleaded guilty to charges of stealing over the car theft. The 18-month jail term knocked Abbott for six.

That was a shock to the system, I must say. Didn't expect it at all. At the most, I thought three months. Next shock we got was when we were told we were heading for the notorious Fremantle Prison. To say we were both scared would've been an understatement. I was shitting myself, as was Hood.

Jackie says, 'It shook him and I know he was scared, but he's kinda tough on the inside. So he did his time well, but hard. He often shared this during the visits at Freo.'

Abbott's first memory of Fremantle and its stark limestone surroundings is clear:

> *On arrival at the prison, we were led into the reception area, strip-searched and given prison greens to wear and then led to the cell-block area in single file with the others who were on the bus with us. At the age of 19, it frightened the life out of me. At that time, I was certain I wouldn't do wrong again. If my visit to Fremantle was a short, sharp shock for a few months and then to a farm, I'm sure I wouldn't have fucked up again. But, after months in there, being accepted by most and getting accustomed to the place, the fear subsided.*

But on day one in Main Division (the collective name for Three Division and Four Division), Brenden and Hood faced the unknown and were not happy about it.

> *On entering, we were told to stand on a line that was painted on the concrete floor and then individually were called into the senior prison officer's office. I recall while standing there, thinking how similar the place looked to jails I'd seen in the movies. The suicide net [strung from railing to railing in the middle of the long multi-storey building] was a concern. Hood and I were given a cell to share, which was a relief. At least I knew I didn't have the worry of someone trying to fuck me on my first night in jail. After being shown our cell, we were told to head into the yard. Main Division held about 130 inmates and, when we walked out in the yard, about that many pairs of eyes were on us. Newcomers were easy to spot and it wasn't what I'd call a comfortable feeling. We both sat down to try to take it all in. I was thinking, How the fuck did I get myself in this situation? It'd be a fair comment to say Hood was feeling the same way. As all caged animals do, they pace up and down. Humans are no exception. So as the saying goes, when in Rome ... Hood and I started to pace.*
> *Within ten minutes of being in the yard, I was approached by a bloke who asked if I was Brenden Abbott. At first, I thought drama was coming. But then he identified himself as: 'Ian S, I was at Darlington Cottage with you.' Well, that came as a relief, as did the fact that I knew someone there. Ian had been in Freo*

for some time for armed robbery and helped Hood and me in learning the ropes. He also helped get me a job in the prison tailor shop.

An ally and a good job. It was a positive start in the tiny, twisted world of Fremantle Prison. Just outside its massive walls lay the 20th century. Inside was a harsh, unforgiving convict culture, more consistent with a hundred years earlier. 'Fremantle was a real shit-hole. Some of the screws were right pricks and some would scream at you as if they were some fucking drill sergeant. It amazes me that some of them were never sorted out outside the prison.'

With no running water, toilet facilities consisted of a 15-litre paint tin, emptied daily. Water came in plastic bottles; and all meals were eaten in cells, sometimes with a dinner companion.

I remember one night waking up because of a cockroach having a feed from the corner of my mouth. Old Papillon would've been rapt. He'd never go hungry. [In the 1973 prison escape film Papillon, based on a true story, Steve McQueen eats insects to survive.] ... Days after my arrival, I scored a job in the tailor shop, thanks to the help of Ian. Later, I worked in the cook house. At first, I thought it was a bad choice, especially when my first job was washing pots. But I soon moved on to being a cook. The days flew by and eating well came with the territory.

And yet he still couldn't help himself. Pushing a food trolley down to Main Division, a guard stopped Abbott for a random search and found a block of cheese. Abbott cursed himself. He lost the job and was marched to solitary for seven days.

My first experience of solitary (chokey, it was called) came as a shock. Being a smoker at the time didn't help. Solitary confinement was done in an area of the jail called New Division. In the cell, you had a plastic shit bucket, a plastic water bottle and a Bible and, worst of all, no smokes. The sudden withdrawal from nicotine was the killer and had you spinning like a top for the first few days.

A bed pack made up of a thin foam mattress, two sheets, three blankets and pyjamas was handed to solitary inmates at dinner time

(4.30pm). At breakfast at 7am, the pack was exchanged for prison greens, flip flops and food.

After breakfast, inmates cleaned their shit buckets and then showered under the eye of two prison officers. They remained in their cells for the rest of the day, aside from an hour of exercise, but, if they stopped walking, the session ended abruptly. Abbott reckons some guards made an elaborate routine of enjoying their cigarettes in front of him, just to rub it in. The time alone turned his mind inwards.

After long stretches of isolation, you tend to question your state of mind, due to certain thoughts. I've had some terrible ones, usually based on revenge. Due solely to the boredom, I started to read some passages from the Bible, but found that as boring as doing chokey itself.

Jackie:

Broke my heart having to see him caged up and not be able to help him. As I was already living at Thelma's, I stayed on along with Diane, and we waited for [Brenden and Hood] to do their time. We wrote endless letters.

The girls spread a blanket out on Thelma's front lawn and listened to music on a cassette player while writing to their men. Diane was pregnant with her first child, and Jackie again had a job at Miss Maud's.

Abbott's fears in Fremantle – where he was shoulder to shoulder with the state's most dangerous criminals – gradually faded as he found his place in the system. But he grew bitter. 'Those first few months in Freo were a hard time for me. I believe if I was released after a couple of months, the fear of returning would've been enough to keep my nose clean. I missed not being with Jackie more than anything; she was forever on my mind. She wrote just about every day and visited each week. It was obvious she was doing it as hard as I was.'

Hood got a transfer to a prison farm after a few months. But the conspiracy charge hung over Abbott's head from the petrol stealing matter. He stayed in Fremantle.

People wonder why I am a bitter person. I was dirty on the world over it and even dirtier when convicted some months later

[31 March 1982] when I received a three-year sentence with a one-year minimum. During this time, a prison complex was built at Canning Vale. I was on one of the first buses out there. The place was a luxury compared to Fremantle, but, regardless of the improvements, I was still in jail doing extra time for something I was innocent of. By now, the fear of jail, especially that of doing it in Fremantle, had disappeared. I had spent an extra four to five months in jail when my appeal against the conviction for the conspiracy was heard. The conviction was quashed. Finally, I was deemed innocent, as I'd always stated.

Judges Wickham, Wallace and Kennedy allowed Abbott's appeal on 5 August 1982, on the grounds that the trial judge erred on several issues. The way the remission system worked, he needed to spend only a month at most in a work-release centre or minimum-security facility, and then walk away. But Abbott wanted out instantly. He didn't care that it meant reporting to a parole officer for six months. After a special sitting, the parole board approved Abbott's release and ordered him to live with his sister Janet at Brownlie Towers in Bentley, a State Housing Commission building destined for notoriety. Compared with Fremantle, it seemed like a five-star hotel.

Brenden says, 'Jackie was waiting for me at the front gate. And, as she drove me away, I gave the place the finger, sure I'd seen the last of it.'

Chapter Five

1982–1986

In spite of his intelligence, at 20 years old Brenden Abbott possessed few brains. Jail had not turned him away from crime but towards it. The odds of him returning to Fremantle Prison within a couple of years were high. He went on the dole and, he says, picked up some casual work with panel beaters and working on cars.

His mate Rabbit remembers it this way: 'The day he got out of jail, he was jumping out of his skin. We said, 'Sit down mate, have a smoke.' But he couldn't stay in one place. He wanted to go to Belmont Forum, into town, somewhere where there were people.'

Jackie says of those first weeks that he 'was just out scheming with his mates'. Abbott himself reckons the only trouble he got up to after his release involved knocking off petrol from some service stations at night, with help from Hood.

One place in particular didn't have any padlocks on the actual pumps and just on the other side of the door into the premises, on the wall, were the switches for the pumps. We were able to slip a piece of wire through the gap of the door and its frame to turn on the switches, fill up the car or cars and then switch the pumps off again. Finally, the owner worked out why things weren't balancing out and set it up so that you could no longer get access to the switches.

But Abbott's days as a petty criminal were almost over. He wanted quick, easy dollars in his pocket, having forgotten Fremantle Prison all too soon. He returned to Jackie and to the same social circle, including Jackie's brother, Terry, and Hood. Terry tried to impress his sister's boyfriend, telling him how much cash he used to carry on the night run for Miss Maud's. He thought they still carried out the same procedure – and adhered to strict instructions not to challenge armed robbers. This convinced Abbott and they began watching the area at night, waiting for the pair of restaurant employees to appear on the cash run.

> *And sure enough, it was as Terry said. A bloke and a chick of about 18 to 25 did the run and followed the exact route each time. We went to do it one night, had it all planned and at the last moment we called it off due to a loss of nerve. A few nights later, the temptation of the quick dollar got the better of us and we decided: 'Fuck it, we'll do it.'*

It was a turning point. Abbott, young knockabout revhead and petty thief from the suburbs, was about to cross a line and become a violent criminal, prepared to put people at physical risk for the sake of cash. But he didn't see this boundary as he crossed it – parking his Torana at the edge of the Perth Supreme Court Gardens and hurrying towards the city.

> *There were four of us involved and all were to get an even cut of the booty.*
> *The four were Hood, Allan W, Terry and myself. Hood and myself hung around the corner of Hay Street and Barrack Street and waited until the pair carrying the bag were near the bank. I realised I'd seen the bloke with the bag somewhere before. As Hood and I sprinted past them, Hood grabbed the moneybag as I shouldered the bloke carrying it. We kept that pace up while heading towards the Supreme Court Gardens and, you wouldn't believe it, the bloke we snatched the bag from was giving chase. He was right on my heels when we got to St Georges Terrace. Luckily, the traffic flow on St Georges Terrace was stopped at a red light. It was here the chap chasing us gave it up, but did so because he spotted a cop car at the lights and headed to them. A car next to the cops had two brothers in it and, as the bloke was*

giving the cops the mail on him being robbed, these two heard it and promoted themselves as a couple of deputies.

Meanwhile, Hood and I were just about through the Gardens when he had to stop. He wasn't too fit. I was telling him, 'Come on, we can't stop now, we've got to get back to the car.'

He gave me the bag and said, 'You go, I'll be right behind you.'

I got to the car and started it up and waited for what seemed like minutes for Hood. I couldn't wait any longer and then got out of the area. In that time, the two brothers who were next to the cops had driven down St Georges Terrace, heading east, and turned right at the first street. As they did, they've spotted our car turning right from the street behind the Gardens. Just as I got on to Riverside Drive heading east, the two brothers came alongside and told me to pull over. They continued to follow before they obviously made their way to police headquarters, which we had just passed. Hood and Allan, who I didn't recall seeing when we made our way into the Gardens, eventually got away from the area and managed to sit back and watch the area get swamped with cops.

Meanwhile, I knew we had problems. The car we were in was mine and the registration plates just happened to be a dead giveaway as to who owned the vehicle. How fucking stupid. That surely deserves the goose of the century award. I had to get rid of the cash. Other than that, they've got nothing on me, or so I thought. My second mistake was taking Terry with me to hide it. It didn't take long for the cops to get a car to my mother's place, where I was staying. Jackie was staying there on this night. Heading home, Terry and I were rehearsing our story. No sooner had I pulled up at home than a detectives' car has got there. They both had their guns drawn. Jackie came out to the front porch to see what was going on, only to see Terry and me being arrested.

At CIB headquarters, we were put into separate rooms and the interrogation commenced. This, I'd been through before, but, for Terry, it was a new experience. I was sticking to the story, because I knew the consequences of a conviction on this one. Surprisingly, they didn't interrogate me long and I was left in a room alone for what seemed like hours.

When they did return, they knew the story, had the money and then took a sample of the dirt from under my fingernails. I thought I was a shot duck. I still hadn't learned by then that you should never make a confession or sign the dotted line. I had this false belief that, by confessing, it goes better for you on sentencing. Yeah, fucking sure it does.

We all fronted court the next day and it was remanded to another date. Bail was set, but I couldn't get surety and was sent to Canning Vale remand centre. It came as a shock one evening when I was told I was being bailed. I had no idea Jackie was going to do it. I was under the impression that, without the cash or assets, there was no chance of being able to bail me.

By chance, Abbott knew the Miss Maud's employee who he shouldered out of the way to steal the cash – they had served time together in Fremantle. This fact initially put that unfortunate individual in the picture as well, but, after a lot of explaining to suspicious police, the reformed character was eventually cleared of involvement in the $12,500 robbery.

Abbott knew serious jail time loomed and bail was only a brief reprieve. Jackie lived in a Canning Highway unit in Como, not far from the legendary Raffles Hotel – a live-rock venue, among other claims to fame including its ownership by a colourful Sydney identity. Abbott, now hanging around with Coops and brother Glenn again, moved back in with her. His mood turned dark.

Jackie:

They let him out as long as he stayed with me and reported in for his parole. And that's around the time of that big party. The next day he was going back to court, and he knew he was going back inside for at least three years. He was really angry the night before and he got really ... not drunk, but he had a few beers and he got really aggro with me when he got home. I said, 'What are we supposed to do? All this pressure, you're always going to jail. Am I supposed to sit back and wear it all the time and just wait?' He got really angry and punched my arm and he dislocated my bloody shoulder. Had to rush me to the hospital. It was a one-off, but he knows I'll never forget it.

Abbott:

Prior to sentencing day on the bag snatch, I contemplated doing a runner and was running hot to make a dollar. I thought, Fuck it. I was going away, anyway. If I could make a decent quid, I'd cover the surety Jackie put up and head out of the state. Doing armed robberies was out of the question back then. I considered that type of crime far too heavy and serious for me. Only the bad bastards did that sort of shit was [my] thoughts on that.

As time drew near to the sentence date, the stress was starting to take its toll on both Jackie and myself. We had some heated moments as it drew near to that date. One night, I went out to make a dollar on my own and I should've been back in a number of hours with the goods. Things didn't go to plan and, after hours of hanging around to pull it off, I gave it a miss. Jackie really gave me the third degree when I got home with the news that I didn't do what I intended. She went on and on about it and made accusations that I was seeing other women. No matter what I said, she went on about it and made mention of an ex-girlfriend and eventually I lost the plot. I ended up punching her as hard as I could in the shoulder. It was the first time I'd ever resorted to actual physical violence on Jackie, or any girlfriend, and, yes, I felt like a cunt for it. I ended up taking her to hospital because her shoulder didn't look right. On examination, it was slightly dislocated and was put right without much ado, as Jackie claims.

The ugly incident stopped Abbott in his tracks. He had never thought of himself as the type to knock women around. It helped him reach a decision about the coming day in court. Abbott says, 'Come court day, a few days prior to my 21st [8 May 1983], I decided to face the music and entered a plea of guilty, believing I would've been sentenced.'

Jackie remembered his determination to be prepared for Fremantle this time around:

The night [before court] he went over the road and nicked someone's TV out of the sports shop to take in with him. He said, 'I won't be long.'

'Where you going?'

'Don't worry, I'll be back in five minutes.' He came back with this TV. 'Where'd you get that from?'

'Just went over that surf shop over there. I saw it in there the other day. Thought I could use it in jail.' [He] took a tape recorder and a box of tapes as well.

Abbott:

> *Since the last time I'd been in Freo, all the cells now had power.*
> *I turned up to court with a colour TV and a portable stereo*
> *under each arm. The copper at the desk was stunned and said,*
> *'You can't come in here with that.'*
>
> *I said, 'What do you expect me to do with it, take it home?*
> *I've got to front court soon.'*
>
> *With a few grunts and moans, he took it from me and I was*
> *placed in the cells.*

He was sent to Canning Vale remand centre until sentencing on 24
June 1983, when Judge Hammond dryly noted of the bungled
robbery that: 'The whole enterprise came to nought in the course of
the very evening.' Abbott was seen by people who knew him, used his
own car as the getaway vehicle and took an even more inexperienced
accomplice with him to hide the money; he deserved a cream pie in
the face from Miss Maud herself for such a slapstick routine.

His lawyer, Ross Lonnie, took a deep breath and addressed the bench:

> *I do not for one minute think that you are going to be granting*
> *probation. What I am saying is that he obviously has a bad*
> *record; he has done something when he was on parole. But I am*
> *asking you to consider a minimum term ... There is good in*
> *Abbott and I would like him to have the opportunity of coming*
> *out as soon as possible.*

Judge Hammond disagreed, finding 'very little encouragement to be
gained' from Abbott's criminal record. He sentenced him to four
years' jail with a 22-month minimum. Abbott was furious, but
remained outwardly calm.

> *After sentencing, I was sent to Freo again. The sentence was a bit*
> *steep, I thought, as some armed robbers were getting sentences*
> *much the same.*
>
> *It'd be fair to say that, because it was some well-known,*
> *influential person whose takings were stolen, it had some input*
> *in the sentencing. Hood and Allan received the same sentence*
> *and Terry ended up with the least. For Terry, the jail sentence*
> *took its toll. He spent a large chunk of it at a farm. The stress of*

jail on him had most of his hair falling out in clumps. I made life hard for myself doing this stretch and ended up doing months of chokey for making a cunt of myself. Blaming everyone but me for my current predicament, as many young blokes tend to do. Some pay the price and end up digging deeper holes for themselves and some have ended up with a life sentence. The relationship with Jackie was a rollercoaster ride, but we kept in touch through that time and she did visit on occasion.

Months after arriving at Fremantle, Abbott moved to the medium-security prison Canning Vale. Stabbie was a couple of years younger than Abbott and had been one of the first inmates sent to the prison when it opened in June 1982. Stabbie loved cars and shared a lot of Abbott's interests, particularly a thirst for speed and thrills, and they struck up a friendship while working in the mechanic shop. Stabbie had robbed a coffee shop with a .22 rifle, shortly after becoming a father at the age of 17. The thin, blond handsome lad had originally been sent to Fremantle, but even prison guards insisted after two days that he go to Canning Vale, or be eaten alive in the yard.

Within weeks of arriving at Canning Vale, Abbott got 28 days in solitary for bashing a paedophile. After racking up internal breach after internal breach, his file was marked 'management problem'. Abbott says, 'Eventually, management had had enough of me. I was my own worst enemy. They sent me back to Freo.'

And straight to the 1A yard with other problem prisoners. Months later, Abbott finally started to calm down and earned a downgrade in his security rating to medium, resulting in a transfer to Bunbury Prison, in the state's southwest.

This complex was far more relaxing than the other jails I'd spent time at. I was employed in the mechanic shop and my mechanical and panel-beating abilities became known by the screws and the superintendent. I was always kept occupied working on cars. After some months, I put it to the instructor of the workshop about the possibility of getting my own car in to work on. He took it up with the superintendent and it was approved. The instructor, Mick Salmon (no relation to John), I got along with quite well and he was more than happy to pass on his knowledge and skills. I had my car [the LC Torana] in there for some time and, when it left, it was in good condition. Even gave it a change of colour.

Jackie remembers Abbott's time in the country prison for different reasons:

> *Brenden got to work on his Torana in the prison, and spray-painted it green. I remember one visit which Brenden will have a smile about. It was raining when I got there, so they put us in a small room with two chairs and a table, and closed the door, no guard or cameras, so Brenden thinks it's an opportunity to muck around a bit. Well, we got a bit heated, as you can imagine, when the bloody door opens and an officer walks in. The screw had a chuckle and left, leaving the door open. We had a laugh. It's all an adventure.*

A taste of Jackie switched a light on at the end of the tunnel. Three months before his sentence ended, Abbott's security rating changed to 'open' and he moved to the West Perth Work Release Centre.

> *I scored a job at the vegetable markets through a friend and worked three days a week. The money was good, but the hours took some getting used to. I'd be up at 3am and finished the day around 5pm. Those at the centre who were unemployed were allowed to go into the city CES to check job boards. Prior to getting employment, I made several visits to the CES. Jackie had picked me up not far from the work-release centre. She'd drive to the CES, where I had to get something signed that would verify I had been there. Then we'd shoot off to her place in South Perth where I'd do some shooting off in another form, then back to the centre again.*
>
> *On the last month of a sentence at the work-release centre, it was possible to get day leave on the weekends. The first few weekends, it started with one day's leave, then two days, then to the point where you could spend the whole weekend, including overnight. You had to submit a plan as to where you'd be, as well as the sponsor's particulars. The first opportunity to get leave, I decided to spend it with Jackie.*
>
> *She picked me up from the centre and we headed back to her place. For some unknown reason, she had the dirts on about something and started on at me over some bullshit and I decided to split the scene and head out for the day somewhere. I learned later in life that walking out when arguing with a woman isn't*

the best way to handle the situation. I've always preferred to leave the scene when they start carrying on.

I didn't see Jackie again that day and made my way back to the work-release centre by the deadline. The screw asked where I'd been. Naturally, I said, 'With Jackie.'

He informed me that they had received a phone call that I wasn't with my sponsor. He gave me the opportunity to contact Jackie to sort out the misunderstanding. I called Jackie and told her someone had called the screw at the work-release centre, saying that I wasn't with her today. She said she had made the call. I couldn't believe my fucking ears. And the next response I got from her had me seeing red. I asked her to deny that she had made the call and that I'd been with her for the day. She refused to do it. It wouldn't be the last time I'd feel the brunt of Jackie's vindictiveness from her moments of jealousy. For years, I've heard stories about blokes' wives or girlfriends playing a big part in them being arrested and doing time. I myself would experience that in years to come.

As a result of not being with my sponsor for the day, I lost all remaining leave privileges until my release. Next time I saw Jackie was about five weeks later when released. On my way to her place, I couldn't find a sports shop to buy a baseball bat. Instead, I ended up forgiving her, but could never forget. Not long after my release, she had gone to London for what was initially a holiday. My parole conditions restricted me in following. I wasn't able to cover the costs, anyway.

Jackie:

I had also decided to start planning a trip to London, much to Brenden's annoyance. I always kept in touch with him via mail. Missed him terribly, but I was determined to get on with my own life. Got a job as a security officer with Argus Shield security company, then trained as a store detective, which I became quite good at, so I was reluctant to return to Perth.

Abbott:

A week after my release, I quit the job at the markets to work for a construction company called John Holland. The Gloucester

Park trotting track in Perth was being rebuilt and Hollands had the contract. I started as a labourer then moved on to driving a roller, a huge square water tank sitting on rubber tyres. It was a boring job, almost ten hours a day driving around the track for weeks on end. The foreman must've got bored watching me going around the track all day, because one time he pulled me up and said, 'You know, you can go around in the other direction.'

The job paid well and helped me get back on my feet again, as well as wasting much of it on my car. I still owned the Torana and, with the money I was making, I dropped a V8 engine into it [the 253 admired by Rabbit]. That wasn't a cheap exercise and it was illegal.

After Jackie took off to England, I was seeing a number of women, as well as having the occasional visit to the brothels. I've often heard people refer to these places as houses of sin, but, for all the times I've been inside them, I never witnessed anything untoward. Back then, the precautions used in brothels weren't as they are today and it was probably through a visit I picked up the clap for the first time. The worst part about that was that I had to contact the women I'd been seeing around that time. Surprisingly, they were fine about it and their tests proved negative. Well, that's what they told me. It was a mild form of an STD and the course of penicillin sorted me out.

In a few months, the job was completed at the trotting track and I was given the opportunity to be transferred to a job in the northwest, where bridges on a Bicentennial road project were being built. We were housed at a construction camp not far from the work sites. The area was about 140 kilometres from the nearest town, Port Hedland. I drove up there and, after a week or so, I regretted it. I'd just got out of the nick and here I was in the middle of fucking nowhere, no nightlife, no women, and I was surrounded by blokes whose favourite pastime was to drink piss every day after work. No wonder I was depressed. It was like being in the nick again.

The one good thing about the work camp was the weekend. One of the blokes at the site, nicknamed Flea, asked Abbott to drive him in to Port Hedland. He knew the bar manager at the Walkabout Hotel, near the airport, and wanted to catch up with him. Part of a chain through northern WA and the Northern Territory, the Walkabout complex included a motel, a disco that doubled as an indoor cricket arena during the week, a restaurant and cocktail bar, a sportsmans bar and the public bar. An instant regular, Abbott struck up a friendship with the bar manager, Lou Miraudo. After slogging out on the highway all week, he went straight into town on Saturday mornings and drove back on Sunday nights, weary and partied out.

Well, it was inevitable I wasn't going to last long in that job. Lou offered me a job at the hotel, as well as accommodation in the staff quarters, not long after I first met him. I scored the company of one of the women in town, so it was just a matter of time before I'd pull the pin.

One morning, after I'd driven all the way back to the campsite from Port Hedland, I decided I'd had enough. I was going to give a week's notice after the day's work. I had breakfast in the mess and then was driven out to the work site with a few of the other workers. Then, while sitting in the roller waiting for the engine to warm up, I decided, 'No, fuck this, I've had enough.' I waved the foreman over and told him to take me back to camp; I've had enough and I'm out of here. He found the whole thing amusing. The manager back at the camp didn't, though, and didn't have much to say at all. I packed my gear and headed back to Port Hedland.

The first job I had at the pub was as yardman, then on the door at the disco on the Friday and Saturday nights. Then I was a barman in the sportsmans bar for the Wednesday-night women's darts competition. I'd never had any experience behind the bar and the women soon picked that up and started to have more fun than just the darts, at my expense. I picked up the job – and some of the women – in no time.

Some weeks later, Lou offered me the job of the disco manager on the Friday and Saturday nights. I was a little sceptical about taking it at first, but after some assurance from Lou that it wasn't difficult to do, and that he'd show me the ropes, I took the job.

I picked it up in no time and at first thought it was the best thing since sliced bread, but eventually the hours and the drama that came just about every night – with dickheads who couldn't handle their piss – took the gloss off it. At one stage, I was employed in numerous jobs at the hotel. A barman on the

Wednesday night, disco manager on the weekends and during the weekdays I was the gardener. Some time later, I also performed the role as duty manager a few times a week.

Abbott also attracted attention from the law. After the robbery of a Perth burger bar, Hamburger Hill, Abbott heard he was a suspect, and says he immediately contacted Perth CIB to advise them of his whereabouts. They referred him to South Hedland CIB.

I contacted them and said I'd be in the following day to speak to them. I had nothing to be concerned about, other than them coming out to where I was working and fucking that job up for me. The arse I spoke to assured me that they wouldn't come to my work and agreed to see me the following day.

But the detectives turned up the same day, while Abbott, Lou and another man were smoking a joint in Lou's room.

Getting interviewed while stoned wasn't the most pleasant experience ... The first thing I made clear to the jacks was how pissed off I was that they came to my work after being given assurances that they wouldn't. I expected them to try to bust us over the pot – the staff quarters reeked.

After the interview, I was sure I would be sacked, so I fronted the general manager about the visit and told him of my past jail stint. I told him, 'If that is going to be a problem, I'll pack my bags and be out of there.'

He said, 'If you were arrested, I would have fired you. Seeing as that didn't happen, things remain as they are.'

I really didn't have an opinion of the general manager prior to that day, other than it being known among the staff that he had a drinking problem. But from then on, I thought he was OK.

Lou would remember the pub as being 'our life' in and out of working hours. There was nowhere else to go, and it had a pool and an indoor cricket pitch. 'Brenden was good at cricket. We both were at the time. We used to play against a lot of the patrons. We had good nights. We were undefeated for a while.'

Abbott became captain of the indoor cricket side, the Jabbers. Life was good.

I was soon allocated living quarters that were a bit upmarket from the standard staff quarters. The pay was excellent, food and accommodation was included, couldn't get much better – except I still longed for the company of Jackie, even though female company was never an issue.

Jackie:

He tried to bribe me to come back from England. I was saying, 'You're here one year, gone the next, you want to get married, but you can't stay out of jail long enough. What sort of life am I going to have? Settle down and get a job, or I'm going.'

I went for nine months. He kept ringing, and made plans to come over, but I was coming back anyway because my mum was getting remarried. I got back, and he said, 'I'm working at Port Hedland. I'll leave a ticket for you at the flight desk.'

So, when I flew back from England, I was out to 4am at a nightclub with my brother. The plane left at 6am. Then I flew up to Port Hedland. From London to the Walkabout Hotel. What a culture shock. I was jetlagged, but I was in the bar working the same night.

Lou:

Jackie came up to Port Hedland once. I know he would give her a lot – money, presents. He was smitten. I would say, 'She's just bloody using you.' I think he didn't want to believe it. As much as he became a mastermind in later years, in his early days, when it came to Jackie, he wasn't. He used to talk to her a fair bit on the phone. I think she liked Brenden, but I don't think she ever loved him. He liked to play the field, and be the Casanova type.

Then their idyllic Walkabout life began to fall apart. Lou and the assistant manager plotted a coup against the general manager, based on the theory that, if head office in Perth became aware of his drinking problem, they could both be promoted at his expense. Part of their plan was that Abbott would become bar manager, but he wasn't impressed.

I was made aware of their plan and made it clear I didn't agree with it and told them that, as it was, they pretty much ran the show, anyhow. But they went through with it and eventually it all backfired. The general manager got his marching orders and his position was filled by a manager from the Walkabout Hotel at Gove in the NT. He made it clear who would be running the joint. He made me the assistant bar manager and put me on a salary, which took a chunk out of my previous weekly earnings. He allocated the gardener's job to his fiancé, who wasn't a bad sort at all and she knew it; had the general manager by the balls. Many other changes came about that had Lou and the assistant manager kicking themselves.

Jackie had returned from England [in October 1985] just prior to the new manager's arrival and I paid for her to fly up. She was doing some bar work during the weeknights when the indoor cricket comp was on. Living in Port Hedland wasn't for Jackie and after a few months she headed back to Perth to live. Not long after, I handed in my resignation and returned to Perth, not because I wasn't happy with the job; it was so I could be with Jackie. A decision I regretted making not long after leaving the place – some months later, Jackie decided she wanted to go to live in England and shipped all of her property over. I almost followed and was prepared to jeopardise my parole. A month or so after she departed, I obtained my passport and was in the process of selling my car [the beloved Torana] when Jackie decided the move to England wasn't such a good decision and returned to Australia. She claimed she was doing so because she didn't want me breaching my parole.

Jackie:

I was pregnant and went back to Perth for an abortion. I said, 'I'm not having kids yet. Get real.' Then I moved back to Perth and he followed. That's when he went back a month or two later and did the [Walkabout Hotel] safe, and then came back again. I flew back to England in January [1986]. He wanted to know why I wanted to go back. I said that I had told my other brother Tony that I would go back, and I've still got my bedsit to sort out, and pack my gear and bring it back. So I went back for three months, and I think he went over east while I was back in London, and our plan was to meet back [in Perth] around his birthday in May.

Abbott says he never knew of the pregnancy, which he attributed to an English actor Jackie told him she met while over there, who was in the film *Top Secret*. And he's not saying anything about the theft of a safe at the Walkabout in the months after he left.

Jackie returned to Perth from London for the second time around May 1986. She stayed with Abbott, at the home of Coops and his girlfriend in Perth. Shortly after, Abbott and Jackie moved into a house together in the hills suburb of High Wycombe.

Jackie:

He went and did a big job out at Carousel [shopping centre] somewhere, a real nice furniture warehouse. He backed this truck up in the middle of the night and unloaded a whole houseful of furniture, because we had nothing when we moved in. It was really expensive stuff. We were there three weeks and we got news that Glenn had been locked up in Longmore for the first time. [Brenden] lost it. The memory of him being in Longmore sent him right off. He wasn't one to lose his temper, but when he did ...

[Brenden] came to me for a couple of grams of hash, and said, 'I'll go and give it to Glenn in Longmore, because he's a mess.'

I said, 'All right,' but then said, 'No, you're not taking any gear in there; if you get sprung, you're gonna go, and then you're back to jail.'

He lost it, big time. He tore up the whole house. He went around with a baseball bat [Abbott says it was a log splitter] and smashed all the furniture. He was close to Glenn then. My brother was there and saw it. We were standing there, horrified. We said, 'What did you do that for?' It's like he took all the frustration from when he was in Freo and just let fly. After that, I was a bit wary. I said I thought it would be a good idea if he went and stayed at his mum's. I cleaned up and then we had to get rid of all this smashed-up furniture. We moved out of there and I got a place in Scarborough and I said, 'You're not moving in until you can grow up.'

Abbott:

In the time Jackie was away, I'd bought myself a pup that was a cross between a bull terrier and a blue heeler. A beautiful-looking pup that was white, other than two black ears and a black patch over one of its eyes. In the time I had it, I really got attached to it. It was going to turn out to be a good dog. [He named it JD, and then just Jack, after Mr Daniels, not Miss Jackie Lord, as some of his mates assumed.] For some reason, Jackie wasn't too keen on it and I think the feeling was mutual. The first night I'd slept with her after she came back from England [at Coops's house, in Belmont] he climbed on top of her and pissed over her.

Not long after Jackie returned, we rented a house in the suburb of High Wycombe. Her brother Terry also moved in. The place was unfurnished and as I was never one to have the burden of lugging household furniture around with me everywhere, and with Jackie's furniture still months away from arriving from England, I went shopping in the early hours of the morning after window-shopping days earlier with Jackie to get her approval. I managed to acquire some of the furniture required to make the place homely. In a few more days, the house would've been completely set up, all new and good quality.

Wasn't long after moving into this house some filthy cunt knocked my dog off out of my car. I'd just stopped into the Belair Tavern on Great Eastern Highway to catch up with [stepfather] John Salmon. It was just a quick stop, in and out in a flash. My pup was asleep on the passenger's seat when I left the car and locked it. John convinced me to have at least one beer with him and I was straight out after to find the quarter glass window had been opened and the window wound down, but no dog. I've had stuff knocked off before, but stealing my dog was a real kick in the stones.

Around the same time, Glenn was pinched over something and was placed into Longmore and I was unable to bail him out. By now, I'd become closer to Glenn than any other time before. As a kid, he was more a burden, as little brothers are. Hearing of Glenn being locked up in that shit hole, I knew exactly how he'd be feeling. I was just about on my way to visit when I had a row with Jackie unlike ever before. It was triggered by her not handing over something I wanted to take into Glenn that would help him cope with the depressing surroundings. After that row, we moved out of the house and we lived separately, but still saw a lot of each other. The relationship was basically on the rocks, but, over time, things started to improve again.

Glenn was released from Longmore in the following days after fronting the Children's Court. It wasn't until a year or so earlier that Glenn had become involved with me in some of my activities. He used to go out thieving with mates around his age and it was only a matter of time before they all came undone. The stuff they were stealing wasn't worth it and they were stealing from people who didn't have much themselves. I wasn't going to start preaching to Glenn about what was right and wrong and that 'crime doesn't pay' shit. He was destined to take the same path, so, instead of him learning the hard way, I took him under my wing. He was making more money than he ever had and soon had himself his first car and was enjoying the fruits that money brings in life. Glenn was also doing the odd job with others and occasionally by himself.

Glenn Abbott shared his brother's love of fast cars, as Jackie would recall:

I remember one time, Glenn drove a brand-new [Nissan] 300ZX through a showroom window. Stole it, joyrided it around Perth, took us all for a ride. Then they ended up in this huge car chase and wrecked it. He parked it around the back of Thelma's at 141 Surrey Road, Rivervale. We'd rocked up in a car and I says to Brenden, 'Bloody hell, where'd you get the ZX?'

And he says, 'It's not my bloody car.' He says to Glenn, 'Are you stupid? What did you bring it here for?' He freaked out: 'Get rid of it, get rid of it.'

And the times they used to use my car. I had to put me foot down about it.

Abbott:

That 300ZX was supposed to be stolen while I was present. But Glenn, with someone else, decided to collect it without me. When I turned up to my mother's place with Jackie, the 300ZX was parked in the backyard. I was dirty that Glenn brought it to Mum's. That type of car was brand new and just didn't look right in that suburb, even less so parked at the Abbott house.

The day after Abbott's fit of rage, they all moved out of the High

Wycombe house. The tension remained and Jackie wondered just who Brenden Abbott was some days. She found herself a unit in Scarborough, near the beach, and kept Abbott at arm's length.

Just down the road, then hero of the people and local-boy-made-good Alan Bond did all sorts of deals to secure a slice of prime Scarborough beachfront, bulldozing history to make way for a shiny high-rise five-star hotel, Observation City. Jackie got a job there soon after it opened and even Eileen Bond's hideous decorating couldn't dampen her enthusiasm for the place.

Jackie says, 'It was all new then. And I loved the beach. I had a little dog I would walk over there every day.'

Only a suburb away, in North Beach, Abbott moved into the games room connected to the garage of his friends David K and David's girlfriend Kathy R. He rarely went into their house, happy to remain in the garage working on his Torana.

I'd known Kathy for some years, as well as her brother Mark R. In the past few months, I started to see a lot of Mark through going to the same karate school. Glenn, Coops and Phil F were also in the same karate school run by a bloke named Laurence Junior, and often travelled together to the dojo twice a week. Other nights during the week, we'd often get together for training at Phil's house. Phil and Mark had been doing it for some time. They were both brown belts and I found training with them a bonus and I was learning the art at a quick rate.

Laurence Junior was a second or third Dan black belt and would give special attention to my training. He encouraged me to take part in a number of tournaments. The first one didn't go so well and I soon felt the after-effects of a kick under the rib cage. The second tournament involved competing with other academies. I did better in that one and, if I'd won the fight, I would've been fighting for first place in the next fight. I'd never been one for contact sport, but the karate I enjoyed doing, maybe because you're more in control of what's going on.

Abbott found a job again, and Jackie saw hope in the new stability.

This was when we were settling down. [I told him,] 'You've got to stop breaking and entering.'

The guy we went on this boat trip with, he was doing the

*Blackwood [River Classic] thing as well; he gave Brenden a job
without a [tradesman's] certificate, at the Caltex on Canning
Highway [in Como, an inner Perth suburb]. We all went on this
boating trip. I was working out there on the pumps. He had me
out there in little skimpy shorts to try to get the customers in,
right? And Brenden was the mechanic. So it was perfect. There
were two of us girls out the front. Brenden had a well-paid job
as a mechanic. We both were doing well. I was working at the
[Scarborough] nightclub in the evenings. We were making really
good money.*

Abbott remembers it differently:

*She was a fucking angel, wasn't she? Jackie can talk some shit at
times. I was only working as a mechanic for three days a week, cash
in hand. Rabbit was also working there as an apprentice mechanic.
I was collecting the dole and also doing the odd job [crime].*

He got a new blue heeler puppy he named Rock and Jackie took some
photos of Abbott playing with his new little mate. But his joy was
short-lived. Working on the Torana at David K's house one day, he
heard the snarl of an angry dog. David's bull terrier had got hold of
Rock and killed him. Jackie remembers, 'It was only a few months
old. He was a bit disappointed. He liked that little dog.'

While Jackie held on to her picket-fence dreams, Abbott quietly
returned to his old ways.

Diane Abbott recalls,

*I'm sure Jackie's told you about his late-night shopping
expeditions. She woke up one morning and came through to the
kitchen. She walked back and noticed a shadow in the lounge
room. She turned on the light. She said it was just full of TVs,
stereos, microwaves.*

Jackie wasn't surprised. 'Blow me down if he couldn't bloody
help himself.'

Chapter Six

1987

After Abbott left Nollamara CIB's back door swinging in the breeze in December 1986, the slow wheels of the justice system eventually caught up with the parolee's change of status.

In February 1987, the parole board suspended his parole and then, in May, cancelled it. The month before, he had arrived back in Perth from Wollongong with his property investment financing plans with Lou high on the agenda.

He also caught up with friends, Jackie included. Their complicated relationship took a new twist with the news that her current beau was an Australian Federal Police detective.

Jackie:

[The detective, who is not named for legal reasons] came to see me because they found seeds when I brought my gear back from England. I'd gone over there to try to get away from all this. My brother had put a matchbox of marijuana seeds in my luggage and Customs found them. So [the detective] came to my home in Mullaloo and searched it. For some reason, [he] kept hanging around because he said he quite liked my company. Looking back now I know that [he] was fishing for information about Brenden.

She admitted later that going out with the detective was 'weird' for her. 'Brenden said to me, "What are you doing on the other side of the fence?"'

'I said, "Well, you've got to try everything."'

Abbott took a more pragmatic view: 'She was just stringing him along to save her arse [over the cannabis seeds].'

On 3 May 1987, he booked into a $42-a-night room at the Windsor Regency Lodge on Great Eastern Highway, providing details of a Ford Falcon with South Australian plates and using the ID of his old comrade Che. Che remained a loyal supporter of Abbott's and happily handed over his identification for use while on the run.

A few days later, Brenden and Jackie drove to Geraldton for a long weekend. Jackie packed her camera and they stopped on the side of the highway. She propped it on the bonnet and set the timer for a picture of them together, racing over to stand beside Abbott, the highway stretching off in the distance behind them.

For the picture, Jackie smiles broadly, sunglasses propped lazily on her head and wearing short shorts and singlet. He pulls her close, scowling behind aviator-style sunglasses. Abbott is solidly built and wearing a Jim Beam T-shirt and jeans; he looks watchful and belligerent, but insists he was feeling relaxed. Asked what his reaction would have been if a police car had appeared on the horizon, he said, 'I'd be cool, calm and collected; I had ID.'

On 15 May, after Brenden and Jackie returned to Perth, he again booked into the Windsor Regency, this time driving a Ford Laser. Then, on 28 May, the fugitive hooked up with Stabbie. Abbott knew he needed cash reserves to remain a free man and set up the Wollongong business venture. He put a long-held theory to his mate and Stabbie didn't hesitate. Fast money and pumping adrenalin suited him. They drove to Belmont to see Peter Lievense, Abbott's old mate from Darlington Cottages, and cooked up a plan. The next morning, just before opening time, Abbott and Stabbie would hold up a bank. They needed a driver and some tools. Everything else, including guns, was covered – although Stabbie admits there was no elaborate planning and preparation. 'The Belmont job wasn't planned until the Thursday night. It was an entirely spur-of-the-moment decision and the whole thing was put together that night.'

Earlier, on 21 May, a ram raid on WA Guns and Ammo in Maddington netted handguns worth $10,000 – an ominous sign that automatically put the armed robbery squad on alert. Abbott later denied stealing the guns, but admitted seeing them laid out on a table and selecting what he wanted. As well as the guns for the planned bank job, he also tucked away a .357 Magnum. The six months on the run had clearly changed him. Mates who saw him in this period noticed he seemed constantly alert, but calm. And his earlier misgivings about being armed had evaporated.

In those months between his exit from Nollamara CIB in December 1986 and his reappearance in Perth in May 1987, he started learning how to make himself invisible. And he had taken to firearms, believing they were essential to his continued freedom. In the process he was turning into one of the 'bad bastards' he had previously feared. Now someone could get hurt.

'Which bank?' Peter asked.

'That's the one,' Abbott answered, sending up the response to the Commonwealth Bank advertising slogan.

Typically of Abbott, this bank robbery would be different. He believed he'd hit on the solution to the hurdle that stopped most bank robbers getting more than a few grand from the tellers' drawers. He knew that the big money in a bank is kept under lock and key. But if they could be there when the time-delay lock released on the bank vault – just before opening time – then they could get their hands on serious money. All they needed to do was get in there and control the staff, to ensure they didn't trigger any alarms. It couldn't be any more technically difficult than fixing those trucks out on the Nullarbor.

Lievense dropped Abbott and Stabbie off near the bank after the adjacent Belmont Hotel closed its doors at midnight. They cut their way into the bank ceiling through the roof, all the while monitoring police frequencies in case they triggered any silent alarms. They dozed off in the air-conditioning duct and woke in the morning to the sound of a bank courier arriving. The getaway car had been taken care of, says Abbott. A Cordia turbo was dropped off just after sunrise while they were waiting in the roof.

At 8.45am, when all the staff were present, it began. Abbott, wearing a balaclava and overalls and armed with a .45 pistol, dived through a ceiling panel. Stabbie passed down the shotgun and then jumped down. Abbott took control of the staff: 'Everybody down. We only want the money. We don't want to hurt anybody and we don't want any fuckin' heroes pushing buttons.'

Stabbie grabbed the assistant manager and steered him in the direction of the bank's treasury while Abbott kept watch over the other staff. Loud threats and abuse were common themes in witness statements taken later and staff had good reason to be terrified – both weapons were loaded.

Abbott:

During that robbery, one offender outside the vault area accidentally fired off a round. This bullet travelled under the carpet for some distance. The other offender let a round off in the vault area. The evidence was that both shots came from Stabbie's gun – this was wrong.

From where Stabbie stood, it looked as though Abbott had shot one of the staff. He said, 'I was convinced I was going to see this guy's head pasted across the floor. Even Langdon was shitting himself. He was wearing a bloody pink shirt.'

Mr Pink Shirt was Karl Langdon, a bank teller, future high-profile footballer for Subiaco and West Coast Eagles, and strident Abbott critic.

Suddenly, an unrelated burglar alarm at a shop next door convinced Abbott and Stabbie that police were on their way. They ran for the door, taking $112,730, sprinted to the Mitsubishi Cordia and sped off down the road. It was Western Australia's biggest bank robbery and also the first ever 'drop-in' bank robbery in the state – and possibly the nation. This added a new dimension of terror for bank staff. Abbott showed they could never be safe, even with the doors locked and alarms on; this new method of robbery played on the minds of Australian bank staff for years.

After hearing a blast from the Cordia's horn, Peter left his house and met them in his own car at the pre-arranged rendezvous, the Travelodge Motel on Great Eastern Highway. The Cordia was dumped at the motel car park and the trio's next destination was Room 31 at The Raffles Hotel in Applecross. The cash was then counted and divided up. Abbott and Stabbie each got $49,000 and Peter received $15,000.

But Lievense later insisted in his police statement:

I grabbed a couple of grand and said I was going to grab some more later because I didn't want [his girlfriend] Lisa to know what I had done. I took Brenden from there [Raffles] and dropped the shit in the river – the tin and the bag. It was off Guildford Bridge. Stabbie went home with half the money.

After the dumping site was later discovered – complete with tyre tracks – and reported in the media, Abbott gave Peter an extra $300 to buy himself some new tyres. Hours after the robbery, Peter Lievense went to a car-hire business in Rivervale. Abbott felt prosperous. He told him to hire something flash, like a red Porsche. He settled for a black BMW.

Jackie:

We went to Mandurah in the BMW to ditch the shoes and clothes. Then we went horse riding in Mandurah. I remember, because I cursed that bloody horse. I couldn't ride the bloody thing; it wouldn't go.

On the Sunday after the Belmont job, Lievense drove Abbott to Tame Street, Dianella, to look at a Toyota Land Cruiser advertised for sale in the newspaper. Abbott paid $6,000 on the spot for it. On Tuesday, 2 June, he dropped by Peter's house and told him he needed to leave town again. The robbery had created a lot of heat and, sooner or later, the police would come looking for him. Wisely, Abbott chose not to tell Peter his actual destination, instead telling him he was heading for Darwin.

Meanwhile, Jackie was speaking to the police. One source says she spoke to them because she found out about the girl Abbott slept with in Port Hedland. Abbott says of her involvement, 'An important lesson in life, that one. And costly.'

Jackie:

Looking back now, I know that [the AFP detective] was fishing for information on Brenden. He said, 'You obviously know Brenden very well. Do you know if he did that bank job?'

I thought, I wouldn't tell you if I knew. You never tell a cop anything. That's what Brenden used to say. He said something about Brenden getting a motorbike. And I said, 'No, it's a four-wheel drive,' because I knew Brenden had done the job and was heading up north.

[He said,] 'Ah, it was a four-wheel drive, was it?'

The morning after the job I heard Brenden on the phone

*saying, 'Pay cash for a Toyota.' And, of course, they had other
information from Peter that he was heading for Darwin.*

Someone led the police to Lievense first. And that someone was
Jackie. They raided his home on Wednesday, 3 June 1987. Police –
and Lievense – alleged in court that only $2,354 was found in a red
carrier bag in a cupboard at his home. But Jackie says, 'He didn't get
two grand for being getaway driver, he got 15. Brenden told me.'
  Stabbie remembers,

*I knew some shit was happening when I heard on the news that
a 25-year-old man had been arrested for the Belmont job. I knew
Peter was 25. My phone rang five minutes later. It was Brenden.*

Abbott:

*I was having a counter meal at the pub in Marble Bar [1,500km
north of Perth]. Next on the TV news was a story that someone
had been arrested over the Belmont robbery. I suddenly lost my
appetite. I phoned Stabbie. He was spinning out, claiming he's
being followed everywhere. I phoned Peter. I can't recall the
whole conversation, but knew straight away by his tone of voice
he was up to no good. I gave him info I was on the coast road,
I believe, south of Karratha. In fact, I'd come up the inland road.*

He stopped at the Walkabout Hotel in Port Hedland, but police were
a step ahead of him. They visited the day before to speak to the
manager, Wayne Halligan. Perth detectives contacted South Hedland
CIB's Detective Sergeant Mick Conchie, who knew that Abbott had
previously worked there. Conchie asked Halligan for any history on
Abbott. Halligan found Abbott's old payslips and ran off some
photocopies. Conchie told him, 'We've got a bit of a hunch that
Abbott's coming up the Gunbarrel Highway. We could have a visitor
tomorrow. What time does reception close?'
  'Nine pm,' Halligan told him.
  The detective asked Halligan to get the hotel receptionist to advise
Halligan of all check-ins.
  Abbott remembers,

On reaching the Walkabout, we booked two rooms. The chap

who was with me [Jamie J, another associate] booked a room for two. I later went in and booked a single. The Land Cruiser was parked outside the room my friend was in (the room booked as a twin). It was a difficult night to get to sleep. Being in the middle of nowhere, I figured the best option was to fly out. This wasn't available until the next morning. I could only hope that what I told Peter would give me time.

They booked in just before 9pm. The receptionist forgot to advise her boss of the two separate late arrivals.

Halligan remembers what happened the next morning:

I walked over to the dining room at 7am and walked past them. One was in sunnies, had jet-black hair and a leather jacket. I kept smiling and walked into the kitchen. I asked the waitress to go out there and check – casually – if she knew anyone. She came back and said, 'No,' and I said, 'What about the guy in the jacket?' and she said, 'Ah, yes, he used to work here. Brenden Abbott. Isn't he wanted?'

I checked the list and so I knew the two rooms they were staying in. There was a two-door Land Cruiser parked outside one, with a bull terrier with a studded collar in the tray. I could see a satchel or something under a blanket in there. One of the cops said later, 'If only you'd known there was 32 grand in there. And the dog would have licked you to death.'

The officer's supposed casual comment about the amount of cash turned out to be crucial. Halligan was confident that he had the figure right but couldn't remember which officer made it. Conchie denies it was him, which is fair enough. After confirming Abbott's identity, Halligan maintained his composure and went to the office and got their room records. He recalls,

Abbott had rung Mackay in Queensland something like 13 times, about three numbers, [Abbott denies this] but the other guy hadn't made any calls. I tried to track down the cops and eventually got hold of John Skeffington, who was then OIC of South Hedland. I told him we had Brenden Abbott sitting in the dining room. He said he would try to rustle up some troops, but the CIB boys were out on an early-morning drug raid. About

7.30am to 7.40am, I walked past the pool and was watching to see what they were doing. They drove out – without having paid, I noticed – and then turned into the airport a couple of hundred metres away. The police went to the airport and showed the staff pictures, but they didn't ID Abbott. There were two flights leaving: Darwin via Broome and Perth via Karratha. While the police were at the airport, other police came through our kitchen door. The Toyota returned from the airport, and when [Jamie J] came into the reception, he got a gun behind the ear as he was about to start flipping through the Yellow Pages.

Jamie came back to pay the bill. He was pushed to the floor and handcuffed, taken into the office and handcuffed to a chair.

'Abbott was with you?'

'Yes.'

'You took him to the airport?'

'Yes.'

'And which flight is he on?'

Silence.

The detectives headed to the airport, but just missed Abbott's flight. (Wayne Halligan later received $2,000 reward money, but police told him he wasn't the only civic-minded citizen involved; the reward for the bank robbery was ultimately split five ways.)

Police in Perth prepared a reception committee. When Ansett Flight 347 reached Perth, the last person to hit the tarmac was Brenden Abbott. He warily tagged along with the other passengers as they walked towards the terminal, his hand straying inside the leather jacket. Suddenly, the passengers parted and a man with a gun confronted him: 'Brenden Abbott! Freeze. Police. On the ground now!'

Abbott withdrew his hand from inside the leather jacket. The pistol was in his luggage anyway. He went to ground, as ordered by Detective Sergeant Barry Lehmann.

The prick couldn't help himself. I was on the ground getting cuffed, a handful of hair was grabbed, he pulled my head up and slammed it into the ground. I was lucky I turned my head to the side, otherwise I would've had either a broken nose or at least a few teeth missing. Stabbie wasn't arrested until after I was.

Stabbie remembers, 'Later, Mum rang and said, "They've got Brenden." They picked me up two hours later. In hindsight, they had nothing on me.'

Stabbie was interviewed for this book but declined to comment directly on what happened after his arrest for the Belmont robbery. (He would speak about the robbery only on condition he was not named, hence the pseudonym 'Stabbie'.)

After hauling Abbott into the airport terminal, the detectives went to the baggage conveyor belt and found a carry bag containing clothing, a large amount of cash and a birthday card that read: 'To Brenden, wishing you all the best and future happiness always. Love Always, Jackie. Happy Birthday 25.' Another bag containing clothes and pistol was also seized. Abbott denied knowledge of either bag and the detectives took him to CIB headquarters.

Abbott claims he spent about $11,000 in the six days between the robbery and his recapture, plus another $6,000 on the Land Cruiser. But that still left about $32,000 – the same amount the unnamed police officer at Port Hedland had said was in the bag in his casual remark to the Walkabout manager. But in court, the prosecution said the bag contained $16,000.

Abbott:

What would be of interest was a photo shown to me during my evidence. This was a photo taken by police at CIB headquarters after my arrest. Come trial day, it was alleged I had $16,000 in my bag upon arrest. The photo I was shown appeared to show more than $16,000. This has stuck in my mind. I've questioned the coppers' tactics – surely they wouldn't make such a fuck-up.

At police headquarters, Jeff Beaman from the break squad finally asked Abbott some questions about the Homecraft break.
Beaman:

He was alert and he was very intent on listening to what was said. He was cautious and answered the questions we put to him. He made sure he understood what was going on, so he had his wits about him.

They told him the Ozone Parade unit contained only $3,000 worth of the goods. Beaman says he asked Abbott, 'Do you wish to make a statement in relation to this matter?'

> *ABBOTT: 'No, I'll never go to paper. Can the charges against Jackie be dropped? She's not a crim. I'm the one who did the break. You've got me. You only charged her because I ran off.'*
> *BEAMAN: 'She was charged because she admitted committing the offence.'*
> *ABBOTT: 'Can you do anything about it?'*
> *BEAMAN: 'No.'*
> *ABBOTT: 'What about the washing machine I gave my mother? What will happen to her?'*
> *BEAMAN: 'Did she know where it came from?'*
> *ABBOTT: 'No, all I said to her was "Merry Christmas". She's innocent. You've got [the others] for the break. That's enough. If I hadn't kept any of the gear, I would have been all right. Besides, this break doesn't worry me at all.'*

Alongside armed robbery, it didn't look so bad. Detective Beaman then questioned Abbott about the Maddington gun-shop ram raid. Abbott insisted that he did not do the break, but he knew of some guns in the river. He asked to speak to Stabbie and then agreed to take the detectives on a drive.

> *The only reason the cops were shown where the guns in the river were was the result of a deal. They intended to charge me with numerous electrical store break-ins. This was only an agreement with [Stabbie]. That was why they let me speak to [Stabbie] briefly alone. I told him what I had to gain from it. The cops' priority was to get the guns off the street. As for the others that were sold, no way was I assisting with that.*

The armed robbery squad's Detective Sergeant Ian Brandis was next in line outside the interview room. Criminals had slung mud at the hard-nosed veteran detective for most of his career. None of it stuck. Abbott says he told Brandis nothing. Brandis later tendered his notes of the interview in court, which concluded:

> *ABBOTT: 'Whatever's in the bag is all that's left of my share.'*
> *BRANDIS: 'How much is there?'*

ABBOTT: *'I don't know.'*
BRANDIS: *'Are you prepared to give me a statement about the receiving of the gun, the robbery of the bank and the taking of the Mitsubishi car?'*
ABBOTT: *'No way. I've said enough. You've got enough to hang me, anyway.'*
BRANDIS: *'You'll be charged with the receiving of the gun, the unauthorised use of the car and the robbery on the bank. Do you understand that?'*
ABBOTT: *'Yes.'*
BRANDIS: *'Is there anything else you want to ask me?'*
ABBOTT: *'Who dobbed me in?'*
BRANDIS: *'You know I can't tell you that.'*

The search of the bags seized at the airport also yielded personal papers and identification for Che and ID in the name of several of Abbott's other mates.

A detective reinterviewed Stabbie. He took two detectives to a shed at the rear of a house in Arbon Way, Lockridge, where they used boltcutters to gain access and found a blue bag containing $39,000, which was the balance of his $49,000 share. The cash appeared to add up, everyone police arrested was locked up, and internal investigators had no reason to go anywhere near the case. In 2003, when the WA Police Royal Commission shone a light into the dark crevices of the CIB, the Belmont robbery was not on the list.

Stabbie had been two months short of completing 32 months of parole when he committed the Belmont robbery, which added nearly three years to his jail term. He walked free in November 1995. Then, after years of circles in the exercise yard, he finally went straight.

A month or two before the Belmont robbery, the R&I Bank near by was also robbed, and Brandis attributes this to Abbott, whom he remembers as 'a very cold, calculating person – one of the coldest I've ever dealt with. He's a deep thinker. He's very confident in his work because he puts so much planning into it. He doesn't do things on the spur of the moment. He does his homework.'

Abbott was not charged over the R&I robbery, but, at this point, he barely cared. While on parole, he'd escaped legal custody and now faced charges over a big break and an even bigger bank robbery.

I recall two of the detectives at that [subsequent Belmont robbery] trial seemed a little concerned. After I was sentenced, I was put in the prison van. They ushered the screws or cops running the escort away. I was sitting in the back of the wagon and they quietly said, 'We aren't going to charge you over the R&I robbery.'

After a few months to stew in his steaming Fremantle cell, Abbott twitched with anger when the truth finally dawned on him in the dock of the Supreme Court with Peter Lievense. (Stabbie had already been sentenced.) Abbott was going back to Fremantle while Lievense got bail. Abbott lunged across the dock at his old mate. In her article 'Violence erupts at court hearing' (*West Australian*, 2 December 1987), veteran court reporter Margot Lang reported that Abbott hissed, 'I wish I'd never met you.'

Abbott recalls,

One of the dumbest things I've ever done in my life was the attack on Peter Lievense in the dock. Days prior to this, Stabbie was sentenced to 12 years for the robbery. At the time, neither of us (Stabbie and myself) knew how we came undone. What was clear, though, was Peter was lending them a hand. I felt responsible for our undoing, because I had assured Stabbie that Peter was OK, a good friend of mine. Some kind of payback was needed. 'I wish I'd never met you' was a misquote. In fact, what I said was: 'You'll wish you never met me.' It was an act of stupidity. I've learned that any intent on doing paybacks is best kept to oneself and sorted out in other ways.

Police separated Abbott and Lievense and Abbott was taken back to the cells. In handcuffs and leg chains, he was bundled into a van and taken back to Fremantle. The following year, Lievense swallowed six years' jail, with a minimum of two years. Shortly after, he stood up and gave evidence against his old friend, telling the court he was just giving a mate a lift. The Court of Criminal Appeal, to some extent, agreed. His sentence was reduced to two years, with a nine-month minimum.

Abbott recalled,

He was wrapped in cotton wool for his entire sentence and did it as a 'trusty' in the Armadale police station. He was given new identification when he was released.

After the incident in the dock – and from then on – Abbott went to court fully shackled in the company of two burly prison officers. The kid with the crooked grin was gone for good now, replaced by an angry, bitter and dangerous man. Glenn still shadowed him, having managed to follow his brother to Fremantle. He even earned himself a prison nickname – 'Michael Jackson'.

> *That name came about from a bank robbery Glenn was convicted of in 1987 or 1988. He was convicted due to a fingerprint left on a glass screen in the bank that suggested it was him. During that job, the offender wore only one glove and, when some of the blokes in Freo got wind of that, a little Michael Jackson singalong was created for Glenn that went: 'If you wore another glove, you would've beat it, beat it.'*

Violence and humour were two of the main preoccupations in the tiny world of Fremantle's inmates, but the summer of 1987–88 was different. The dry, strangling heat magnified the boredom and the bile. The threat of violence hung in the still air. Abbott had a full court calendar and intended fighting every charge, with potential decades in Fremantle ahead of him. Jackie visited. She and her mother received $7,500 reward money for their role in his Belmont conviction. She says,

> *I told Brenden about it [talking to her detective boyfriend] when I went to see him after he was locked up. He said, 'Did you tell that [cop] what was going on?'*
> *I said, 'No, I swear I didn't.'*

The woman Brenden Abbott loved most in the world – along with one of his best mates – had betrayed him and ruined the most lucrative crime he ever committed. Now the system had reclaimed him and the adventure was over. He swore to himself to never trust anyone again. And, as Fremantle Prison's summer of hell began, he embraced the darkness, the heat and the violence waiting to erupt.

Chapter Seven

1988–1989

Instead of drugs hidden in body cavities, the 135,000 people who now visit Fremantle Prison each year usually bring questions and cameras. They stare in awe at the limestone relics and the graffiti, poetry and art left behind by the thousands of men who wasted large parts of their lives here.

Tour guides retell the events of January 1988 in hushed tones. Some were prison guards, and some were here on those two terrible days. As chilling as the tours are – especially by candlelight – the sights and stories of a tourist treasure cannot recreate the long-gone pungent odours of a crowded prison filled with angry men.

On 4 January 1988, the unmistakeable institutional smell Brenden Abbott knew so well hung heavily in the air. Pine disinfectant used to wash down the floors in the divisions each day mingled with the polish applied to the old jarrah floors. The stale body odour was constant, particularly in the remand yard. Six hundred prisoners – double its approved capacity – sweltered within Fremantle's walls. The temperature topped 42 degrees that day and was 10 to 12 degrees higher in the limestone kilns known as cells.

The trouble began at the 7am 'first unlock'. A prisoner in Main Division, Bruce S, was slow to leave his cell and got a hurry-up from a warder. The inmate knew his abusive reply meant trouble, but, as one ex-prisoner says, 'People start whacking people for very little reason. The hotter, the more trivial.'

Bruce and the warder locked horns, resulting in the former being dragged, kicking and yelling, to an observation cell in New Division. He remained upset and hostile; word spread that the warder had bashed him.

Later in the day, the prison's chief officer spoke to New Division's senior officer and said he thought the inmate should be moved out of the cell.

The prisoner entered Main Division's exercise yard, where other prisoners held a meeting. They demanded to see the superintendent, but settled for an examination of the prisoner by medical staff, which confirmed the presence of marks on his face and neck.

Abbott:

It was through negotiations between a few inmates and the screws that resulted in Bruce S being brought back. Everyone was on edge and a decision was made to keep most of the inmates who worked in the prison industries in the exercise yards that afternoon. After hearing what he'd endured, it was decided a riot was on. I couldn't help myself and voted myself in, as did Glenn and about 20 other blokes to begin with.

When the inmates huddled together in conversation in Main Division and Two Division, worried warders requested the presence of the feared Metropolitan Security Unit. The request was refused.

Abbott says of the unit,

These jokers were the so-called elite screws who would also carry out normal duties as screws. When they played their MSU role, they'd don their blue overalls, black baseball caps and tough-guy expressions. There was animosity between these screws and the run-of-the-mill screws. One lot chewed gum, while the other thought they could chew rocks.

Two Division inmates stuffed a note inside a tennis ball and threw it across to the exercise yard in Three Division: 'We're out at the moment. Don't leave us posted. Reply straight away.'

Soon after, the ball sailed back: 'Two Division, hang on. Stay cool. We are in the process of deciding. Give us 3.30pm. We won't weaken. Just give us time.' Handwriting experts later identified the author as one of the ringleaders, notorious rapist Paul Stephen Keating.

A decision was made to put all prisoners back in their cells, but confusion gripped prison officers. Three Division inmates were allowed into their cells about 3.40pm to unload their gear. They counted the number of officers in the division and, when they returned to the exercise yard, their plan was clear. But, when they were called in for dinner, landing by landing, there was a terrible 'mistake':

> Our defence was that we were only carrying out as we were ordered. Some screws would say over the loudspeaker, 'Right, G and H inside.' And on this day we did. It was just a misunderstanding. We all thought he said, 'Riot.'

The call for G and H was also Abbott's cue. He saw a despised prison officer nearby on the phone and thought to himself that the man would soon be in trouble. It was his job to disable any officers at the gate to allow other inmates to storm the narrow barred barrier.

> In front of me were about six inmates who were none the wiser as to what was about to unfold. But the cleaners, who were dishing out the meals, were clearly wound up and ready to rock and roll. As I came through the gate, I made out I was about to reach for a plate, but I quickly spun around and with the base of my palm, landed a forceful blow in an upward strike on the jaw of the screw on the gate. The impact dropped him to his knees and then I held the gate open, yelling, 'Go, go, go.' The rush through the gate caused a bottleneck at first, but soon the numbers were coming through and what followed can only be described as utter mayhem.

The despised officer Abbott had seen then tried to flee to the doors of the division, near the phone he was on. Abbott swears he saw a senior prison officer push this officer back through the division doors and then lock them.

> Next thing [the despised officer] was surrounded by a sea of green and everyone was trying to land a fist or boot into him. The wooden tables were turned up and the legs disappeared in a flash. A screw who was standing directly behind the tables just put his hands up and casually walked to the end doors that led to New Division. Not a finger was laid on him because he was respected by most inmates.

Some inmates grabbed the stainless-steel buckets of boiling tea and water that were sitting in readiness for the evening meal and threw them over some prison officers. It made the concrete floor slippery and one inmate tried to throw the contents of his bucket, only to slip and land heavily on his back – a moment of comedy noted by many in the pandemonium.

> *Prison officers on the upper landings retreated through the doors to Two Division, while others came down the stairs, only to be overpowered. Screws from Two Division had come through the A and B landing's large wooden doors and started to head in our direction. Some of us headed to take them on and, in doing so, put ourselves in the line of fire from those behind us who decided to use the steel plates as projectiles. The screws retreated back through the doors. We soon overran the division and the screws were out, or so we thought.*
>
> *No sooner had the division been taken than other inmates not involved in the initial plan made plans of their own and started to torch some cells. My understanding was that Main Division was to be taken first and then, when One Division and Two Division were taken, we would burn the whole place to the ground. Some of us actually went upstairs and tried to put the fires out. Some were screaming out to those lighting fires for them to stop, but it was all in vain. Before long, the place was well ablaze and we had to withdraw to the yard, once every cell was checked to make sure no one was left locked up. Taking hostages wasn't talked about in the planning either, but, like the cells being torched, others had their own plans.*

Of the 12 warders in Three Division, five were caught on the ground floor. The fire added to the confusion, allowing the inmates to take control. Fifteen prison officers were injured in the ensuing clashes. A ringleader, armed robber Gary Roser, would later tell a court, 'My immediate concern was that the MSU were in the division, flogging prisoners over the meetings we had had that day ... it was just mayhem. There were prisoners everywhere, plates getting thrown, people screaming.'

David Gaudie, a prison officer for only two weeks, was beaten senseless, dragged into a cell and locked in with another officer. When he came to and saw the smoke, he thought the worst. But, because of a bad gash to his head, the inmates released Gaudie shortly after they seized control. After the fire spread, five other warders were taken from the cells and led to a corner of the Three Division exercise yard.

Roser later told a court, 'I heard some prisoners say, "Let's belt the screws."

'I then turned around and yelled out to all the prisoners, "Nobody is to touch these officers."'

Roser, with about seven other inmates including Brenden and Glenn Abbott, warned the guards not to move or their safety could not be guaranteed. One of the warders later told the *West Australian*, 'All we could do was sit and talk to them [the prisoners] and be as friendly as possible. We assured them nothing would happen to them and hoped to Christ we were right.'

Abbott:

The scariest thing about the riot was the sight of men who had totally lost all self-control. The manner in which they carried out some of their attacks on the screws was sickening to watch. It was like a school of sharks in a feeding frenzy. It's a wonder that any of the screws weren't killed or more seriously injured. Most didn't deserve what was dished out to them. In fact, some were quite reasonable in their dealings with inmates.

As prisoners and hostages faced each other in the exercise yard, the roof of the burning cell block exploded, showering the yard with sparks.

When I went back out there, I spotted that [the despised officer] had been claimed as a hostage. I was quite surprised to see he'd come through the attack pretty much without a scratch. He had a few bumps and welts, but that was about all. It was probably because he had so many attacking him at once that no one was able to get a decent hit in. He looked like a worried man, though.

By 5pm, thick smoke poured across the port city. The rioters barricaded themselves in the exercise yard, pushing a fridge and benches against the grille gate. Inmates threw rocks, lumps of asbestos roofing and iron bars at firemen and yelled, 'Let it burn, it deserves to burn.'

Firefighters managed to save more than three-quarters of the prison, despite the difficulties in reaching the fires. The flames licked at the polished jarrah floors and beams but they were slow to catch alight. Shadows lengthened around the prison, now surrounded by police, who quickly took over the situation.

> *Police negotiators were brought in and sat up on the bank that overlooked the yard and proceeded to pick out people to be charged and put their negotiating skills into practice. I was approached on numerous occasions to guard the screws, but I didn't want anything to do with that. I didn't believe they should have been in that position and I also didn't want to be seen by the coppers as one of the people preventing the screws from leaving the yard. I talked to some of the inmates who were in the vicinity of the screws for a brief period and that was all.*

As night fell, 135 inmates remained on the loose inside Fremantle's walls. Only the five hostages prevented the Metropolitan Security Unit and half the city's police force from storming the yard. The prisoners' lawyers later told a court there was no plan to riot and take hostages. The rush to the Three Division gate was spontaneous; the fires lit by unknown prisoners acting alone; and everyone in the prison – including the guards – had no choice but to go into the yard. There, they were held by armed police who never asked or told the warders to leave. The prisoners were hostages as much as the warders.

'So it is all just a big misunderstanding?' incredulous prosecutor Ron Davies asked ringleader Paul Keating.

'I am telling you now, Mr Davies,' Keating replied gravely. 'It hurts me, too.'

The tensions simmered after darkness fell. Another group of prisoners, not involved with the hostages, stockpiled rocks and bricks below the prison's north wall. Warders split the group in two and, at 9.45pm, mounted a baton charge. They shouted, 'Stay against the wall or you will be shot.'

The inmates wisely complied and were led away by the warders. In another part of the prison, the remaining 360 prisoners not involved in the situation were locked down. Police negotiators, headed by Bob Kucera (later a state Labor minister), began the task of saving the lives of the five prison warders.

Inmates held aloft sheets with messages written in charcoal. They demanded face-to-face communication with the Attorney-General, Joe Berinson, access to Corrective Services executives and a promise of no physical retribution against rioters. Most were convinced it was only a matter of time before the Special Air Service regiment, based at nearby Swanbourne Barracks, stormed the prison. But no one was going in yet. The exercise yard seemed likely to turn into a bloodbath if the crisis wasn't handled properly.

At 1.30am, warders in riot gear entered the prison and soon all areas were secure, except for the Three Division exercise yard. No one slept. The long hot night dragged on. The yards had water, but no food. A hostage recalls, 'First thing in the morning was the danger period, when they wanted food. Their spokesman warned the negotiators that, if food was refused, they would leave us, walk away and let us suffer for it.'

The police weren't sending out an order for a mountain of hamburgers without something in return. The breakfast cost one hostage, followed by two cartons of cigarettes for the second. The three remaining officers ate breakfast while negotiations continued.

Late in the morning, nearly 19 hours after Brenden Abbott delivered his upper cut at the Three Division gate, Police Minister Gordon Hill broadcast a message to the prisoners over the radio, assuring them of fair treatment. The last three hostages were released and the prison retaken. Enraged, prison chaplain Father Robert McGregor told waiting reporters that the jail was unfit for animals. 'It is 10 or 12 degrees hotter in there [the cells] and it was more than 40 degrees outside on Monday. If they kept animals in conditions like those, the RSPCA would have been up in arms years ago. The tragedy is it [prison] creates problems instead of solving them. Some very angry people are created in there.'

Attorney-General Joe Berinson bubbled with fury at the chaplain's criticism: 'The preacher's comments are totally inaccurate. Conditions are sub-standard, but the fact remains they have considerably improved since the Labor Government was elected in 1983.'

Abbott:

Some hours after the screws left the yard, the inmates were taken out in small groups at a time, walked through the burned-out shell of Main Division, out to the front compound of the divisions, and then through a gauntlet of screws all the way into Two Division. Glenn and I managed to stick together and were placed in the same cell. I was certain some paybacks were coming, if not then, in the days that followed. Nothing eventuated, but, for months, there was a lot of tension in the air and everyone – screws and inmates – were on edge. All the inmates previously held in One, One-A and Two Divisions prior to the riot were moved into New Division. In the days that followed, most were moved to other jails.

I was charged with six counts of deprivation of liberty, and two counts of assault. It was alleged I was seen guarding the screws held in the yard and reported as having a length of timber in my hand while doing so. Utter crap. I was never guarding the screws nor did I ever have a weapon of any sort in my hand. One of the police negotiators, who was on the bank overlooking the yard, claimed in his evidence at the riot trial he was able to recognise me from his dealings with me during an investigation some years back. He claimed he spoke to me over matters while I was in Perth CIB headquarters. The thing was, I'd never had any dealings with him whatsoever. The time he was talking about was when everyone was pinched over the electrical stores. I was never in Perth CIB headquarters – I was hiding under a bush at the front of someone's house.

The second assault charge was also a case of mistaken identity. It related to an assault being carried out on a screw on the C and D landing soon after the initial rush. The evidence the Crown led on that assault was basically the testimony of the screws: about six claimed they saw me belting the screw across the head with a length of wood; about seven screws said they saw Glenn doing it. There was even evidence given that I was seen by a number of screws on the A and B landing while the assault on this particular screw was taking place. The exact section of the C and D landing where it took place was also in dispute – evidence given showed no one was quite sure where it happened.

The Crown's ploy worked – they knew they didn't have a hope in hell in getting a conviction with just one of us charged, so they charged us both and managed to convince the jury that Glenn hopped into this joker first and then I'm supposed to have had a crack at him further along the landing. Not long after the riot, the prison authorities decided to set up a special handling unit in New Division. I believe it held a maximum of 12 blokes who they felt were the ringleaders of the riot. If they'd had room for

14, Glenn and I would have joined them. Even at this point in time, I was considered a security risk by the powers that be. My court appearances had me surrounded with extra security to and from court and I was transported by the MSU.

The *West Australian*'s legendary crime reporter Cyril Ayris toured the prison on 5 January. He described the exercise yard as like a bearpit in a third-rate zoo, with inmates lying on concrete or pacing like caged lions. The pungent odours of the previous day were gone, masked by the stink of fiery destruction.

Meanwhile, life and the wheels of justice slowly turned. Two days after belting prison officers around the head, Brenden Abbott prepared for another court appearance, meeting his new lawyer Richard Utting to discuss the Belmont robbery charges.

On Monday, 11 January, Utting represented Abbott in the Supreme Court, and the next day his client and an MSU entourage made an appearance as well. Court documents described Abbott as an unemployed labourer of no fixed address. He was literally surrounded by guards in court – two prison officers, two MSU officers and one uniformed police officer. Peter Lievense could rest easy in the dock that day.

The dog ate Richard Utting's homework. On Monday, he didn't have time for proper instructions; on Tuesday, he didn't have time to interview witnesses; and, on Thursday, he said that notes Abbott made in preparation for his defence were destroyed when his cell burned – then Abbott's new notes 'disappeared'. But they were returned to him on Wednesday by a senior prison officer who obtained them from the consorting squad. Utting was concerned the consorting squad used the notes to obtain a statement from Peter Lievense's de facto wife. He wanted time to investigate; so did Lievense's lawyer. They won their adjournment and the trial moved to March.

Both Stabbie – also charged over the riot, but later acquitted – and Abbott concocted compelling fairytales for their defence, and their stories dovetailed nicely. Stabbie was desperate to pay a $10,000 drug debt, as he had told the court when he was sentenced in December 1987, after admitting the robbery. Abbott claimed he was the drug dealer, and attributed some of the money in his possession to this debt. He also spun a yarn claiming the second robber was actually a mysterious Maori man nicknamed Kiwi. The jury bought none of it, especially with a contrite Peter Lievense to back up the Crown case.

On 29 March 1988, Abbott received a ten-year jail term for charges laid over the Belmont robbery. The judge noted, 'There is little that is mitigating in your personal circumstances. You are now 26 years of age and appear to be determined to follow a path of crime. Your criminal record stretches back some 12 years and involves many convictions for crimes of dishonesty.'

In July 1988, the examination of the prison riot began in Court 41 of Perth's Central Law Courts. The *West Australian* described it as 'the greatest show in WA legal history ... the biggest, longest and most expensive criminal hearing the state has seen'.

The prisoners were less impressed with the proceedings, since they rose at 5.30am each day to be shackled and strip-searched, before a day of stifling courtroom tedium. Abbott took the time to pen a letter to Lou on 25 October 1988:

'Well my good friend, as you'd be aware, I got myself in a spot of bother earlier this year. I'm writing this letter from the dock at the moment while the trial continues. I'm sitting here with another 19, one being Glenn. There's about another month to go before we all know the outcome. All I can say for myself so far is it doesn't look too bad. If convicted, I'm looking at more time than the ten years I've got. I could be old and grey before I feel freedom again. I may ask for a reservation in one of these new old people's homes that are being built. Other than the few problems, I'm fine, still planning ways to make a quick dollar. The plans Glenn and myself have made – you can just imagine what we would be up to ...

'I'm forgetting what a woman looks like, so if you do visit me with your girlfriend, you'll understand why I'll have a fat during the visit. I tell you, it's getting to the stage that some of these new young blokes coming in look like ugly girls. I don't fuck ugly girls. It's when they start looking pretty that things could change. I've had this bird named Sandy call in to see me now and then. She's been the only one, other than my mother, who sees me. I had a few girls call in when I first came in, but after a while they dropped off. They just wanted my body, the using bitches ... Remember Jackie? Well, she's no longer around. What a mistake I made with that one. Should have listened to you, but I was too blind. Mole cost me my freedom.'

Small talk out of the way, Abbott got down to what was really on his mind:

'I do need to speak to you over some important matters. I hope you could make it down as soon as possible. Please come alone, as it's for your ears only.'

Any prison censor knew that the only important matter on the mind of a man doing ten years – with more to come – is escape. But, while Lou was a mate, he was not a criminal, and wanted no part in a prison break. The censors didn't seem interested, either. But they should have – Brenden Abbott was not willing to accept his fate. He slept, ate and breathed escape plans.

The gun posts were the biggest hurdle. A good plan needed to cut the risk of a bullet in the back. How could would-be escapees either avoid the guards' attention or put enough doubt in their minds to keep their fingers clear of the trigger?

Abbott worked out part of the answer during the riot trial. Each prisoner involved was allowed to have several sets of clothes dropped off at the prison. Clothing brought into the prison when an inmate arrived was fully recorded, but the many bags of court clothes were simply hung on racks in the reception storeroom. The inmates were escorted from the divisions to reception, where they would be led in by a reception officer through the shower area to the main reception area, then sat on a bench attached to the wall.

On command, they would strip off their prison greens and put them into pillowcases on the bench. They would then line up naked along a line on the floor, where a prison officer would go through the body-search ritual – present both hands for checks, raise arms, turn around and lift the soles of the feet and then squat. The inmates then grabbed a towel off a stack and walked into the showers. Afterwards, another door in the shower area would be unlocked and they would enter a small change room where the bags with their civilian clothes were hung on a rack. Abbott noted that above the clothes rack were a couple of round ventilation holes about 20cm in diameter that went vertically into the roof. A scheduled two-day adjournment during the riot trial gave him the opportunity he needed.

During the early stages of the trial, the reception screws would leave one clothing bag that contained our civvies in the change room. Often, the screws were asked by inmates to get a different bag to the one they put in there. They soon got fed up with running around and chasing up different clothes bags, so, in the end, they would put all the bags in there. Standing on the clothes rack, I was able to reach the ventilation hole and stuffed some civilian clothing in it.

After returning from court that day, I pulled the clothing out of the vent and a couple of us wore the civvies under our prison greens and took them back to the division. The following day, due to a day off at court, I went and worked in the tailor shop, smuggling the clothing over with me. My major concern was getting sprung with it during one of the surprise searches they'd pull on us now and again, just prior to leaving the division to go to work. Once I got it over to the shop, it was stashed away within the storeroom.

A police security-video recording from 11 July 1988 shows Brenden and Glenn Abbott sitting together on a bench while the older brother puts his shoes on. Glenn keeps his head buried in his chest, glancing at the camera only once, while Brenden is alert and watchful. They are handcuffed together and stand up at the same time. Chains are fitted to Brenden's feet and they shuffle off down the hall to court. A more revealing video, in several respects, was recorded on 20 September. Abbott chats easily with the guards and it's clear he enjoys a friendly relationship with them. As he stands in a cell and strips, he waves his penis at the camera with a sly grin and then covers his face in mock modesty as he exits.

Abbott's theory that his riot-trial prognosis 'doesn't look too bad' was wrong. He received an additional six years prison in December 1988, after being convicted on all counts. Eventually, only Abbott and one other prisoner won appeals against their sentences. His jail term for the riot was reduced to four years, because the Appeals Court ruled that six years on top of a remaining nine years was too harsh for a man his age. Glenn's appeal was rejected and he swallowed the four years he received in addition to the bank robbery sentence.

Only days after the Fremantle verdict, Brenden Abbott returned to the Perth District Court again, on 14 December 1988, two years to the day after his burglary team hit the Homecraft store in Whitfords. The Homecraft manager gave evidence that a stock take revealed $20,000 worth of goods missing from the premises. Detective Bourke explained the raid on Jackie's Ozone Parade unit and related the recovery of the stolen goods, the trip to Nollamara police station and Abbott's surprise exit.

Abbott says he got the electrical goods from David Knapp and Mark Reynolds. They pleaded guilty to the charges in August 1987, each earning a nice stretch in Freo, along with Stabbie's younger brother, and the incorrigible Coops. Since they'd already pleaded guilty, it was a lot easier for Abbott, ethically speaking, to blame them. Abbott took the stand and gave his wide-eyed earnest version of events; the jury retired at 11.37am on the first day. At 6.01pm, they announced a deadlock and were discharged. Another jury reached the same point within a few hours of considering the case again on 29 March.

That month, Jackie Lord found the Lord and became a born-again Christian. Weeks later, on 5 May 1989, possibly through some kind of divine intervention, frustrated prosecutors entered a *nolle prosequi* on the Whitfords charges. In other words, they gave up the case.

Jackie remembers,

[I was] still visiting Brenden every week, my last visit to him was about 18 August 1989. He said, 'You're like the God Squad in here.' I thought that, with all the time he has, he might turn to the Lord and change his ways. I decided I couldn't keep waiting for this man to get out of jail. There was no life in it. So I kind of married my first husband Phil for the sake of breaking ties with Brenden. I told Brenden that I was going to go out with Phil. He asked me if I would marry him in jail in August 1989, and sent me a dozen red roses to show he meant it, as he never bought flowers [Abbott denies there was a proposal]. I was surprised and taken, even tempted, but I knew I had to make up my mind. I didn't visit or write again.

The last matter Abbott had to face court over was the cannabis found in his bags when arrested at Perth Airport. It was dealt with by a magistrate after Abbott pleaded not guilty. He says, 'The bastard found me guilty, and I think I received a fine on that one. More than anything, I was pissed off with getting a drug conviction.'

Meanwhile, the all-consuming task of planning an escape continued. He came up with the idea of fashioning a ladder – to get over the outer limestone wall – using material smuggled from the carpenters shop and metal shop. The plan was to use the seats in the One Division yard. They were to be painstakingly unbolted over the course of several weeks – Abbott had already made a start – and then fastened together with bolts. But the plot was doomed.

During one of my court appearances (maybe the Homecraft matter), while in a holding cell at the Central Law Courts, a bloke who was in the same division arrived on a later escort and gave me the mail that the escape plan had been brought undone. He told me the screws were in the yard that morning with some workers and the slats were hit with a power saw. Obviously, someone felt it was their duty to tell the screws about it. That's a major issue in the prison environment, with so many eyes on you from both sides; it's difficult to keep things dark. Word spreads like wildfire and, before long, the screws get wind of things. But that's just how it is.

Before being moved back into Main Division after it was rebuilt, Abbott began working in the tailor shop and was already working on new escape plans.

At first, I was working on going through the roof of the prisoners' toilet, and then digging through the limestone wall that would have brought me out on top of the print shop next door. It was at a blind spot from the gun posts and the hole in the wall could've only been spotted by someone being up on the roof of the print shop itself or by standing on something in the toilet area in an effort to see above the roof of the toilets.

Digging through the wall may sound like a feat in itself, but it wouldn't have been a real problem. The limestone walls at Fremantle were as soft as chalk in most places. From there, I hadn't yet decided in which direction we would go over the outer wall of the prison. I was already aware we could make it as far as the inner gates area by running across the print-shop roof, then over the main-stores roof and on to the roof of what was believed to be the armoury or the MSU's storeroom. From that roof, it would've required us jumping across to another area, but I wasn't sure if, in fact, it had a roof on it or not. Then it was just a matter of a small hop over the outer wall to freedom.

The roof of the inmates' toilet was what I considered the main hurdle to overcome at first, so I focused on that for the meantime. We would figure our route of exit from the prison during that time; if it required us making ropes to scale a wall, we were in the right place to do so.

Going through the inmates' toilet had to be set up in a way in which I could remove the asbestos sheeting of the toilet cubicle's roof and then be able to replace it quickly. Once I'd set that up, it was a matter of then cutting through the corrugated-iron roof before being able to work on the limestone wall. Because it would require working on the corrugated iron and the wall over a period of time, the asbestos sheeting, once put back in place, had to be done in a way where it wouldn't catch the eye of any screw during a ramp [search] of the tailor shop. Not only were the screws a worry, I didn't want other inmates who worked in the tailor shop to notice it. It was a process that would take time. But time I had plenty of and I knew I wasn't leaving for another jail in the near future. The first few days of the riot trial preliminary hearings I attended and it was fortunate I did. We were able to not only hear some of the evidence, but also view some of the photos tendered as exhibits, one of which was an aerial photograph of the prison complex, clear enough to show me there was indeed a roof to jump on to from the MSU storeroom (to reach the outer wall). Made my day, that did.

The tailor shop usually had about 15 to 20 inmates working in it. A prison officer and a civilian instructor would be rostered to supervise and, generally, the officer left the inmates alone to get on with their work. If the officer was called away to other duties or had the day off – which happened several times a month – only six to eight inmates were allowed to work. Abbott was always among the group. By now, several inmates were in on the new escape plan.

When the opportunity was right, I'd go into the toilet after the head count was done, and would stay in there not much longer than one would take to have a long shit. If anyone was heading in there, I'd get the mail from one of those in the work area. The screws' toilet was in the same area and they had to walk past our cubicle to use it – there was only a half-door on the inmates' toilet and that made it possible to be seen in it.

That plan was put on hold not long after going to work. So far, though, I'd removed the dowelling that ran around the edge of the asbestos and pulled the nails out that held them up. With a drill bit, I made a countersunk hole in the dowelling in a few places so it would hide the head of the screws used to hold it back in place. Then, with a smaller bit, I made another hole big enough for the screw's thread to go through the dowelling. The screws were screwed into the holes left by the nails to hold the dowelling back in place. Once it was up, I used some putty to cover the head of the screw and painted over the putty. Easy enough job in normal circumstances, but it was far from normal there. This had taken months to complete and I predicted it was going to take many more yet just to get started on digging through the limestone wall.

One day, out of the blue, someone in Main Division approached me asking if I wanted a hacksaw blade. I thought he was just talking shit, but told him if he could get hold of one I'd take it. He then pulls it out from the sleeve of his jumper and gives it to me. It was unused, I couldn't believe my luck. I had no plans to use it, but it could be useful. It was smuggled over to the tailor shop and stashed away.

Not long after that, dwelling away while sitting at my sewing machine and staring up at the windows to my right, I realised the blade could come in handy sooner than I thought. I'd come up with another idea to get out of the shop on to the print-shop roof. The row of windows in the tailor shop ran along the top of the southern wall. The base of these were about ten feet from the floor; the actual windows would've been about four to five feet high. Directly below one of the windows that could be opened was the inmates' fridge. It had crossed my mind – and surely that of many others over the years – that, if only it was possible to cut one of the bars, you could get out of the tailor shop, then possibly over the outer western wall to freedom. It seemed an impossible feat to cut the bars without being noticed by the screws. From their office, they couldn't miss you, but, when only the one screw was working in the shop, he would always sit at the desk next to the phone where there was a blind spot.

The tailor-shop instructor was a Macedonian man who had migrated to Australia in the 1970s and had worked in the prison for many years. He was a tailor by trade and Abbott's ability to learn quickly impressed him.

> *He [the instructor] was a nice bloke. We got along quite well and we would often chat about anything in general. I actually enjoyed the work and soon learned from scratch how to make all the garments the shop produced. The instructor saw that I was keen to learn the trade and was more than happy to pass on his expertise. In time, I was able to make any item and use any of the machines in the shop. Speciality jobs were handed to me, including measuring up fat bastards who had nothing that would fit them when they came in.*

Abbott's skills were in hot demand and he was soon making garments to order and design. The only restriction on the fashion-conscious inmates was the colour – prison green – although kitchen workers were allowed to wear white. Abbott would exchange his handiwork for canteen items and cannabis, which was rife in the prison. But his new skills and friendships also delivered far more important benefits.

> *The instructor had an interest in the property market and he would often chat about it if you got him started. His other liking was reading hardcore stick books. That type of reading material was floating around everywhere in prison in those days. Now you're lucky to get hold of a Penthouse. Since the introduction of female screws working in men's prisons, they've clamped down on that type of reading material. I think the instructor had a similar problem at home with his wife.*
>
> *Often when we were escorted over to the tailor shop, he'd be standing at the entrance with the door open. Before we'd go in, we had to place our carry bags into the cubicle shelving just outside. Now and then, he'd get eye contact with me and then eye my bag to see if I had any stick books. I'd found in the past that if I gave him a stick book – the more hardcore the better – he'd disappear into his office and study every detail of the photos and pretty much ignore the goings-on in the shop. I figured this could help out in what I had in store for the future and held off bringing over more. I got hold of as many hardcore books as I could and snookered them for the right time.*

In the tailor-shop store room were racks holding rolled-up garments that had been cut out and were yet to be assembled. Each roll had every part of the intended garment and sizes were marked with dressmakers chalk. Years before Abbott's arrival, the tailor shop had produced other garments, and material from those days was still in storage. They included grey drill-material aprons and navy-blue overalls, which happened to be the same outfit worn by the MSU.

I soon figured that wearing these when running across the roofs would deter a trigger-happy screw in a gun post. There would be no way I could get away with knocking them up without being seen; the blue colour would catch the screws' eyes like a red flag to a bull. Not only that, I'd never made overalls before, anyway. The idea of wearing the overalls came to me early in the initial escape plan. Pulling it off was still some time away, so I figured I'd just ask the instructor if he'd teach me how to make them. He said he would, but some other time and I left it at that. As time went by, I hit him again with it.

Finally, when things were quiet one day, he showed me how to put them together. After running through the steps on one pair, he left it with me to go it alone and told me to grab a couple of pairs from the store to knock up. I grabbed about seven pairs, one size to fit me, the others were one size down. I raced through making them and showed him about three pairs I'd made, the others I made I hid back in the store. The ones I showed him included the pair that was my size and, as I would later learn, the same size as the screw working in the shop for that roster. I distinctly recall him saying that day how a pair of those would be good for whenever he goes fishing.

I also had to make the hats to go with the overalls. These weren't a real issue; I'd already been knocking up the baseball-type hats by modifying the prison-issue hats for inmates. A number of blokes were getting around with these and the instructor actually pulled me up about making them. He didn't really make an issue of it, but I thought I'd best pull up before someone did. The ones I made to use with the overalls, I coloured black with a permanent black marker pen.

I wanted to go even further in making the escape outfit look the real thing. The MSU uniforms also had embroidered badges on their hats and on the top of both sleeves of the overalls. These consisted of the WA Coat of Arms, [featuring a swan] and the words: WA PRISONS DEPARTMENT.

It was by chance that I noticed a couple in a drawer in the screw's office. He would always keep it locked; I thought I had no chance of ever getting my hands on them. The drawer was a part of the instructor's desk, just a few feet from the office door. While standing there asking for something one day, I noticed the drawer open and saw the badges in it. Then, on another occasion while at the door, the drawer was open again and, since he had his back turned, I managed to swipe one.

Each outfit would require at least three badges. No way was I able to get that many, there was only about two in the drawer as it was. So in using canvas and paints, I spent many hours of the nights in my cell trying out my artistic skills. They turned out pretty good, if I do say so myself. I made at least eight of these. There were definitely three who were going over the wall when the day came.

Abbott sewed the badges on to the hats and hid them in the tailor-shop storeroom. The area was supposed to be permanently locked and out of bounds to prisoners but he says it was never locked during the day.

The instructor was never involved or present when the ramps were on and he would always lock up the storeroom at the end of every day.

As for sewing the badges on the overalls, I thought that would be too risky. That would require those to be hidden as well, not as easy to do as the caps. The other pairs I put in the store were hidden among the rolls of overalls yet to be put together. The plan was to get super glue in the meantime and stick the badges on when it was time to go.

By now I had just about everything in place; the major obstacle was cutting the bar at the windows. Continuing with that depended on the instructor or the screw being on his own and with the six to eight inmates being in the shop. The identities of those inmates had a bearing, too. I was, however, able to influence the instructor into which inmates he'd call over, but usually I could only manage this for the afternoons on the days he was on his *own. Cutting the bar when just a screw was in the shop seemed an unlikely task; but, luckily, not all of them were on the ball.*

When the opportunity did arise to chop away at it, I'd keep the instructor occupied. Sometimes it'd be the stick books, other times, I'd just stand at the door of his office and chat with him. Then there were the times I'd use an oil stone that was kept in his office for sharpening scissors. I got it off him, and put it on the table next to the office door. I would sharpen up mine and others' scissors while at the same time, yarn away with the instructor as he sat in the chair next to the phone. Meanwhile, someone would be standing on top of the fridge sawing away at the bar, ever so slowly to keep the noise down, and watching me the whole time. If the instructor – or sometimes it was the screw – went to make a move out of his chair, the bloke doing the cutting would get the mail and jump down from the fridge. We had some close calls. When I was sharpening the scissors on one occasion, the instructor hopped up out of his chair unexpectedly to make his way out into the shop. I quickly moved into his office, asking him for the large bottle of oil on top of the cupboard behind him. This oil was for the sewing machines and to top up the smaller bottles floating around the shop. My sudden move startled him as much as he did me when he hopped up; that was the nearest he came to springing us.

When the bar was being worked on, the other inmates would be busy on their sewing machines to help cover the hacksaw noise. With the machines working overtime, I couldn't help feeling that all this sudden work would create suspicion. Even the cleaner would get in on the act, banging things as he swept the floors. At times, it was difficult not to smile.

Coincidentally, the cleaner at the time was Bobby Thorton, a well-known Perth tattooist who had applied Abbott's first piece of ink when he was a teenager – a winged serpent on his shoulder.

Leading up to the escape, about four people I trusted and thought would come on board were invited. When asked, none needed time to think about it and were in. They all started to work in the tailor shop, but many pulled out as it drew closer to the time to go. I guess during the quiet moments in their cells, the fact there were two gun posts to run between may have played a part.

Abbott, too, had his doubts about whether they could make it out alive. At night in his cell, quietly smoking a joint, worst-case scenarios would drift across his mind as he stared out of the barred window. But he decided to take the chance of a bullet in the back.

When stoned, the paranoia works overtime and many a night I was awake until the early hours. It tends to make me think of all the things that can go wrong; it even had me feeling they knew it was to go down and they'd be ready for us when we were running across the roofs. The following day, when I was no longer stoned, I'd just tell myself I shouldn't be smoking the shit while I've got this on the go. But, as soon as more pot was available, I'd do it to myself all over again.

As the planning continued, Abbott harangued a detective to return some sunglasses and a scanner that were seized from him at Perth Airport, and the detective eventually dropped them off at the prison.

The scanner was signed out to a visitor and I gave instructions that it be dropped off at the same place where I'd earlier organised a bag of my clothing to be left. Inmates were able to buy small AM/FM radios through the prison canteen and it was possible to modify their circuit boards to enable them to tune into the local police frequency. I managed to get hold of two radios and made the modifications. I'd used scanners in the past when up to no good and they'd saved my arse a number of times. I figured that having something similar for the escape would be a great help once over the wall.

Some months prior to the escape, a young bloke by the name of Aaron Reynolds had arrived at Fremantle Prison. He'd been recaptured after escaping from Bunbury Prison some weeks earlier. Not long after arriving back in Fremantle, he started working in the tailor shop. Another bloke, Willy M, had also started to work in the shop just prior to the escape, was on remand over a murder blue [linked to his alleged involvement with 'Hungry' Jack Van Tongeren and his racist group, the Australian Nationalists Movement] and was looking down the barrel of a 20-year stretch if convicted. When he became aware of the go, he wanted to be on board. Who could blame him? By then, those who were initially in on it had pulled the pin. One of them later changed his mind and was back in, only to change his mind again some weeks later. He continued to work in the shop though and I thought he'd probably change his mind again when the go went down.

When Aaron got wind of it, he also wanted in, which I thought wasn't a bright move. I even tried to talk some sense into him; he was only doing 18 months max, but he insisted on being part of it. It wasn't up to me to stop him if he wanted to go. To prove that he was determined to be in on it, he insisted on having a chop at the bar when the next opportunity arose. But he almost fucked it completely with his eagerness; the first time he was working on it, there was a snap and the distinctive sound of a hacksaw blade hitting concrete. I didn't have to look to see what he'd just done and couldn't help thinking, You useless fucking goose. I was keeping the screw occupied when that went down and was sure that was the end of that hacksaw blade. Luckily, it wasn't the case, only a small piece had broken off and we were still in business.

I had doubts about letting him have another shot, but told him to take it easy, just relax and take it slow, for fuck's sake. He got the message. Aaron managed to get more of the bar cut than anyone else; he had some heart and guts about him, but the grey matter was still scattered, as is the case with most at that age. Over just a couple of sessions, he cut well over three-quarters of the bar. I figured two more cracks at it and we were on our way, but things happened sooner than expected.

On the morning of Friday, 24 November 1989, the tailor shop had both the instructor and a screw in the shop and all inmates employed as normal. I had no indication that either was to have the afternoon off until being called over to the workshop after lunch. The instructor had some personal matters he needed to sort out. The screw working in the shop that afternoon had been rostered there for the last month or so and wasn't shy about having a chat with inmates. He was easygoing and caused no dramas. I figured we were able to go to work on the bar while he was here.

I got the hacksaw from the stash spot in the store and gave it to Aaron. I then stood in the doorway and started having a yarn with the screw in the office. Aaron was up on the fridge and went for it. He was at it for about ten minutes when I heard a slight crack, but it wasn't the hacksaw blade he'd broken again. He jumped down from off the fridge and hung around the sink area next to it, giving me the nod. I cut the conversation with the screw and made my way over to Aaron and looked up at the bar.

It was obvious to a blind person it was cut. What made it so obvious was it wasn't straight. The bars are under tension and, when cut through, they bow – something the screws wouldn't miss at all. I never expected to be going over the wall that day, but, the bar being as it was, I felt to leave it another day would only have the whole plan come to a crumbling heap. It was now or never and I told Aaron we had to go now or we may never get the chance.

Willy also got the mail, and, for the next 15 to 20 minutes, I was busy getting the overalls, civvies, hats, radios, plastic bag and $20 cash from where they were stashed. As for sticking the badges on the overalls, I didn't have the superglue and there wasn't time to sew them on. Just had to go without them. While I was getting all this together, Aaron and Willy were on their machines and another bloke in the workshop was busy talking to the screw in the office, after I asked him to keep him occupied.

Aaron then got on top of the fridge and I passed him all the gear and he tossed it on to the print-shop roof. Then the cut bar was pulled aside and we each took our turn to squeeze through the bars on to the print-shop roof. Once on the roof, we moved to the left to be out of sight of those in the shop and stripped off our prison greens, put on our civvies and then into the overalls. Aaron and Willy were already in their overalls when I realised the pair I was putting on weren't my size. I said to them that one of you have got mine. But my pair weren't there; they were probably at the screw's house or in the bastard's boat.

I had to settle for a pair a size or two too small. They were a tight fit to get into and the leg hem sat some way above my ankles, but this was not a time to worry about one's vanity. As all this was going on, the adrenalin was flowing and my heart was pumping overtime.

Once we were all dressed the part in uniforms and caps, I put my radio in the plastic bag and rolled it up and put it into the front of my overalls. Willy had the other radio and put it in his pocket with an earphone from it to his ear. I then moved back towards the windows of the tailor shop to look in. By now, there were a couple of inmates standing at the door talking to the *screw; he wasn't on to being a few short yet. I then crept along the roof of the print shop in the direction we needed to go. The roofs of these shops were slanted on a 45-degree angle, and the further I crept away from the tailor-shop windows, the higher up I was. Bit by bit, I was able to view the gun post to my north. I was getting too far away from the other two and still wasn't able to clearly see the gun post or the screw who was in it.*

I gave up and made my way back to the other two and told them I wasn't able to spot the screw in there unless I was almost to the end of the print-shop roof. I said, 'Fuck it, we'll just go for it and hope for the best.'

They agreed and, on the count of three, we all bolted. I was in front, Aaron a close second and Willy close to his heels. We leaped off the print-shop roof together, about two or three metres down on to the prison's main store roof. With the three of us hitting it, there was an almighty bang and I felt the corrugated-iron roof buckle. The stores roof was also on a 45-degree angle and we were running uphill to make the next jump. The next roof we landed on was flat iron; a few metres along that and we were on to the MSU's store, or the armoury roof. A few more metres along that roof, we had to jump across a gap and on to a small roof. This area was the stepping stone that I had doubts about some months ago. I distinctly recall that jump; my foot just made it on the top of the wall as I jumped across, then on to the small roof. Then it was just a small climb over the actual outer wall and on to a roof that came off the wall on the other side. Jumping off that, I was out of the prison. Aaron was a split second behind, but there was no sign of Willy.

There was a story going around that he broke his ankle, but he sent me a letter that explained that was not the case. I was happy about the fact we escaped when the [tailor-shop] instructor wasn't on, though it doesn't mean I wouldn't have done so otherwise. Obviously he would've copped some flak over it, especially with them seeing Willy's attire. Somehow, none of the gun post screws or screws at the front gate area actually saw us. I saw a re-enactment of the escape on Australia's Most Wanted some years later. It showed the gun-post screws giving us a wave and we returned the gesture. Like fuck we did. I was too occupied to even look that way, but I was listening out for the distinctive sound of a rifle going off.

After leaving the prison walls, we ran through the large car park directly west of the prison. Once we got closer to the Fremantle CBD, we stripped off our overalls. I unrolled the plastic shopping bag that had the radio in it and we casually strolled into Freo's main street, which had a few MTT buses parked in it. We jumped on one but the driver didn't have change for the $20 note I had. He wasn't due to start his route for a few minutes, which gave me time to break the note at a nearby shop. I sat down on the bus, pulled out the radio and tuned into the local police frequency. The bus started its route and one of the first streets it took ran directly next to Freo Prison's north wall. The prison sirens were going off and I heard activity on the police frequency relating to the escape before I lost radio reception. After some distance, we got off and walked down a street that brought us to Stirling Highway. We sat in a Hungry Jack's store and bought a burger and a drink while I pondered our next move.

I found out years later that Willy miscued his jump and landed in between the front-gate area. He wandered around looking for a way out ... He said he got more of a hard time from the detectives who interviewed him than the screws. We would've only had about 15 minutes' head start. But, when it comes to a jailbreak, any head start is a good head start.

Munching on his Whopper, Reynolds grinned like a schoolkid, but Abbott's jaw was set, his mind already analysing their available options and resources. And he swore to himself for at least the second time in his life: 'That's the last fucking time.'

Chapter Eight

1989–1990

The events in Brenden Abbott's life over the next six weeks changed him forever, and etched a new criminal legend in the Australian psyche – the 'Postcard Bandit'.

For the first time, Abbott reveals – in his own selective detail – what happened in that chaotic summer of 1989, when he came to the conclusion that, to remain a free man, he needed to vanish and reinvent himself.

After their bus ride, Abbott and Reynolds spent hours on foot. They ended up in affluent South Perth in the early hours of the next morning, where they stole a Holden Commodore. Later in the morning, they called in to see one of Abbott's mates, after scanning the street for police surveillance.

I went through the yard of the house behind his and jumped the fence. He was surprised when I shook him awake. He then shook my hand and congratulated me. Without asking, he was up grabbing his wallet, saying, 'No doubt you'll be needing some cash.' He gave me about $100, apologising for not having more. I commented that this was far more than I had before. From there I quickly departed, with him wishing me the best of luck. Next stop was Warwick shopping centre. I arranged with the person who'd been holding my clothes and scanner to meet me in the car park. He soon pulled in and parked, still in the

Commodore. I pulled alongside his car. Within seconds, I had
the bag in the car and an extra $500 and we parted.

The fugitives kept a low profile in the following days, sleeping on the beaches north of Perth, grateful that it was summer. The first thing they had to do was to get some 'tools of the trade' so that they could pull a job and get some cash.

In the early hours of Wednesday, 29 November 1989, the Max Williams gun shop in Rokeby Road, Subiaco, was burgled. The thieves peeled back a sheet of roofing and stole two shotguns. At 2.50pm that day, a stolen Holden Commodore stopped near the ANZ bank at the Innaloo shopping centre in Oswald Street. Two men with balaclavas, overalls and shotguns ordered staff and customers to the floor. When a staff member reached for an alarm button, one bandit warned her she would be shot. The other bandit collected $6,672 from the teller drawers and they escaped. The stolen Commodore was found abandoned a few streets away.

While back in Freo, I often thought of scenarios of being on the run
and the idea of lying low in the bush appeared to be the best option.
*   Staying with people was far too risky, especially anyone that*
was known by police as being a friend. Staying with family was
totally out of the question.

On 1 December 1989, the *West Australian* warned: 'More hold-ups feared with escapees at large'.

The same day, somewhere on the eastern seaboard, a Japanese tourist named Masao Ayuda took his first breath of Australian air, pondering his options for the next two months. He'd have a look around the Gold Coast first, kick up his heels for his 31st birthday in two days' time, then perhaps a package tour. The guy at the airport said they were a good bet; plenty of chicks from Tokyo signed on for them. Masao was exhilarated; Australia was going to be an adventure.

In Western Australia, about three days after the escape, they headed to the seaside city of Mandurah, south of Perth.

In the days following, we scored cash [ANZ Bank robbery] and
went on a spending spree at another camping store in a suburb
of Perth. It was probably the owner's best sale for a month. He

was alone and the shop was empty of customers. On the counter were boxes of buckshot shotgun rounds. We stacked up the gear on the counter and, as it was checked and rung off on the till, Aaron proceeded to take it out to the car. A few boxes of buckshot were put in the gear, unknown to the owner. After the sale was almost complete, I thought I'd put it to the owner for a few boxes of the shotgun rounds. Wouldn't believe it, he sold me a few boxes. With the laws so strict when even buying ammo in WA, I thought I'd be pushing shit uphill buying them without a licence. But, with the cash we were spending, the more the merrier, he was thinking. We were now pretty well set up for a decent bush camp. There were still a few other items to get, though.

Initially, we camped just outside of Armadale [29km from Perth] near the base of the Canning Dam. On a trip to the central shopping area of Armadale, I was recognised by a fucking screw. You wouldn't fucking read about it. Some time after going back to Fremantle for the Belmont job, there had been a new screw who had a tendency to openly stare at me. I often felt like asking him what his problem was. His look wasn't one of animosity and the way he dealt with me was civil. After a few weeks of weighing me up, he realised I was approachable and civil. It was then I became aware of his obvious interest in me. It turns out he was a courier for the Commonwealth Bank and on the morning the Belmont branch was robbed (that I was convicted of) he had rocked up doing his delivery just after. He believed that, if he was a few minutes earlier, he would've been there as the robbery went down. On this day in Armadale, he was using an ATM. I was walking past with something I'd just bought for the campsite, and our eyes met. Naturally, you can imagine what I thought. I know what he thought, something like: 'Fuck!'

I just gave him a half-smile and proceeded around the side of the building, and he followed. I turned to face him and put down what I was carrying. My loose-fitting oversized T-shirt wasn't tucked in and hung over the waist of my pants. I quickly put my right hand under my shirt and made it look like I was reaching for something in my waistband. I didn't have a fucking thing there, other than my cock, a few inches lower. But the move worked and he suddenly put his hands slightly up, around shoulder height, palms facing me, as if to say: 'Whoa, I'm not going to do anything.'

All he said was: 'You've caused some drama.'

I said, 'Like what?'

And he said, 'Back at the jail.'

I then said, 'Well, we aren't back at the jail now. It'd be best if you'd just fuck off.'

He also thought that was a good idea, since he no doubt thought I was armed, and proceeded to walk towards Albany Highway. I knew where he was heading. Living in Armadale some years earlier at Coops's and Val's house while I was working at Pinjarra, I knew where the local cop shop was.

In a mad rush, I had to find Aaron at the shopping complex not far from where I was. I found him and said, 'We have to get to the car now and get out of here.'

I explained the meeting with the screw as we headed for the car. As Aaron drove the car out of the car park, we turned right towards the cop shop. I bobbed down in the passenger side and, sure enough, there was the screw, almost to the cop shop. But, as we passed him, it seemed he had second thoughts. He turned around and headed back in the other direction.

After we eventually got all the required gear – as well as a camera which Aaron seemed to have a liking for – we headed down south to a camping area next to a river near Dwellingup. On the way, we passed through the small town where the infamous police station photo was taken with Aaron leaning on the fence. I thought it may have been a good snap for the album, but never expected it would end up in the hands of the cops. When we got to where we planned to spend a week or more by the river, the campsite took a half-hour or more to set up.

We had two shotguns with us and put one each under two sleeping bags that were rolled out in the tent. Later on, as night set in, I went and caught some marron for dinner (freshwater crayfish – a food source I often would eat when staying in the bush around Perth in times that followed). We'd already eaten a few (undersize at that) and we headed back to the water's edge to catch some more. Heading back to cook the fresh catch, this cunt has to spring from behind some bushes with his torch on us, telling us to: 'Hold it there!' frightening the life out of both Aaron and myself. Even the marron we had shit itself.

It took a moment to realise they weren't cops, they were fisheries. We were catching marron out of season, or undersized, or both. We were breaking the law. I mean, how fucking dare we? Anyway, they took our names and addresses and vehicle reg. I gave the name of a friend who later got a fine in the post. They searched the campsite and the car for marron, but there weren't any to be found, other than the ones we'd just caught and the shells from those we ate. One of the inspectors asked if we were in the army, I guess because of the short hair. Anyway, we played it cool and they fucked off. The campsite was packed up in a matter of seconds and we were out of there. In the days that followed, we headed north to Lancelin and eventually back to the spot below the Canning Dam wall, downstream some 100 or more yards [from their original camp].

It was while camped here that I started to change my appearance. I shaved the top of my head, leaving hair around the back and sides. The part of my head that was shaved was white as a ghost and I spent hours getting sun on it to give it some colour. It's amazing how it changes one's appearance. I got the idea from adverts I'd seen in newspapers for Ashley & Martin. They show before and after shots of a bald bloke, then with a head of hair. Some days later, I caught up with someone who knew me very well. He didn't recognise me until I spoke, even then it took a long look before he jerried that it was me. Do it properly and it can fool the most observant person, do otherwise and you'll stand out like a pimple on an arse. After I'd done myself up this way, I felt far more comfortable in getting around Perth during the day. Aaron had dyed his hair black and looked much different himself. We started to stay in some motels after the changes to our appearances.

They spent a night at the White Sands Hotel in Scarborough, where Abbott stood idly at the window and took a picture of the nearby and far more luxurious Observation City, Jackie's former workplace and the former jewel in the crown of the now-disgraced Alan Bond.

A few days before parting WA, my dick got the better of me and I attended a brothel in the Perth city area. I think it was called the Scarlet Garter. On this night, my disguise was the balding guy. I spent an hour with a young English girl who was touring the country and using the gold mine she obviously knew she had to help pay the way. She wasn't a bad-looking sort at all. As she led me out the door, she told me, 'Be careful and don't get yourself caught.'

That caught me by surprise and the expression on my face drew a smile from her. I gave that place a miss – as well as any other brothel in Perth – from then on. Well, for a few years anyway.

On 12 December 1989, a Mitsubishi Cordia turbo was stolen from Hastings Street, Scarborough. On 14 December, a Holden Commodore was stolen from the Karrinyup shopping centre in Perth's northern suburbs and driven to the Whitfords shopping centre, a few minutes' drive north. One man waited in the car while another entered a TAB with a shotgun. He threatened a staff member and a customer and appeared very nervous. He waved the shotgun wildly and took some convincing that they had only $4,048. At 2.20am on Saturday, 16 December, the paths of Brenden Abbott, Aaron Reynolds and the WA police finally collided.

It was the early hours of 15 or 16 December that an incident went down which led me to think leaving the state would be a good move. I was driving a Cordia turbo along Hepburn Avenue and turned right to get on to the Mitchell Freeway. At that intersection was a set of lights. I was halfway across the intersection waiting for the few cars heading in the opposite direction to go past, before being able to do the right-hand turn. I stalled the car and had to use the screwdriver to start it. In that time, the lights changed to red. Since I was in the centre of the intersection, when the car started, I continued the right turn.

As I got on to Mitchell Freeway, a cop van gave chase and turned his lights on. I pulled over and had intended to play it by ear and explain I'd stalled the car. Aaron was playing up big time.

He said, 'What the fuck are you doing? Just gun it, we can outrun them, it's just a van.'

I had no doubt whatsoever that the Cordia would, but to do so would only indicate to the cops that there's something amiss.

I was going to attempt to talk my way out of it. If it looked like things weren't going my way, I'd be dropping the clutch and out of there. A cop got out of the van and walked towards the Cordia from behind. Watching him in the mirror, he seemed casual in his demeanour as he approached and then looked as though he was heading to the passenger-side door. On telling Aaron this, he pulls the shotgun up off the floor and chambers a round. I decided it might not be in everyone's best interest to hang around. I was out of there. The next off-ramp was Warwick Road and I took it to get into the side streets to lie low for a while, and use the scanner for its purpose in situations like these.

I turned left on to Warwick Road and then into the first right and, as I did so, a fucking pursuit car was heading towards me on Warwick Road as I did the right. It followed me. Because I wasn't familiar with this area, I wasn't going to get boxed in. I then turned another right and stopped the car. The pursuit car came around to the left side of the Cordia as I reversed and it clipped my left mirror.

At this time, Aaron lets go with the shotgun. I head back the way I came and see the cop van heading towards us. Aaron lets another round off while hanging out the window, pointing it in front of the Cordia at the oncoming van. I realise I'm with a loose cannon. After a few side streets and having no idea where I was, it was time to leave the vehicle because there were no cops following. Get out while the going's good. I parked the Cordia in a driveway of a house and jumped a few fences. Aaron was right with me, carrying both shotguns. The scanner was left behind, as well as some other things, one being my baseball cap and a roll of film.

Next thing was to find some cover and lie low. We'd come on to another street and by now could hear sirens. A shrub in front of a house caught my eye. It was halfway between the front of the house and the street. In the carport of the house was a car with its boot open. In a flash, I cancelled that idea. With all the activity going on around us, I hid under the bush, as did Aaron, the shotguns with us. Then there were cop cars cruising that street and, next, cops on foot walking around us. I thought we were fucked. They were at the bush with their torches shining at the base of it. As luck would have it, they didn't see us. I couldn't believe it.

After waiting a while, I buried the shotguns in a sand heap on someone's front lawn, with the intention of collecting them. Just after that, we heard a car coming down the street at a snail's pace without its headlights on. The cops were still in the area. We *made for cover again. This time, I got between a house window and a wall that had gaps in it, a trellis-like thing. Aaron squatted near the front door of the house, with some cover from the road. He was only metres from me and we could see each other. We were next to a lane at one point and we actually heard whispering from the house opposite. The cops were lying in wait in case we walked through the lane.*

We sat it out there until after sunrise, when we saw a bloke walking along the street in his work garb. Aaron and I caught up to him and made chit-chat, asking where we could catch a bus. He pointed us in the right direction and the bus we caught took us all the way into Perth to the main bus terminal. It was full of people going to work. I copped stares, since I'd left the cap in the car. I wasn't able to cover the melon and the bald head was well past having a five o'clock shadow. If anyone asked, I would've just said it was a party joke. After getting into the Perth bus station, a cap was the first buy. I realised that, after last night's episode, the heat would be on, big time. Helmets and motorbikes were the next targets.

At 11am on 16 December 1989, a motorcycle was stolen from a city car park and, a short time later, a second similar bike disappeared from the car park of Curtin University in Bentley.

We collected the two shotguns that night and I think it was the next morning that we headed east. The bikes we had were the same type and colour. I'd had very little experience in riding road bikes, but I got the hang of it in no time. We both had duffle bags that hang over the seat behind the rider. We had a two-man tent and sleeping bags, and slept on the side of the road until we reached Adelaide.

While in Adelaide, Aaron called in to see some relatives. Understandably, they didn't want to help out. The SA police were soon aware of our presence in that city and paid Aaron's relatives a visit. It soon came to my attention that the law knew we were on motorbikes, days after we parted with the relatives. I told Aaron, 'Now you know you can't trust those relatives.'

On Thursday, 21 December 1989, a man wearing a wide-brimmed khaki hat – just like the one Abbott wore in pictures taken at the

Dwellingup bush camp – walked into the National Bank on Dequetteville Terrace, Kent Town. He wore a thick black moustache and carried a blue bag, which landed on a teller's drawer. She looked up, straight down the barrel of a sawn-off shotgun. He ordered her to fill the bag, and then exited with $8,000, fleeing in an early-model Commodore. Abbott and Reynolds arrived in Melbourne on 22 December, where Abbott decided to visit a long-lost relative of his own: his father, Brian.

My father lived in the western suburbs of Melbourne and I had decided to pay him a visit the night we arrived in the city. We hoped that we could find somewhere to lie low for a while (by myself maybe, but, for the two of us, highly unlikely). Just as we came into the first built-up area of Melbourne from the west, we stopped at a caravan park and got a cabin for the night. I then looked up my father's address and rode to his house while Aaron remained at the caravan park.

It was 1972 when I last saw my father. I often thought about what to say to him when I met him again. I had no ill feeling towards him for his departure all those years earlier. All sorts of things were going through my head on the ride to his house. What would his response be to seeing me? Would he know I'd escaped from prison? If so, would he call the cops on me? How can I trust him if I don't know him? I soon found his house and pulled up at the gate. I turned the bike off and, when I was about to walk through the gate, I couldn't bring myself to go any further. I got on the bike and headed back to the caravan park. I told Aaron I had a quick chat with him and he told me he couldn't help out. I didn't know any other relatives in Melbourne and knew no one else there. My eldest brother in Alice Springs, David, I didn't really know too well. My eldest sister, Janet, I wouldn't ask for any help.

The only other person I knew who might be of help was Che. He was living in the town of Temora in New South Wales. The last time I'd seen Che was late 1985 after returning from Port Hedland, though I had still been in touch with him since, via the phone and the occasional letter. I knew Che would help if he could and I put it to Aaron about heading to NSW. He didn't need persuading. What else or who else could we turn to? Any plan was better than the one we currently didn't have. The next day (Christmas Eve), we made our way to Temora and got there late in the evening. Che had no warning of our arrival and, as it turned out, wasn't aware of my escape from prison. He was actually based in Wagga Wagga, but was in Temora for Christmas with his family. Aaron and myself were taking a few of them for joy-rides on the bike.

While we were in Temora, Che, Aaron, Che's sister Louise and myself went to the RSL for dinner. I still was getting around as the balding guy, but much of the time was wearing a golfer's-type cap; a bit more classy than a baseball cap. I wasn't paying as much attention to having it look the part due to the cap. But, in the RSL, there are no hats allowed and the waitress asked me to remove it. There was an odd look from her when I did.

We stayed in Temora for a few days and Che offered to help us get accommodation, preferably in Wollongong [which Abbott was familiar with from his time there working at the pub with Lou]. We decided the bikes had served their purpose. We'd been lucky not to be pulled over for the entire trip. We had to go to Wagga [on 27 December] for two reasons: to catch the train to Sydney and for Che to sort out matters where he was currently living. Aaron took care of getting rid of the bikes and rode them into the Murrumbidgee River. It was the discovery of the bikes on the following day after we left for Sydney that brought the spotlight and cops to Che's parents in Temora and the story of the two escapees and stolen bikes. This news wasn't greeted warmly.

After our arrival in Sydney, we stayed in a real dive called the CB Hotel, a backpackers on Pitt Street. The next day [28 December], we headed to Wollongong and, after a day or so, Che arranged to rent a flat for us. After we got the flat, I shaved off the remaining hair. Maintaining the balding-guy look got to be too much and it had served its purpose. Next was getting the power on at the joint. Unlike other states, getting the power on wasn't as simple as it sounds, especially if you haven't got ID. Using Che's name was out of the question, but, before we could get over that hurdle, we were on the move again. There was a write-up in the local paper and, when Che rang his parents, we knew we had to part company and leave the flat we'd just paid bond for. Che was to go back to Wagga to help police with their investigations. He wasn't able to tell them anything, aside from the fact that we were *heading for Sydney [on 30 December]. By the time they got that info, Aaron and I were halfway to Adelaide again.*

On 20 December 1989, Masao Ayuda paid for a tour bus package trip at Adventure Passport Travel, beginning at Surfers Paradise on 28 December. Sitting on a bus bound for Adelaide on New Year's Eve, he drank in the views, thrilled by the wide brown land opening up in front of him.

Abbott:

On one of the meal stops on the bus ride to Adelaide, I got talking to a Japanese tourist on the same bus. I'd been doing a Japanese language course while in Freo. Though I knew some of the language, I was far from being fluent. We spent the remainder of the trip to Adelaide trying to have a conversation. After a few days in Adelaide and sightseeing with Masao, Aaron and I decided to join him on his trip around Australia. It was a great way to keep ahead of the law and also to experience a holiday after the years locked up. As well as that, to see and do things most of us wish to in our lives. The money to cover expenses for such a holiday was in abundance.

In Adelaide on Tuesday, 2 January 1990, a lone bandit entered the robbery-prone National Bank branch on Dequetteville Terrace, armed with a pump-action shotgun. He calmly threw a bag at one of the tellers, ordering her to fill it. 'Keep filling it up. I don't want to hurt you. I just want the money,' he told her.

He fled with $19,500 and jumped into a stolen red Commodore. The same day as this robbery, Abbott and Reynolds – or 'Walter' and 'Peter' – got on a bus with their Japanese travelling companion. It was heading for Uluru in the Northern Territory. And, all the while, Aaron's camera worked overtime.

Abbott:

At that point in my life, my main objective was to remain free, but enjoy life to the full, since it could come to an end at any time. But, unlike Aaron, I had some idea of how to avoid situations that could result in being captured, much of which one would call using common sense. We all caught a coach to Ayers Rock and spent a few days at the resort there.

On 4 January, WA police named Brenden James Abbott and Aaron Raymond Reynolds as the state's most wanted men. The latest theory put Abbott in Sydney. The tourist cover story was working out nicely. Back in Perth on 7 January, Jackie Lord married her new boyfriend, Phil, as a way of 'cutting ties' with Abbott, she says. Because what might happen, she thought, if he decided to come knocking on her door again? But Jackie was a long way from Abbott's thoughts.

The following day [5 January], we all left on a coach for Alice Springs. On arrival, we booked into a hotel. Masao booked two rooms in his name because I was concerned about not having any ID. Masao had a room to himself. That night, we called an escort agency and the girl they sent out provided her expertise to the three of us, one at a time, while the other two were in the other room.

From Alice Springs, I believe Masao's next planned stop on his travel itinerary was Cairns. For some reason, Aaron and myself decided to fly to Darwin. Could've been that Masao was to go to Darwin anyway, but by bus. Whatever, we covered his airfare to Darwin. Before we left for Darwin, we still had both shotguns with us. One could be broken down and the barrel could be removed from the breech. But, with the other, this wasn't possible. We decided to leave that behind. We hid that one in the base of one of the single bed ensembles. As far as I know, it's still there today.

Arriving in Darwin, we then booked into the Atrium Hotel. It was there that the photo was taken of me in the swimming pool with the hat on and holding up the glass. While in Darwin, we took a flight in a light aircraft over Kakadu's twin falls and Jim Jim Falls. We landed at Jabiru and did a tour to the uranium mine and to the Croc Hotel before flying back to Darwin. On another day, there was a trip to Darwin's crocodile farm.

A few days later, we headed for Cairns and checked into a hotel called Acacia Court. The accommodation here was a part of Masao's itinerary around Australia. He wasn't able to get a triple room, so we got two rooms on the same floor. Masao and Aaron went off and rented a small Suzuki-type four-wheel drive and were checking out the surrounds of Cairns, snapping away with their cameras.

That night, we called the services of the local escort agency after the barman at the Acacia Court gave us the drum on a good-looking blonde piece doing the rounds. He had her name and the agency she worked for. I was soon up at my room waiting for the knock at the door. After an hour or so, Aaron was her next visit. I don't think that Masao was in on it this evening. After I'd had my fun with her, I headed back to the bar for a few more hours before crashing for the night. Aaron and I were to share a room and Masao had his own. Aaron was still occupied and I assumed he must've extended his time with this bird. I don't blame him. She was a stunner, as the barman said she was. That night, I crashed in Masao's room.

Come morning, our breakfast was delivered. Well, Masao's was – I had to go to the other room. Our breakfasts were delivered at the same time and leaving to go to my room, I spotted two breakfast trays on the floor outside the door and the woman who delivered them walking off. She had been at the door knocking for some time. I told her he'd be asleep because he had a late night. After I almost kicked the door in, he finally woke up and answered the door. I took our breakfast in and find he's got a bird in bed with him. It wasn't the blonde piece that we both saw, but an Asian piece. She soon got herself dressed and made her way home. Then I find out he'd paid her for the night, as well as the other one from earlier on. I wasn't impressed with the money he had paid out and I blew up over it. The final outcome was that he wanted to go back to Perth. We split the remaining cash and later that day was the last I saw of Aaron. I knew he wouldn't last long as a free man.

That evening, I was back down to the cocktail bar and was getting the third degree from the barman and the night-security guy. As it turned out, Aaron had not just called for the services of two girls – it was three or four. In between, he was back at the bar charging himself up with booze and shooting his mouth off and these two blokes smelled a rat. They said that Walter told them his hair was really blond, even that his real name wasn't Walter. There was even talk about Aaron's conversations about police and crime. At one stage, he brought down one of the two-way radios we had, to see if he could tune into the one the Acacia security guy was carrying.

I couldn't believe what I was hearing. All I could really come up with was to claim that Walter has a habit of bullshitting to big-note himself. It was obvious these two weren't buying it and knew something was amiss. I soon left the bar and headed back to my room and took some time to get some sleep. I'd decided that I'd be flying out of Cairns a day earlier than planned. Masao was a little surprised about the urgency. We flew to Brisbane later on that morning and made our way to the Gold Coast and booked into a room in a Broadbeach motel.

That same day, 11 January 1990, Aaron Reynolds dropped West Australian police an enormous hint about his recent arrival back in town by trying to rob the Westpac branch in Osborne Park with another former Freo acquaintance, Craig Atkinson. But none of the staff responded when Reynolds demanded money. He pointed his 12-gauge shotgun at a filing cabinet and pulled the trigger to 'get them moving'. No one did. He fled, empty-handed. They were more successful at the ANZ bank in the adjacent suburb of Innaloo.

That night – coincidentally, just a street away from Thelma Salmon's home in Surrey Road, Rivervale – Perth armed robbery squad detectives stormed a house and arrested both men. A few days later, prison officers found Reynolds swinging in a cell, but managed to cut him down in time. 'ESCAPEE HURLS CHAIR IN COURT' and 'PRISONER KICKS OUT IN COURT' were among the headlines he earned in the following weeks and months.

Reynolds would eventually serve another nine years in prison, mostly at the medium-security Albany Regional Prison, on the south coast of Western Australia. In 1999, authorities deported him to the UK, a place he hadn't seen since he left aged six, when his parents' bitter break-up led to him coming to Australia to live with his father, who remarried.

Reynolds returned to Perth just once, via satellite from the UK. His face flickered on to the screen in the WA Police Royal Commission on 22 January 2003. He proceeded to tell the truth behind the armed-robbery confession that had landed him in prison in the first place.

Reynolds had bashed a supermarket employee during a robbery in Heathridge, a northern Perth suburb, on 21 May 1988. He got six years with a four-year minimum after police found him hiding in the bedroom of a Glendalough unit on the same day. He was taken to Wanneroo CIB, which, just like Nollamara CIB, was nothing more than an old house in the suburbs. Reynolds told the commission that immediately after his arrest, he was 'good copped, bad copped':

I didn't tell them what they wanted to know and, at one stage, one policeman had a silver gun and a tissue that was – he was pointing around the room, pointing to my head, saying that, 'It's quite easy, we can organise for you to be shot.' I was also – some time had elapsed and I was taken into the adjoining room and was electrocuted [electrically shocked with a stun-gun] by about, I don't know, two or three people.

Reynolds says he only had about $600 on him and this was seized by police. About another $7,000 was stashed in a shoebox on top of a cupboard in a Malaga house. Part of his statement that day, which he said was 'virtually written for me after I'd been electrocuted', reads,

Went to bed. Next day I bought an Odyssey Buggy from Rick Gills in Main Street. Michael and Daniel were with me. I bought a motorbike, bought a car, a red Torana.

MR PETIT: 'How much did you pay for the Odyssey buggy?'
[The police record of interview quotes Reynolds as saying he paid $12,000. But at the Royal Commission, Reynolds flatly denied he paid that much.]
REYNOLDS: 'It was between $1,200 and $1,500. There's no way that cost $12,000. Impossible.'
MR PETIT: 'How much did you pay for the motorbike?'
REYNOLDS: '$1,000.'
MR PETIT: 'How much did you pay for the Torana?'
REYNOLDS: '$3,000'.

On 24 January 2003, a police witness codenamed L4 told the Police Royal Commission, 'I walked into the detectives' office and I zapped Reynolds with the stun-gun twice in the back.'

But this courtroom vindication was little consolation for the luckless career criminal; the venue for his live satellite appearance was Chelmsford Prison, where he was doing time for breaking and entering.

On 11 January 1990, Abbott and Masao Ayuda booked into the Golden Rainbow Motel, Broadbeach – probably around the same time Aaron Reynolds displayed the appalling lack of aptitude for crime that would see him still behind bars 14 years later.

Abbott:

'Just days later, through a contact in Perth, I was made aware of Aaron's arrest. On hearing this, I parted company with Masao. I gave him an address in Perth, because he wanted to send me a copy of the photos he had yet to get developed. He eventually did, prior to finding out the true identity of Walter and Peter.'

In Tokyo in June 1990, the Japanese National Protection Bureau of the Foreign Affairs Ministry visited Masao Ayuda. He explained that he thought Walter and Peter were engineers on holidays. He saw no guns and knew nothing about any bank robberies. These guys joined up with him on his holiday. They enjoyed a few drinks, a few laughs and met plenty of girls. After a second interview months later, Ayuda was left to wonder just who Walter and Peter really were.

Abbott:

After parting company with Masao, my funds were getting low. The few days on the Gold Coast had me feeling the place would be ideal to hide out, but I needed to top up in the cash department and soon. I decided against doing this in Queensland for a number of reasons. One, I wasn't familiar with the place and, two, if I'm going to hide out here, I don't need the authorities having an interest in me. But the latter would change some years later. Before departing Queensland, I bought myself a wig from a Gold Coast shop and a pair of reading glasses.

There were stories that Abbott dabbled in a theatrical make-up course during those long years in Freo, but he says this was false; his skills were all self-taught and he believed he could develop other disguises to allow him to melt into a crowd. Reynolds the walking neon sign was no longer attracting unwelcome attention and Masao was on a plane back to Tokyo. The holiday had ended. It was time to plan the next phase.

Alone at the motel in Broadbeach, Abbott took stock. To stay free, he had to walk away from his family and friends, at least for now. It meant a completely fresh start, no baggage for the first time since he'd hit that girl with a bike pump. If he could re-establish the anonymous existence he had built in those months after his exit from Nollamara police station, then he was confident he could get the cash he needed to maintain it. And this time, no one else could ruin it for him.

His mind turned back to Western Australia. Glenn was on his own,

Above: David, Janet, Diane, Brenden and Glenn Abbott at Mount Isa in the early seventies.

Below: The Abbott kids with 'Mum's new scooter' at Heavytree caravan park in Alice Springs, around 1971.

Inset: The real thing! Brenden pictured in the outfit he won in a yo-yo competition at Belmont in 1975.

Above: 'Me, Graham and Coops at Raffles Hotel.' Perth, 1978.

Below: Rebels with flaws … 'Che' and Abbott in 1979.

Above left: Abbott with Jackie Lord at her flat in 1977 …

Above right: … and on the beach together in 1986.

Below: Abbott's hot V8 Torana.

Above left: A little time for some reflection …

Above right: A rock and a hard case – Abbott and his puppy, Rock, in 1986.

Below: The empty highway – with Jackie en route from Geraldton just before the arrest for bank robbery.

Above left: Fugitives Abbott and Reynolds outside South Australia Museum of Natural History.

Above right: Reynolds lives it up at the hotel pool in Darwin.

Below: The birth of the 'postcard' myth … Aaron Reynolds poses outside Dwellingup police station in December 1989.

Louise Laycock, mother of Abbott's son James.

Above left: Abbott, Reynolds and tourist Ayuda at Alice Springs, 1990. 'Aaron had just bought a new remote controlled camera.'

Above right: Abbott and Ayuda at Uluru in January 1990.

Below: A fugitive's best friends – false passport, air tickets, sunglasses and greenbacks, ready for the Thailand jaunt.

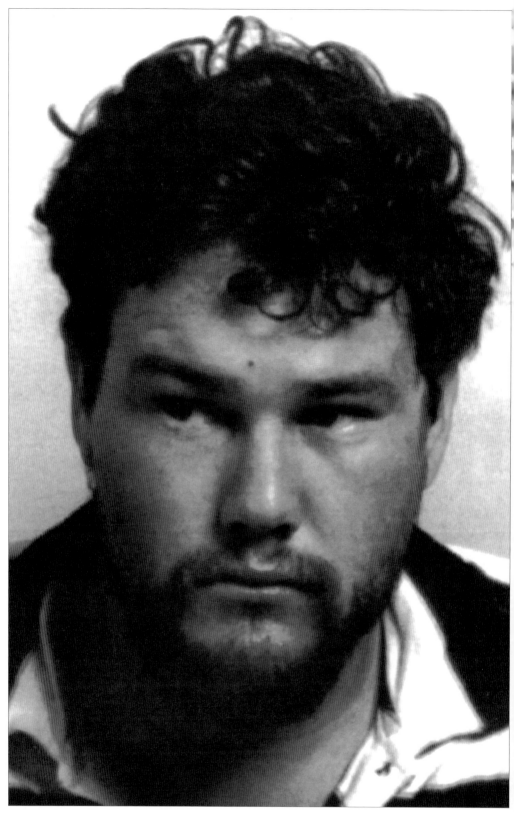

A mugshot of Glenn Abbott.

climbing the walls in his cell in Albany Regional Prison over his brother's successful escape. He needed to get word to him to try to keep it together until he got out through the gates, not over the wall. The cops would put plenty of pressure on Thelma, and his other siblings and extended family, but there wasn't much he could do about that, aside from steer clear of them. They'd understand. And staying away from Western Australia made a lot of sense. It was the only state actively hunting him.

Queensland police, on the other hand, were oblivious to him. And Abbott loved the Gold Coast. The weather, the women and the beaches were sensational. The language practice with Masao could be handy in a place so popular with Japanese tourists. But Gold Coast living was expensive. To set up a base here, he needed plenty more cash behind him.

Abbott put on his reading glasses and baseball cap and headed for the sand at Kirra Surf Club, already making plans.

Chapter Nine

1990–1992

Louise L was a pretty young thing in her mid-twenties, all blonde curls and knowing smiles. But not far below the surface lurked trouble. Her mother, Judy, remembers that her daughter met a man and a woman in a Kombi van who persuaded her to join them on a trip to Queensland. Louise packed up her gear in Sydney and went off on her adventure.

Judy:

The Kombi van people went back to Sydney. Louise was left up there. She then worked for another couple up there [Tweed Heads, NSW]. And how I met them, I was in the Grafton bus accident [20 October 1989]. I was going up there to bring [Louise's son] Timothy back to give Louise a break. [Four days later,] when I came out of Grafton Hospital, I was taken by car up to the house of these people. The night I came out of hospital and went up there, she went out. She told me that she was working at a club, I think the Twin Towns, as a waitress. It was a 24-hour place. There was a little flat and [the couple] and I were left there with Timothy. The next morning, Louise still wasn't home, and the guy came down to me. He told me she'd taken an overdose of tablets with vodka or something and she was in hospital. So we had to go to the hospital and get her. They didn't even put her in rehab or anything.

I think she then took up with some other guy for a while and he was a drug user. They came down to Sydney together and then when she went back up again she met this [other] guy, Pete. He took a liking to Louise. And that wasn't long after my accident that she met him. [Around February–March 1990] we picked up Louise and this guy from Pendle Hill station, right where I live [in western Sydney]. They were coming down from Queensland with Timothy. They came down not long after Christmas. [Pete] cared that much for her that he wanted to get her away from these people. The night after they came, we had a barbecue. He was introduced as Peter Holden. I liked him; I thought he was a nice guy. He wasn't like the other losers. I didn't know what he was into at that stage, but I think she did. He had dyed his hair. It was a funny colour. He tried to dye it black; it looked like a wig. The guy that I was with at the time got on with him really well. They were laughing and joking out there doing the barbecue. He wasn't nervous at all. He was the opposite.

'Peter Holden' was, of course, Brenden Abbott. Shortly after he parted with Masao Ayuda, he based himself on the Gold Coast at a holiday unit in Tugun and met Louise on one of his discreet sojourns just across the border into Tweed Heads, in New South Wales. Abbott recognised Louise's need for rescue and happily played the hero. Initially, he kept her at arm's length, careful not to arouse her suspicions about his true identity. And, from very early in the relationship, he disappeared for weeks or months at a time. Of early 1990, he will only say, 'After a few weeks and numerous train trips, I was back in Brisbane and then back on the Gold Coast.'

But Abbott did more than stare out of train windows at that time. On Australia Day, 26 January 1990, a man dropped from the ceiling of a Westpac branch on Torrens Road, Woodville, in Adelaide, at 8.55am. He had gained entry the previous night by cutting through the corrugated iron roof.

A bank security camera captured the moment. In the black and white image, there is absolutely no mistaking the eyes peering out from the balaclava. The overalls look bulky, as though the bandit is wearing other layers of clothes underneath. A cord runs between the balaclava and overalls. The bag sits on the bench and his hand grips a pistol, pointed menacingly towards the floor. A single outstretched hand, just visible over the top of the teller's box, is a pitiful sight in the face of such a threat. This man was ice cool.

He walked away with $25,000, but the hardest thing for the staff was his promise to return, because it sounded as if he meant it.

Louise's mother continues, '[Brenden and Louise] stayed until they found a house in Blacktown. I would call over there every second night. I knew who he was by then. In the meantime, she fell pregnant. He wasn't there all the time. He more or less set up the house for Louise so that she would have her own little place with Tim [her son]. It was lovely. He bought her a dog. I think Thelma still has that dog [Ben]. He was only a pup when he bought him and brought him down for Louise.'

Abbott later left Ben at his mother's home in Perth, saying he'd return for him in six weeks. Thelma says the dog often sat in the driveway to wait for his master. 'It made me cry,' she says.

Judy continues:

Louise said, 'He's into something, Mum, because he carries a gun.' And then when she told me, she said, 'He's told me all these stories, but I don't believe him.'

We didn't believe it at first, but then when [a friend] saw it in the Australasian Post [an article containing the pictures taken in the summer of 1989], we actually believed it. He treated her well. I know he robbed banks, but he had good values. She had the stability she needed. He looked after them. He looked after Tim, who wasn't his son. When she was very close to having the baby, he didn't really want to be coming backwards and forwards. He didn't want her to be on her own, with Timothy and a new baby. So they moved into my place, Louise and Tim. He was away for months at a time then. He came when she had the baby. He was at the birth. He came to my place and we went to Grace Bros and bought all the baby stuff. And then we went to the hospital. He provided for Louise. He gave her money to furnish the house with ... He was a proud father.

Brenden Abbott forged several other key relationships early in 1990. Earlier, after he first arrived on the Gold Coast and was pondering his future, he rented a holiday unit in the suburb of Tugun for four weeks. He bought a second-hand racing bike for transport, avoiding cars and relying on buses and taxis for longer trips.

Most mornings, I'd ride to the beach at Kirra surf club and soak up the sun and take a swim. Most lunches were at a restaurant in Coolangatta. There were trips to the cinemas and I generally explored my new surroundings. I had most evening meals at different restaurants around Coolangatta and occasionally up at Surfers Paradise. After about a week, I made new friends with some Japanese guys in their early twenties. They were mad surfers and some of them were on 12-month working visas and hadn't long been in the country.

Abbott had met them during a morning swim at Kirra and they had a drink afterwards at the Kirra Hotel. Between their broken English and his broken Japanese, they struck up a conversation that would blossom into friendship. Over the next 12 months, they would provide a crucial safe haven for Abbott. They were constantly on the move up and down the Gold Coast, changing rented units regularly.

Sometimes, I'd be away for a few months and, on my return, I'd go to where one of them worked to find their new address. To them, my name was Peter, but they pronounced it Peeta. Shinichi Sato was the one who appeared to call the shots and organised the numerous apartments they rented.

Shinichi worked for most of his stay at Ataka, a Surfers Paradise Japanese restaurant. In the years to come, I'd eat there often. I'd go to parties they'd throw and would usually be the only non-Japanese there. I never felt uncomfortable and they never asked my business, which was something I liked about most of the Japanese I met. There were times when they wanted pot – 'huppa' they'd call it – and I'd chase some up. Eventually, after socialising with their group, I met another Japanese guy by the name of Koichi Fujieda. He was also in the country on a 12-month working visa, but he never did a day's work.

After Shinichi went back to Japan, I spent a lot of time staying at Koichi's places. He was a quiet one who kept to himself and was another mad surfer, as well as a keen fisherman. After he left the country, he returned some months later, but could only manage a three-month visa the second time. In the whole time I

*associated with the Japanese, none were the wiser of my true
identity. But it didn't take long for Shinichi to figure out I was a
shifty character.*

As 1990 progressed, Adelaide detectives' suspicions grew that
Brenden Abbott was playing a major role in the crime wave hitting
the city's suburban bank branches. As promised, the bandit returned
to the Woodville Park Westpac on Torrens Road, on 25 May 1990. A
bank officer told police,

*I heard a loud, confident voice say something like: 'Don't worry,
this is just a hold-up.' He nudged a lady out of the way ... and
placed an open bag on the counter, and he was holding a
shotgun. He then loaded the gun by sliding his right hand up and
down the underside of the barrel. I started handing over money.
He said, 'Hurry up, I haven't got all fucking day.' I then placed
bundles of $50, $20, $10 and $5 notes and loose notes on the
counter. He was sweeping the money across the counter into his
bag. He had tight-fitting black vinyl gloves. [He then said,]
'You'd better answer the phone. That'll be your security ringing.'
I think I handed him about $8,000. All I can remember after that
is he said something like: 'It beats working for a living.' I
activated the hold-up alarm after I handed him the other notes.
He seemed very arrogant and sure of himself and didn't appear
to panic.*

The bandit walked away with $26,000 – exactly $1,000 more than
the previous robbery there in January. And then, on Monday, 18 June,
another robbery at the branch netted just $2,600. Three days later,
the National Australia Bank in Morphett Street, Adelaide, was also
robbed. Two masked men, armed with a shotgun and a pistol,
climbed from the ceiling into the women's toilet. A staff member
found them and they chased her back into the main banking chamber.
One fired a shot into a steel cabinet and they escaped with several
security deposit boxes. A second shot went off when a young man
walking past the bank was threatened, but no one was hurt. They
drove from the scene with a third accomplice, who, moments before,
spoke to a parking inspector, perhaps explaining that getaway cars
were, in fact, entitled to park in loading zones.

Detectives said they believed the robberies were linked, but didn't publicly name suspects. On 28 June 1990, the *West Australian* ran a story under the headline 'WA ESCAPEE COULD BE IN SA: POLICE'.

It was exactly 9am on 23 July 1990, and the staff at the Commonwealth Bank branch at the West Lakes shopping centre in Adelaide were trying to find enthusiasm for the Monday-morning rush only 30 minutes away. A supervisor walked over to attend to the restocking of the autobank. A shotgun butt shattered the glass of the front door and a hand reached through and unlocked it. Tellers preparing to open up for the day pounded suspicion buttons.

Two men in balaclavas – one in green overalls, the other in blue overalls – charged towards the tellers' entry door. They ordered staff to the floor, stuffed their bags with $55,000 then fled. After a few seconds of stunned silence, some staff members got up and looked out the window; one began yelling the registration number of a Mitsubishi Star Wagon that picked up the bandit.

On 25 July 1990, *The Advertiser* in Adelaide reported, 'Police have declared a series of five Adelaide bank robberies a major crime. A police spokesman said similarities between the robberies made it likely they were committed by the same people. Three of the robberies targeted one bank, the Westpac bank in Woodville Park. Others were at the Morphett Street branch of the National Australia Bank and the Commonwealth Bank at West Lakes. WA prison escapee Brendon James Abbott is a suspect in at least one of the Woodville Park robberies and the Morphett Street hold-up. In these two robberies, thieves dropped into the bank from the ceiling. Abbott was convicted in 1987 of a Perth robbery using the same method.'

Years later, advances in technology led to a piece of forensic evidence from the West Lakes robbery pointing in Abbott's direction, but it wasn't conclusive. Adelaide Detective Sergeant Sid Thomas also picked up a promising trail to Abbott's suspected South Australian associates, but was still looking for answers on the cases nearly 15 years later. The official police estimate of the number of banks Abbott robbed in Adelaide that year is ten, plus the Kent Town robbery in December 1989. Abbott tacitly admits he was active in Adelaide, but won't say anything more. He doesn't need to, since essentially all the Adelaide detectives ever had was one partial fingerprint, countless abandoned getaway cars and the fact Abbott once leaped from a Perth bank ceiling.

Brenden Abbott's plan to remain a free and anonymous man was panning out nicely. He safely commuted between South Australia and

Queensland without attracting specific police attention. He had a steady supply of cash, disguises that never attracted a second glance, safe places to stay and even a steady relationship and a child on the way.

And he stayed well away from Western Australia, where the Perth armed robbery squad was still peeved one of their best collars of recent times was swanning around the country. They'd found the roll of film in the Mitsubishi Cordia abandoned after the wild freeway chase. It contained shots of Abbott and Reynolds at the Canning Dam campsite, shots of Perth, the Dwellingup campsite and Reynolds with a cheeky smile leaning against the fence of the Dwellingup police station. Weeks later, when Reynolds returned to Perth and was arrested in Rivervale, he was carrying a second roll of film – part two of their summer odyssey, covering their time in Adelaide, Uluru, Alice Springs, Darwin and Kakadu National Park.

For months, these pictures remained plastered across a board in the squad's office – a constant reminder Brenden Abbott was a free man. Months passed without fresh local leads and the situation seemed hopeless. Three weeks after Aaron Reynolds's last appearances in Perth courts, detectives Geoff Maloney and Jeff Beaman discussed new tactics in their hunt for Abbott. They needed to get his face out there; get the public looking for him in case he quietly slipped home. Maloney called Helen Winterton, police reporter at the *West Australian*, and, on 25 September 1990, on page 3, she breathed life into a legend with a story headed 'High time on the run for escaped robbers': 'A holiday on the Gold Coast, aerial tours of the North-West and expensive clothes were some of the trappings of affluence for two of WA's most notorious escaped armed robbers. While police in four states were hunting Brendan James Abbott, 28, [incorrect spelling of Brenden's name occurred frequently in newspaper and police reports] and Aaron Raymond Reynolds, 21, the pair flaunted their freedom and spent money stolen in WA robberies. They were also using the money to pay associates and strangers to make false sightings … After their escape from Fremantle Prison last year, they acted like tourists, photographing their travels across Australia.'

And then, the key paragraph: 'Detectives believe some of the photos were to be sent to their associates as a cheeky reminder of how good life on the run could be.'

The story makes no mention of the 'Postcard Bandit' moniker. That would come later, in *Australasian Post* magazine the following year.

In the *Post* story, the photos became postcards; and they weren't seized by police, they were sent to police by Brenden Abbott, the Postcard Bandit, a larrikin outlaw bank robber. Abbott, incidentally, intended posting a couple of the photographs – but not to police:

> [Glenn] was destined to take the same path, so, instead of him learning the hard way, I took him under my wing. We had this thing between us where we'd flash the wad of notes in our wallets when we'd see each other. I started that off before he was doing jobs with me. He'd often hit me up for money and I'd pull my wallet out and complain that I didn't have much, while letting him see the wad of cash and only give him a 10 or 20. He often called me a tight cunt for not giving him more, though he left that comment until after I'd given him something. When he started earning a quid, he'd flash the wad in his wallet whenever we'd run into each other. The photo that was often shown in the media of me with the wallet full of cash was intended for Glenn. It was a brothers' thing.

The nationally distributed *Australasian Post* article gave Abbott some headaches. A woman sitting in a Darwin doctor's surgery picked up a dog-eared copy and did a double-take on the 'postcards'. She knew the guy as Louise's boyfriend, so she did exactly what Beaman hoped someone would do – picked up a phone and called a detective. The Darwin detective, Dennis Hart, contacted a bureau of criminal intelligence inspector in Sydney, but NSW police took no apparent interest. Hart also contacted Beaman out of courtesy. A couple of months later, Beaman received the phone call he'd been waiting for. A detective from Murwillumbah CIB, just southwest of Tweed Heads on the far northern NSW coast, was investigating an assault complaint. The suspect's name: Brenden Abbott.

Louise's mother, Judy, recalls that, after her daughter gave birth to James Leslie Abbott at Blacktown Hospital in Sydney, on 25 January 1991, Brenden came to her place a couple of weeks later, and the beaming new father cradled his son while pictures were taken. He came back to visit Louise and James regularly, but, even with his life now relatively settled, Abbott was more comfortable on the move. In February 1991, Perth police said Abbott remained their most wanted man. They also suggested that he slept with his favourite weapon, reportedly a sawn-off shotgun, and that he had sired children to different women in different states. An armed and dangerous stud, no less.

Later that year, Abbott hooked up with another old acquaintance from Fremantle, Trevor Wayne Bailey, a hyperactive young Tasmanian. He came to Perth from Launceston, in Tasmania, in 1986, immediately embarking on a crime spree including seven car thefts, break-ins on liquor stores and department stores and a supermarket robbery, for which he was sentenced to five years' jail; he also thumped a cop on the way to court from prison. The angry 19-year-old who arrived in Fremantle got along well with Brenden Abbott. He was finally released from Albany Regional Prison in July 1991 and returned to Launceston. Not long after, Abbott looked him up. Bailey was in awe of a man rapidly becoming a mythical crime figure.

There is little doubt that Trevor Bailey became one of Abbott's accomplices, which conveniently provided a Launceston safe house should Abbott need it. Bailey's release from prison was shortly before another spate of robberies in Adelaide that bore Abbott trademarks. Unlike modern banks, the Salisbury Commonwealth Bank in Adelaide on Friday, 19 July 1991, had a front counter with teller cubicles stretched for miles. At 5.15pm, a Ford Laser screeched from an adjacent laneway and backed through the bank's front window. It came to rest in the middle of the customer queue space. The passenger, in bulky overalls and balaclava, leaped into the tellers' area and stuffed $32,000 into a khaki bag, while the similarly dressed driver kept watch with a semi-automatic weapon. It was over in little more than a minute.

The dramatic modus operandi didn't match any of Abbott's handiwork. But, as Elizabeth CIB's Detective Sergeant Trevor Jenkins would note, 'People just don't drive cars into banks.'

The bureau of criminal intelligence recommended he call Perth. He was soon speaking to Detective Sergeant Geoff Maloney, who agreed Abbott could be involved. The use of the car was different, but everything else about the robbery potentially matched Abbott. The car turned up at a nearby shopping centre. Extensive surveillance of the bank and monitoring of scanners clearly showed professionals at work. Two men believed to be the same bandits returned to John Street, Salisbury, on Friday, 23 August 1991 at 5.20pm, this time to a branch of the National Australia Bank. A staff member later told police,

The three of us were preparing two money cartridges to go into the flexiteller for the weekend. The cartridges were full of money and they were on the counter ready to go into the machine. I heard a crash and glass breaking and looked over to the southern doors. I saw that a vehicle had driven in. I yelled out to the staff to lock up the cage where the money is stored. I then activated a hold-up alarm on my phone. One of the offenders stayed near the car and the other person ran around the counter to the vicinity of the flexiteller. [A staff member] was trying to put one of the cartridges of money into the flexiteller. The person took the cartridge from her and said something like: 'Don't do that'... The person then ran back to the car and both of them got in. By the time I got off the phone to the police, there was a patrol at the back door.

At the Parabanks shopping centre just 100 metres away, the bandits drove the stolen Ford Laser over to a stolen Holden Camira, got out and quickly changed clothes and vehicles. A stunned police officer's wife saw all this unfold. Then she watched the Camira exit one side of the car park as an oblivious police patrol entered from the other side. They escaped with more than $134,000.

Louise's mother, Judy, remembers that a few months later, around October 1991:

Peter [Brenden] said, 'We'll go for a trip to Queensland,' and he bought this car. James would have been about nine months old. They'd been away a couple weeks and came back, and then Louise hit me with the news that she was moving back to Queensland. I was upset, because I was attached to the kids. She moved to Bilinga Beach near the Coolangatta Airport. It was lovely. I saw him [Abbott] there, and that's when I first met [Abbott's friend] Trevor Bailey. They were staying in a unit near by. [Louise] had the house. I think Brenden kept James overnight the night I was there. It was James's birthday. He must have been one.

Abbott and Louise quarrelled regularly and his comings and goings didn't help. Judy says,

She moved from Bilinga because [Brenden] stopped giving her money and paying the rent or something. There was always

*friction. She rented a house with the woman [she met shortly
after arriving in Tweed Heads]. [Louise] was seeing this butcher
from Kingscliffe. Brenden didn't want her there. And [Barry] the
butcher was there one night, and Brenden dropped by. I felt so
sorry for Barry. [He] had to run to his car and went. That's when
[Brenden] had the idea to get Louise away from [the Tweed
Heads woman]. And there was an incident with [this woman].*

Abbott explains,

*I had a run-in with the woman in question. She had separated
from her boyfriend and moved in with Louise. I didn't like the
bitch, she was an alcoholic and she would interfere with our
relationship. I gave her her marching orders. The boyfriend was
happy, because she went back to him. Poor bastard. The
following day, I found out she'd given me up to the cops. The
spiteful bitch knew my real identity, unknown to me. Louise had
no choice but to come clean and tell me that she shared our
secret with the bitch. I was out of there.*

A complaint was made to local police and Detective Andrew Bide from
Murwillumbah CIB investigated. But Abbott left before the report
reached Bide's pigeonhole. Jeff Beaman was livid. West Australian
police at least now knew of the existence of Abbott's young family, but
opportunities to catch him were missed. The bosses didn't think any of
the intelligence warranted action and detectives didn't often get
interstate trips to chase bank robbers. The info going into BCI (bureau
of criminal intelligence) was hard to track and still wasn't
computerised. Surveillance teams, phone taps and phone traces were
out of the question. And one telling remark, published in the *West
Australian*, from an unnamed detective, pointed to the investigation's
central flaw: 'A spokesman from the Perth armed robbery squad said
he had not received information from Adelaide police.'

It wasn't just Adelaide police keeping tight-lipped. No one talked
to anyone. And Abbott laughed all the way to the bank.

After the incident with Louise's flatmate, Abbott says he tried to act
in James's best interests. He wanted both Louise and James away
from the place. Judy says, 'I think that's why Brenden decided to give
her money to buy a townhouse. It was on the Gold Coast somewhere
[Nerang]. He gave her the deposit. Louise was paying it off and I was

helping her.'

On 20 January 1992 – five days before James Abbott's first birthday, when Louise's mother says Brenden Abbott and Trevor Bailey visited Louise at Bilinga – a Westpac bank in John Street, Salisbury, was hit again. When a staff member arrived to open up the bank at 8.20am, he conducted the routine security check and noticed a toilet-cubicle door closed and the light and fan on. The bank officer followed the rest of the procedure with extra care, but nothing else seemed out of the ordinary. At 8.50am, the same bank officer heard noises in the ATM room. An accomplice waiting in a car is suspected of contacting the man crouched in the ceiling, who aimed to jump down exactly when the ATM was switched off for restocking. But their timing sucked.

When the bandit tried to lower himself into the tiny room, he got caught up in cabling, attracting the bank officer's attention and allowing ample time for the hold-up alarm and cameras to be activated. The staff member also warned his colleagues to get under their desks. The bandit stood in the doorway of the ATM room and looked around at the empty banking chamber. Fuck. He ordered two staff members out from under their desks to help him try to get the cartridges out of the ATM. The bank officer says,

> The person yelled out, 'Stop wasting my time, you're wasting my time, get them out.'
>
> I told him that we were trying our best and that the cartridges weren't coming out. After about two minutes, I managed to get one of the cartridges out.
>
> He said, 'Is it full?'

The cartridges had not yet been replenished and the total haul was a pitiful $400. The frustrated robber fled.

Trevor Jenkins didn't need a microscope to see the pattern emerging – in the previous two years, 1990 and 1991, Adelaide banks were hit on the Friday before the Australia Day long weekend, targeting increased cash reserves. This latest attempt came on the Monday before the long weekend. So, on Friday, detectives hid in every bank in the area, each with an open-line radio to minimise the response time of the special tactics and rescue group and police helicopter, both on standby. But all the banks prepared to open as usual and the day passed without incident.

Jenkins grasped at one more chance: The Perth guys had mentioned Abbott was a cricket lover, so he showed the Fremantle jail riot-trial video footage to the STAR Group and sent them to the traditional long weekend Test match at Adelaide Oval.

Abbott says,

> I *never went to any international matches or state games. I preferred to watch games in the comfort of a motel or my safe houses. It never really interested me to do otherwise. Too many people, too many cameras and too much security. There were times while I was on the road, though, I'd come through a town and a local game was on, I'd grab a feed and pull up beside their oval and watch a game. I did attend a major sporting event in Melbourne once – an associate scored a number of tickets for the Jeff Fenech–Azuma Nelson fight. [A record crowd of 37,000 saw Australian Jeff Fenech lose to Ghana's Azuma Nelson for the WBC super-featherweight title at Princes Park on 1 March 1992.]*

Perhaps deploying the 'Starries' was wishful thinking on Jenkins's part, but anything seemed worth a shot to catch Abbott and his crew. Even an act as polished as Abbott's needed only one jumpy accomplice, off-duty cop or heroic bank teller to turn a robbery into a bloodbath. That weekend, the *Sunday Mail*'s Sean Whittington reported: 'One of Australia's most wanted and dangerous men is believed to be raiding Adelaide financial institutions then fleeing across the border into the 'underground' system of the Eastern States ... Described by police as 'cunning and intelligent', Brendan Abbott is believed to go into hiding for several months after a hold-up before resurfacing to raid another bank when his money dries up.

To suggest Abbott waited, junkie-style, until he needed more cash, was a professional insult, but otherwise the theory was entirely accurate. Whittington quoted an unnamed police source: 'After each robbery, he disappears and that's extremely difficult to do unless you have a safety house or somewhere to hide without raising suspicion. It could be a girlfriend, a family, a group of mates. We've been informed Abbott's a thinking man's criminal. He plans his robberies extremely well and covers his tracks like a professional. He's fully aware the smallest clue could lead to his hideout and subsequent arrest and end his lifestyle on the run.'

Brenden Abbott decided to put his professional activities on hold. He deserved a holiday and could afford it.

Louise's mother recalls, 'He actually left the country and went to Thailand. He just wanted to prove he could get out of the country. I said, "You idiot, why did you come back?" It was a game with him, you see. The banks and everything. [As though he was saying:] "I got out of the country! And then came back in again!"'

Glenn Abbott applied for a passport in November 1991 and the West Australian detectives suspected his brother might try to use it. Beaman, who believes Abbott visited Perth in February 1992, alerted Jenkins to the passport issue the same month. But, after the Fenech fight in Melbourne on 1 March 1992, Brenden Abbott headed to Thailand, again playing the snap-happy tourist.

He didn't need to travel on Glenn's passport. Abbott's confidence and skills with false identification had grown markedly over the previous two years and he produced sufficient documents for a genuine passport in a false name or assumed identity. So why didn't he stay overseas?

I did take that trip to Asia. But to leave the country and never return? Well, I never had enough money to do so. I wanted enough to survive elsewhere without having to resort to crime again. Despite what many believe, though they think I stole millions, they forget that I had co-offenders and [they had] no idea of the costs involved as a fugitive. I wanted enough to buy a house, business and citizenship.

So, after returning from Thailand, Abbott intended getting straight back to business. For more than three years now, he'd been a chameleon, adapting to every situation, mapping every exit and eventuality ahead of time. His constant vigilance with personal security brought with it an easy, personable confidence. He explains,

When I flew, I was almost always the businessman, with suit and tie and carrying a briefcase. I always went business or first class. Most people in this part of the plane never ask too many questions. You're last on the plane and first off; baggage was first out, so no need to wait around in the airport; a choice of meals, hot towels and juice before take-off and landing. Drinks

*included in the ticket, probably why I enjoyed a drink in-flight –
get my money's worth. If I did get asked, I said I was a security
adviser. If they continue to drill you with questions, it's easy to
pull them up by suggesting you prefer not to discuss the topic.
For most of the flight, I'd either have headphones on, or, if it was
a long flight, such as to Perth, I'd take a nap. There were times
when I sensed the person next to me thought I was a rude prick
for not conversing. Good.*

*The backpacker disguise was another, depending on the time
of year and which part of the country I was heading to. But
staying in hostels for backpackers, I mostly avoided. The
bumbag was very handy to carry a pistol in. The baseball hat or
the Akubra, and sunglasses, headphones and a wig underneath –
I found this was the best way to wear wigs. They're easy to pick
if you don't have a hat on. They don't usually sit properly on the
top of the head around the forehead. With a hat on, though, you
can have close contact with people and they can't pick it. So I felt
better dressing down when wearing wigs, because, regardless of
the time of day or night, baseball caps don't look odd.*

*At other times, I dyed my hair, either mousy blond or ginger.
The first time I tried it, it turned orange. Had to make another
trip to the chemist looking like a circus clown. Putting on excess
weight also helps change one's appearance. After 1989, I would
eventually put on 20kg. That alone was sufficient as a disguise. I
also grew a moustache. The weight gain wasn't what I'd call
planned. I blame that on the good life and lack of exercise.*

*Once I managed to make up new driver's licences, getting
around in a vehicle of my own was the preferred mode of
transport. The licences could be checked by police and come up
legit. I obtained all the particulars needed of real people's
licences, ranging in all ages and both sexes. [The Northern
Territory Transport Department was the source of the details
and documents.] Once I got around in my own vehicles, I
found it was less of a risk than trains, buses or planes. And
when I was [posing as] your average bloke, I was just a self-
employed mechanic.*

Abbott really believed he was, too – just an average Aussie bloke who
liked to have his head under a bonnet. But the cars were just a sideline
now, a hobby that cost money rather than made it. Just weeks after

his Thailand holiday, on 16 April 1992, Abbott clocked back on for work. But for whatever reason – perhaps success went to his head – he decided to break the golden rule that had served him so well, which was to 'never shit in your own nest'. He knew Gold Coast banks held a lot more cash than Adelaide's. Doing robberies there would draw inevitable attention to him as a suspect and could make life a lot more difficult if things went pear-shaped. But he was confident in his invisibility now. They wouldn't know what hit them.

Clad in a black balaclava, black leather jacket and blue jeans, Brenden Abbott eased a screwdriver into the locking mechanism of the back door of the National Australia Bank's Springwood branch. He carefully twisted it and, when the mechanism clicked open, he strode confidently into the lunchroom. It was 4.10pm. He had a Springfield P9 pistol in one hand and a Slazenger sports bag in the other. On reaching the main banking chamber, he slapped the bag on a desk.

'You, you and you, out the back here,' he said, gesturing to the staff with the pistol. One staff member went around to empty the teller draws. He got upset when she didn't move quickly enough, and the 9mm pistol suddenly discharged.

'Sorry, it wasn't supposed to go off. Should have put the safety on, shouldn't I?'

He shifted his attention to the ATM, addressing the staff member who had been about to restock it. 'Is it open?'

'No.'

'Don't give me that shit; I know you've got the combo.'

The bag was filled and Abbott headed for the door with $203,716 and the farewell line: 'Thanks very much, have a good Easter.'

An informer in Western Australia told police, on 28 August 1992, of his meeting with Abbott. He described the man with Abbott as speaking with an Irish accent, aged 35 to 40 with red hair and a full beard. Abbott carried a scanner and a 9mm Beretta pistol and mentioned that armed robber Gary Roser was supposed to go over the wall with him at Fremantle. All this was very interesting, but the informant didn't tell police about it until three weeks later. He saw Abbott on King Street in Perth's CBD.

Later that year, another 'clue' pointed to an Abbott appearance, although he denies it was him who signed the visitors book at Fremantle Prison – by now decommissioned and replaced by the allegedly escape-proof Casuarina Prison in Perth's southern suburbs. The name in the book was 'B Abbett', the address was 'Nowhere you'd find'. And the remarks were: 'Great to come back and not have to escape'.

If he did sign the book, then perhaps it wasn't him who robbed $140,000 from the National Australia Bank branch at Tweed Heads the next day. Two men with revolvers entered via a side door – tampered with overnight – near the manager's office at the rear of the bank. They ordered staff not to activate alarms or cameras and confronted two employees in the process of refilling the ATM. They told them to put $90,000 from the cartridges into a carry bag. They also ordered staff to empty teller drawers. As they left, one bandit said, 'You've all done well, thank you.'

Both bandits wore full-face motorcycle helmets. The staff told police that one offender did most of the talking, while the other seemed nervous.

Bank staff grew to fear Brenden Abbott's name. Countless evacuations of branches across the country were based on the understandable paranoia that every possum fart or motion-detector alarm could be Abbott or one of his mates. But a significant number of detectives of the era say the banks, for the most part, couldn't even be bothered buying decent new locks, despite repeated warnings from police – particularly in the wake of some of the Adelaide robberies, and then later in Queensland, when Abbott and/or his accomplices switched focus.

In the meantime, Brenden Abbott was content to spend his days conducting surveillance outside banks, and his nights inside them, preparing for a grand entrance the next day. And no one, it seemed, could stop him.

Chapter ten

1992–1994

Every bank robbery is reduced to a clinical, factual description on a detective's computer; a step-by-step modus operandi, crucial to helping establish a suspect list. And, by 1992, Brenden Abbott was usually suspect Number One whenever a major bank robbery occurred in Australia, particularly in Western Australia, South Australia or Queensland. His name was inextricably linked with many such crimes, no matter how unlikely it was that one man would do so many. But there is no doubt the robbery of the Coolangatta Commonwealth Bank branch on Christmas Eve 1992 bore all his trademarks:

> *Rear door lock drilled, previous night*
> *Two bandits enter through rear door*
> *Bandit entry time: 9.20am, shortly before opening, timed to hit teller drawers and ATM cartridges*
> *Alarm failed to activate after door opened, tampered with previous night*
> *Staff used to fill bag, total of $31,920*
> *Getaway car: Datsun 180B, bought November 1992. Buyer paid cash.*
> *Three witnesses estimate bandit height around six feet; five say this bandit was solid; another five say he had a beer gut; and two said he was chubby. Getaway car set on fire.*

But two Abbott staples – scanners and bank terminology – were missing. Not even a wisecrack from the big fellow, who was agitated and pointed a semi-automatic gun at the assistant manager's head. Abbott may or may not have been involved, but Trevor Bailey definitely wasn't. He had other things on his mind.

Louise's mother says of her daughter: 'She rang my mother while she was still living at the [Nerang] townhouse, and asked my mother if she could look after the children. That's when she went down to Tasmania with Trevor.'

Trevor Bailey and Louise Laycock travelled to his mother's Launceston home early in December 1992, after she left Timothy and James with her grandmother in Sydney. Trevor was nervous, and told his mum not to mention Louise's presence if 'Pete' called. Judy Bailey remembers, 'She seemed to care a great deal about Trevor. They were making plans for the future and working out how they could get by between them. Trevor seemed happy.'

Louise Laycock returned to the mainland about a week later; all seemed well with her and Trevor. Years later, when Trevor's concerned mother went to police to voice fears she tried not to face, more of Abbott's movements during 1991 and 1992 came to light:

This Brenden, I knew him as Peter Sims. I think he rang from here one day to make a hairdresser appointment and I overheard him saying his second name and I'm sure it was Sims. In the months leading up to Christmas [1992], he was backwards and forwards here [Judy's Launceston home] probably 20 times. He's slept in my house and eaten in my house. But I didn't know who he was at the time. When he [Trevor] first came out of prison, this Pete kept ringing and that's how we got to know him. He started coming over here and then Trevor would go with him and then they would come back. Well, Trevor would mostly come back on his own. Pete used to ring him at certain times. I remember them coming home and laughing, saying the federal police had been at a gun show [in Launceston in 1991] they were at and [Abbott] was buying guns.

Trevor just always told me to be careful and not to say anything. Trevor told me, he said, 'Mum, don't ever do anything to cross him because this is who he is,' and he showed me the pictures [in Australasian Post]. I believe what was said on TV the other night, because Trevor said that, he [Brenden] would never be taken alive, he'll shoot it out.

Abbott, this time accompanied by another young man, again arrived at the Bailey household to see Trevor on New Year's Eve 1992. Judy remembers they went out with her son for the evening and that, when Louise called to speak to Trevor that night, they weren't home. On 1 or 2 January, Trevor took Abbott and his associate – possibly Glenn Abbott, since he was now out of prison – to the airport. Five days later, Trevor's father dropped Trevor at the airport as well. He gave his parents little idea of his destination, but this was not unusual. The next night, 8 January, he called his mother and said, 'Mum, as soon as I get to where I'm going, I'll give you a call.'

'OK, mate, take care,' she replied.

Judy Bailey never heard from her son again, and eventually reported him missing about a year later and telling police about 'Pete'.

The same day Trevor left Tasmania, Queensland police believed they finally had a lead that would put them directly on the trail of Brenden Abbott. Surveillance began on Louise Laycock at 3/67 Nerang Street, Nerang, on the Gold Coast – the townhouse Abbott helped buy – and on a German man named Hardy Brasche, at 33 Tallebudgera Avenue, Palm Beach, also on the Gold Coast. Brasche, also known as Stephen Rheach, was later interviewed by police, who noted,

He stated that he first met Louise Laycock through another woman who was living with him at the time. He states he had sex with her, but not in a relationship-type affair. He met her at a Christmas party in 1991. Several months after they met, Laycock moved in with Brasche at 33 Tallebudgera Drive. She had the following boyfriends or sexual acquaintances:

1. Pedro, or Peter, a merchant seaman, address unknown.

2. A butcher from Kingscliffe who works at a shop in Murwillumbah. (Surveillance photos obtained of same.)

3. An old fellow.

4. A young Tasmanian named Trevor who had tattoos all over his hands and arms. Described as thin, about 177cm, black wavy hair, acne scars on his face and was a friend of Pedro. At one stage, Trevor went back to Tasmania and got into some trouble over pulling a pistol on some louts, over something to do with a car.

Brasche identified Abbott in Photo Board where Abbott appears at No. 7 as Pedro. He states that Laycock told him Pedro was the father of her son James and that he [Brasche] met him [Abbott] about six times. He used to visit Laycock when 'he

came off his ship' and sometimes stayed the night. He would arrive with a navy-type duffle bag. Pedro talked to Brasche as if he spends a lot of time in north Queensland and said he had a mate with a farm up there. The mate is supposed to have a jeep with a machinegun fitted to it that they used to use for buffalo and pig shooting.

[Brasche also says,] The relationship between Abbott and Laycock was love-hate; whenever they were together they seemed to argue; he did seem to give Laycock some financial assistance, however, she sometimes complained that he did not help her; he does not plonk money around; he dresses well in clothes Brasche described as Country Road; he has never seen him with a firearm; he describes his manner of speech as that of a criminal who has served a term of imprisonment; when at the Gold Coast, Abbott resides in motels. Brasche stated that, should Abbott telephone him again, he will act as though nothing has happened and page Detective Senior Sergeant Gerry Costello immediately. He also stated he would not tell Laycock of his conversation with police.

Abbott says, 'Rheach [Brasche] was a shifty bastard. He tipped me off about the law sniffing around.'

Brasche also told police that, around Christmas 1992, Abbott and Laycock fought over her relationship with Trevor Bailey. Brasche believed Laycock and Bailey were having an affair. On Wednesday, 14 January 1993, Louise rang Judy Bailey to say Trevor stayed with her until Sunday night but he had gone, and left his gear behind. Queensland police running sheets do not say whether Bailey was sighted at Laycock's home by their surveillance. But Launceston Detective Rob King, who ran the subsequent missing-persons investigation on Trevor Bailey, would have appreciated the information, since Louise's phone call is virtually the last known trace of him. Mrs Bailey says Louise promised to call her when she knew where Trevor was. She never did.

Judy, Louise's mother, says,

Then when she came back from Tasmania ... she just said that Trevor had gone. She said it was funny that she hadn't seen or heard from him. My parents [later] rented a house for her in Sydney. Then Brenden and Louise definitely split, because she met this loser [after Trevor] she's with now, and they've been together ever since.

Years later, when Abbott finally went on the record about Trevor Bailey, he first laughed at the suggestion that he had murdered him, and subsequently told Adelaide Detective Sergeant Sid Thomas, 'Are you looking for him? ... I don't think he's around.'

Perhaps Trevor Bailey was even better at invisibility than Brenden Abbott and the possibility he faked his own death by adopting a new identity cannot be ruled out. It's also possible he met a sudden end. Judy Bailey and her family were left to agonise, never knowing if, how, when or why the life of their wayward son ended.

Detective Senior Sergeant Gerry Costello, from the Brisbane armed robbery squad, retained overall control of the Queensland investigation into Brenden Abbott. He knew the suspicions that Abbott was based in Queensland and that he was behind the Gold Coast bank robbery epidemic. In November 1992, Costello arranged photographs of men in 'cowboy hats' standing in front of bus station signs, and then, on 19 January 1993, these shots and some of the 'real postcards' were turned into a photoboard to be shown to robbery witnesses.

At 4.25pm, on 1 February 1993, a man in a baseball cap, wearing reflector sunglasses and with an acne-scarred face, calmly walked into the Commonwealth branch at Palm Beach on the Gold Coast. The back door's alarm cable was cut, but the alarm still tested correctly. The same door had jemmy marks on it, but staff noticed nothing unusual when they opened that morning. The bandit was armed with a pistol with a laser sight, and he put a black bag on one of the desks, ordering staff to fill the bag with cash from tellers' draws and the treasury. The Crown case later stated,

The offender was aggressive and, when the cash was being removed by staff, he became very agitated and was telling the staff to hurry. Before he left, he directed the staff to go to an office. He left through the rear door. Witnesses comment that the offender appeared to have good knowledge of banking procedures; for example, who had the keys to the safe, where the tellers kept the money and where an alarm was. The offender also asked where the bearded Scottish man [the branch manager] was.

By this time, Abbott had enough money to be able to relax again for a while, although still far less than what he felt he needed to set himself up overseas on 21 May 1993 a lone bandit entered the Tugun branch of the Westpac bank on the Gold Coast, about 5.30pm. He escaped with $119,990.

I made a trip to Alice Springs and it was on this trip I obtained some driver's licence laminates and a pile of the data cards they insert into Polaroid cameras, the same as the ones they use in Queensland. On the data cards was an image that I enlarged to make the templates. From then on, I was able to produce NT driver's licences. A short time later, I made a trip to Adelaide to sort out some unfinished business.

Soon after arriving in Adelaide – and before he got down to business – Abbott was perusing a magazine for social options when an ad caught his eye. It was for a local brothel, on the Adelaide CBD's southern fringe, and the name rang pleasant bells. He recalls that it was something like 'Matheson's Daily Planet', and Abbott, a regular visitor at Melbourne's up-market Daily Planet brothel, wanted to see if the Adelaide girls had the same high standards. But, when he entered the establishment early one evening, it didn't look promising.

It wasn't anything flash at all. There were only a few girls and only one was available. I was shown to a room at the rear and I gave her cash for an hour booking, probably about $200. She asked me to get undressed and left the room with the money. She left the door ajar and was obviously coming straight back. No sooner had I undressed than I heard a chime like a doorbell in the room and I saw the girl run quickly past the door to the rear of the house.

At first, I didn't think there was a problem, then a young bloke in his late twenties walked into the room. 'I think you're in the wrong room, mate,' I told him.

He said he was a cop and didn't want to talk to me while I was naked. As I started getting my gear on, he told me it was illegal for me to be on premises used for prostitution.

'I thought they did massages here,' I replied.

He asked me if I was a liar or a smart-arse.

Not helping myself, and showing that I had no fear of the police, I replied, 'You haven't given me too many options, have you?'

His response: 'You're a fucking smart-arse, aren't you?' Then he demanded to see some ID. I pulled my wallet out of my pants pocket while I was putting my shoes on. He snatched the wallet out of my hand and said, 'I hope you've already paid.' On checking my wallet, which had over $500 in it, he said, 'I guess you haven't.'

It was then that I had a flashback and realised how lucky I was. I'd called into a friend's place earlier in the evening. He was into numerous shady dealings, including selling speed. I'd bought a small bag off him the previous day because I often used speed when travelling long distances, particularly between Melbourne and Adelaide at night. On most of these trips, I'd start getting tired when near Ararat or Ballarat, so I would put a small amount of speed in a Tallyho paper, roll it into a ball and swallow it, drinking it down with water. Within 30 minutes, I'd be peaking and start driving again, but it would take me until midday before I could sleep. The speed he sold was very high quality.

I saw him before I went to the brothel and he asked if I still had the bag he sold me yesterday. He had run out of speed and had someone wanting a bag, but he had to drive to the other side of Adelaide to restock and wasn't really keen to do it for the sake of one bag. I gave him the bag, which was in my wallet and hadn't been used, and he said he'd give me another bag the next day.

So, as the copper went through my wallet a couple of hours later, I wondered if my luck would continue. He discovered my fake SA licence and ran a check on the name. While waiting for a response from his hand-held Motorola (the same as one I had), he asked if I had any criminal convictions. I knew there was the one drug offence against the name I was using, possession of cannabis, and I told him that. The response came back over his radio soon after – that person was not of interest. Even though I knew the name on the licence was sweet, my heart was still in my mouth waiting for the radio response. When it came back all clear, I did my best not to show relief.

Another detective entered the room, an older jack who appeared to be running the raid. He told the younger jack to get a statement from me and then he headed for the front door. After he went, I told the younger jack I wouldn't be giving any statements. He started dirtying up and threatening to arrest me for being on the premises, so I again told him I wasn't aware it *was a brothel, I thought they only did massages. I had him fucked on that and he knew it; he wasn't a happy chappy. He told me to wait in the room and he headed to the reception area, I guess to tell the older jack that I wouldn't give a statement. He returned and told me to follow him outside. In the reception area were a few jacks, a couple of girls, a few customers and the bloke who was at the front desk when I first entered the place.*

The jack asked for my car keys as we walked out the door. The car I came in, an LH Torana, was in the brothel's car park. He headed for the driver's side and it appeared he was going to search the car. There were no other jacks in sight. He looked in the window. The only thing in there was on the driver's side floor, pushed up against the brake pedal – my small black leather backpack and in that was my pager, some cash, a scanner and my Caspian .38 super automatic pistol.

I had already decided my next move – if he opened the driver's side door, I was going to king-hit him to the left side of his jaw. If the adrenalin wasn't pumping through my system when he first identified himself, it was now. My heart was pounding. After getting it over him, my next move would have been to grab my backpack and clear out. Fuck the car, the best they'd get from it was my prints.

He then walked to the back of my car and I thought he was going to open the boot. That wouldn't be a problem. He then handed me the keys and said, 'You're nothing but a fuckhead. If you're caught in a brothel again, you'll be arrested.' I quickly jumped in my car and drove out. As I turned on to the main street heading back to the CBD, I saw a couple of jacks escorting the bloke from reception out the front door.

It took some minutes for my hands to stop shaking. I never again visited a brothel in Adelaide. I called escorts to motel rooms instead, which was an expensive exercise, because I'd book a room just to see a girl and then return to another motel to sleep. As for the young detective who called me a fuckhead, need I say more?

As close calls go, they don't come much closer. But it did not deter Abbott from pursuing his 'unfinished business', which is presumably his tacit acknowledgement of pulling South Australia's biggest-ever bank robbery at that time. It was Thursday, 19 August 1993, at the same bank as a previous suspected Abbott robbery, in July 1990. *The Advertiser*'s Bernard Humphreys reported, 'Bandits have pulled off South Australia's biggest bank robbery, grabbing more than $200,000 in three minutes. In a highly professional operation, the gang broke into the West Lakes Mall branch of the Commonwealth Bank, locked up staff, raided the vault and fled the area before police had a chance to react. The state's previous biggest bank heist was in 1991, when notorious robber Brendan James Abbott – who is still on the run – netted about $300,000 in two raids on Salisbury banks. In yesterday's raid, the bandits waited until 4.35pm, when the bank had no customers and then walked to a rear door and drilled its lock. Two members of the gang, brandishing handguns, then herded staff into a lunchroom and locked the door. One staff member was forced to open the bank's vault, where the two men helped themselves to as much cash as they could carry.'

Police swarmed on the domestic airport terminal, following the theory that interstate raiders were involved, but found no trace of the bandits or the $238,000 they escaped with. The following week, another Bernard Humphreys story in *The Advertiser* quoted one of the West Lakes investigators, Detective Sergeant Paul Stalker: 'He said yesterday that investigators developed a "grudging respect" for professional criminals who put a lot of work into their crimes and were then incredibly difficult to trace. "They are like any tradesman who does a good job and, when they do that job, they get accolades," he said. "It's not as if you admire them, but you have a grudging respect for a job well done and well planned." The modern professional criminal was exemplified by Abbott, who played a cat and mouse game with police by sending them photographs of himself counting his loot, but otherwise kept out of traditional crime circles where he could be more easily found.

'"This bloke hardly drinks and he doesn't do drugs or hang around nightclubs … he is not easy to find," Sergeant Stalker said. "But, if they do so many jobs, eventually they have to make a mistake."'

The Adelaide detectives had some strong leads. There were intense surveillance operations conducted on local criminals in the days and weeks after the West Lakes robbery, and, on one occasion, their diligence actually delivered Abbott into their laps.

I'd called into a friend's house in Adelaide for a quick visit. I parked my car in his driveway and walked around to his front door. Just as I got to the front door, I saw a late-model Commodore or Falcon slowly drive past with two jokers sitting in the front. They were both quite interested in me, staring as they drove by slowly.

Straight away, I thought, Fucking jacks? My next thought was that my pistol was in the console of my car. We were on a no-through road and they would have to drive past again.

I knocked on the door of the house, with no intention of going in if anyone answered the door. As soon as the jacks' car was out of sight, I went straight back to my car to leave. As I got into the car, I grabbed my Caspian .38 super, chambered a round, put the safety on and put it between my thighs. I grabbed a spare magazine and put it in my pocket.

Just as I was about to reverse out of the driveway, the jacks have cruised past and again taken an obvious interest in me. When I pulled out of the driveway, they were almost at a stop not far ahead of me.

My mind was already made up. There were only two of them. If it came to a scenario where I had to shoot my way out to avoid capture, so be it. I'd dreaded such a situation for years, but on this day I was prepared to do so. They drove off and I followed them for some distance after, a number of car lengths behind. After a while, I started to think that maybe they're just real estate agents. Their car didn't have the telltale signs of a jacks' car. No two-way aerials or cop rims. I took down the rego of their car and no sooner had I done that than they suddenly slowed down and did an illegal U-turn on the four-lane main road, and passed me going in the opposite direction.

The place I was staying at was only 5–10 minutes' drive away. Looking behind me all the way to see that I wasn't being followed, I arrived and the first thing I did was grab the police radio and carried out a rego check on that car.

I'd done rego checks a number of times in the past with that radio. [Abbott bought a battery for the SA police radio from Motorola in Melbourne. The radio itself had gone missing from the SA police traffic section, but had been logged as returned.] The operator passed on details without drama except on one occasion. He came back saying I wasn't logged on to that channel. I quickly apologised – my mate with me at the time found it amusing – and said I didn't realise I was on that channel

*and would go back to the other. But the operator still came back
and offered to do the check for me anyway. Listening to scanners
for years on end, I got to know the police radio routine, lingo
and phonetic alphabet.*

*After the rego check, I soon had my bags packed and had a flight
booked for Melbourne that was departing within a few hours.*

Times change. People move on. At the Perth armed robbery squad,
Geoff Maloney transferred to the witness protection unit and Jeff
Beaman went to Kalgoorlie as a senior officer at the gold-stealing
detection unit. Not that he gave away the pursuit of Abbott entirely.
The frustrations had mounted; there was another sighting in Perth –
made on a Friday, but not reported to Beaman until the Monday – and
a tale that Abbott's sister Diane met up with him for lunch with her
kids at a Gold Coast Hungry Jack's. When Beaman visited Queensland
on an unrelated extradition matter, he says he tried to drum up support
among Queensland detectives for a national task force to catch
Abbott. But few of them seemed to know much about him and, he
says, weren't really interested. So, while Beaman became familiar with
the finer points of metallurgy and mine security, he couldn't help but
keep his eye out for Abbott. The bastard would pop up sooner or later.

Late in 1993, Detective Sergeant Glen Potter transferred to armed
robbery from division 79, a fast-response group that paired a detective
with a uniformed officer. What intrigued the ambitious young
detective most about his new job was the Abbott case, and the roomful
of boxes that was testament to the squad's lengthy pursuit of the
former suburban villain. Abbott's continued success as a bank robber
and a fugitive embarrassed the Perth CIB as a whole, even though they
could reasonably argue they did their job on the tarmac of Perth
Airport back in 1987. Potter relished the challenge ahead. He says,

*It was clear the case had gone cold. Previous informants were of
no value. Abbott was a man whose associates changed according
to his needs. We took a close look at Thelma and other family
members and we knew that Abbott was in contact with his
mother through a third party. Intelligence indicated he was very
mobile and travelled to various states regularly. And since his
release from prison, Glenn Abbott had effectively vanished. I
thought that, if we could find him, then we would inevitably find
Brenden Abbott.*

On 17 December 1993, a man identifying himself as Jeff Allen and a male companion checked into the Pink Poodle Motel on the Gold Coast. Mr Allen provided ID for an address in Darwin. On 23 December 1993, at 11.30am, an Armaguard team made a delivery to the Pacific Fair shopping centre on the Gold Coast.

Then, on 24 December, Brenden Abbott prepared for all his Christmases to come at once.

He sat in the shade in a garden next to the Commonwealth Bank, wearing headphones and sunglasses, silently cursing himself as he watched a bank officer walk towards him, intent on the morning security check.

'It looks like it's going to be a hot day,' she said.

'I just wanted to get cool, love,' he replied.

The door he was near had no handle, but the bank officer pushed against it firmly and ensured it was secure. She gave the man another look and then came to a decision. She later told police, 'He was very casual in his speech and did not seem worried by my presence.'

She continued on her checks. She warned a male staff member who arrived for work and they went inside together. While he went to the window to watch Abbott, the bank officer switched the teller security screens into 'day' mode.

Abbott says,

Something I missed in my earlier days of surveillance on that bank was someone checking those rear doors. It was due to a slight hiccup that I was sitting there in the first place. I had planted listening devices in the bank the night before. This was extra insurance in case any handiwork of mine was discovered. On this occasion, it was working fine at night when I planted it; range was fine. For some reason, maybe electrical interference, due to something inside the bank coming on, I couldn't pick anything up unless I got close, hence sitting near the door. When she went inside and eventually let another staff member in, a young chap, I heard her say to him something about me sitting outside and to have a look. He came to the window and peeked through the blinds. I moved out of sight and then heard what sounded like a compressor starting up. I guess this was the pop-up security screens. With that going on, it was pointless trying to listen in any further.

While the two staff completed the internal security check, more staff gathered outside, waiting to come in. At 8.50am, the woman suspicious of Abbott put the treasury timer on. Five minutes later, the lock released and she took $100,000 out for distribution to the tellers. The treasury was locked again, but, on Christmas Eve, one of the biggest shopping days of the year, they would need plenty more later. It was going to be a big day.

Abbott:

When I first entered through the fire exit, it was done quickly because it was important to get the drop on all of them. Just as police do on raids, it's of importance to surprise the occupants. People, just like any animals, have reaction times. As soon as someone activates the alarm, the vault is out of the question. On this day, my two-way was clipped on my belt. Somehow it came off while entering. My foot must've kicked the strap, hurling the two-way into the tellers' area. At the time, I wasn't aware of losing it. Wasn't until the staff were under control that I realised I'd lost it. I even wandered outside, thinking I had dropped it outside the door. I was cursing myself out loud when I couldn't find it, saying something like: 'This is a good fucking start to things,' asking the other chap with me, 'Did you see where the radio went?' It took one of the female tellers to point it out to me. I had no idea the strap was missing, or if, in fact, the strap was on it in the first place. [The strap would later be used in evidence against Abbott.]

Staff said this incident was the only time during the robbery that Abbott looked like panicking. With the earpiece plugged back into the two-way again, he checked with the third accomplice outside that all was clear and calmly returned to the script, turning to address the manager:

'Where are the others?'

'I don't know what you mean.'

'Where are the others, don't fuck me around, where are the others?'

'They are over at Albert Avenue [branch].'

'What about the short fat one with the cream top?'

'She's just gone to Coles to get morning tea for the staff.'

'Is it a two-minute or five-minute timer?'

Before this was asked, I wanted to know who the manager was [even though] I knew who he was beforehand. The amount of times I've asked who the manager is in past withdrawals, they seem to never own up. You want to see the looks on their faces when another staff member quickly points them out. Times like that, it's hard not to have a chuckle. When on this day he didn't own up, that's when the pistol was pushed into his chest and cocked. Due to past experience with firearms – especially automatics – I never had one in the chamber. National at Springwood [April 1992] was a good example.

'If you don't fucking tell me, I'll waste you. You're the manager, the staff will do what you tell them.'

A phone rang. The manager leaned forward to pick it up.

'That's a good idea.'

Abbott listened in while the manager bluffed his way through the call. Another staff member emptied the money intended for the tellers' drawers into a bag. Abbott noticed his accomplice's mind wander.

'Don't turn your back on them; you never turn your fucking back on them.'

He then ordered all the staff on to the floor. 'Who's got the keys for the treasury?'

The manager and another staff member admitted they had them, then each of the tellers' keys was collected as well and Abbott led the two key holders into the treasury. Abbott noticed one was the woman from outside. He grinned. 'Jeez, love, I thought you'd blown it for me.'

He ordered the manager to put the timer on. While they waited, Abbott asked at least three times about foreign currency on the premises, but the woman was insistent; pick-ups were twice a week and they had none at the moment. As the five minutes progressed, Abbott ran between the treasury and main banking chamber, ensuring his accomplice didn't stuff it all up. The manager studied Abbott's face, mostly hidden by the big sunglasses, but he did notice Abbott's faded acne scars.

'I know what you're doing, mate. Don't bother, I'll give you a description.'

The timer went off. Abbott looked in at the cash before ordering the manager to put the bundles of $25,000 into an oversized duffle bag.

'I'm going to have a good Christmas.'

'We won't.'

'You'll get over it. What's there, mate? Six hundred, seven hundred thousand?'

The total haul was $781,252. The manager struggled to zip the bag and Abbott leaned over to help him. It looked like his biggest haul yet. The hard work the previous night had really paid off.

'I know this place. I know it like the back of my hand ... I want you all to go up to the morning-tea room.'

Two other staff members who arrived for work during the robbery joined their colleagues in the banking chamber. Apparently, all of Bandit Number Two's lobes were working. While the rest of the staff waited in the tearoom, the manager stood on the landing, creeping down several times, only to be sternly ordered back up. Three minutes after they went up, the bandits vanished. One of the bank officers – the woman who saw Abbott outside, whose faultless observations and courage allowed police to build such a detailed picture of what happened – went to the treasury and activated the alarm. The battery for the alarm box next to the rear fire door was on the floor. And the alarm box – with its own lock – was open. Abbott took the trouble to remove the evidence of his handiwork – no point in tipping off the bank's security boffins as to how he circumvented their safeguards. The leads to the battery that powered the alarm siren were tampered with. And the locksmith who later replaced the fire exit's lock – and the front door, which was also drilled – said he had never seen anything like it.

On Christmas Day, 'Jeff Allen' checked out of the Pink Poodle.

Now Abbott could lay claim to the trifecta – the biggest bank robberies in each of three states. But his record in South Australia was about to be broken; Abbott and his mate weren't the only Australian bank robbers enjoying the festive season that year. Three huge bank robberies in three states in a week: on 20 December, the National Australia Bank, Highpoint shopping centre, Maribyrnong, Victoria – $500,000-plus; on 24 December, the Commonwealth Bank, Pacific Fair shopping centre, Gold Coast – $781,252; and on 30 December the National Australia Bank, Modbury, Adelaide – $478,000.

Detectives needed to confront a new theory. One three-man team doing all three robberies in less than a week was virtually impossible, but one team split into three groups using the same methods adapted for the specific circumstances of each bank? Anything was possible, especially if Brenden Abbott was involved.

As Jackie Lord once noted, Brenden Abbott could be a 'tight git, the tightest'. He was 100 per cent sure no one saw the Mitsubishi Sigma he bought as the getaway car. And he didn't particularly want to torch the thing and draw attention to himself when he could quite easily sell it. Abbott had asked Hardy Brasche to sell a Holden Torana SLR with SA plates – the car the 'fuckhead' detective had failed to search – for him a few months previously, telling him he needed the cash because he was going back to South Australia. Brasche told police he was suspicious. He thought Abbott ran cannabis from Adelaide to the Gold Coast.

So Brasche was equally dubious when he got home from his job as a cleaner at an arts centre and found a Mitsubishi Sigma on his front lawn just after Christmas. Abbott rang and asked him to try to sell it for $1,000, but told him he needed to put a new clutch plate and pressure plate in it first. Brasche thought the car was stolen, but, when Abbott gave him the details of the previous owner to allay his suspicions, Brasche was satisfied. He sold the car for $1,250 to a guy in Kingscliffe on 11 January; Abbott got his $1,000, the clutch parts cost $200 and Brasche got $50 for his trouble. The same day, Queensland detectives commenced 'Operation Braille', aimed at catching Abbott. It was a good name, as the investigators were in the dark most of the time.

The luckless Queensland detectives ordered surveillance on Hardy Brasche's home again on 3 January 1994, but their running sheets do not indicate exactly how long this lasted. Abbott picked up the car sale proceeds from Brasche's house on either Sunday, 15 January or Sunday, 22 January, but either the surveillance had ended or Abbott's merchant seaman disguise as the mysterious Pedro was just too convincing.

Then, in early March that year, Abbott called Brasche and asked him to clean out Louise Laycock's storage shed at Machinery Drive, Tweed Heads. Brasche collected six boxes of clothes, toys and personal items including photos, plus four Commodore wheels. Soon after, Abbott arrived at Brasche's house, repacked the goods and sent them to Louise's unit at Nerang. But all of this fabulous intelligence didn't come to light until police interviewed Brasche on 6 September 1994, and 5 January 1995.

Whatever the reasons for the collapse of the relationship between Abbott and Louise, another overriding concern came to light years later. Detective Inspector Ray Platz told a court, 'Well, we had surveillance on Laycock's premises back in 1992. [Abbott] told me how he had sighted one of the surveillance cars ... As a result of that, he never went back to Laycock again. And I believe I told him I would pass the message on to the surveillance personnel involved, which I did ... He told me that we'd had Louise's place under surveillance because he'd caught one of the cars out. And he said, "Because of that, I had to wipe Laycock and not go near her again."'

Chapter Eleven

1994–1995

Romance isn't easy for a professional fugitive. Brenden Abbott loved his son, but the love-hate dramas with the boy's mother, Louise Laycock, almost cost him his freedom. Jackie was the first to make him acutely aware that trusting a woman could be dangerous; and yet he couldn't help himself, once telling Detective Beaman, 'I've got one vice, Jeffrey, and that's women.'

In Louise's absence, Abbott played the field again but often paid for it, too. For him, brothels were a sanctuary where he could safely retreat and indulge the pleasures of the flesh without the emotional baggage of a relationship. And the girls he saw weren't the kind with tracks on their arms – he told one associate he saw girls in Sydney who charged $1,600 a night. But the self-imposed ban on Adelaide brothels stayed, and it was as much a punishment as a security measure. He knew that he also behaved like a 'fuckhead' that night; bravado in the face of an arrogant young cop was a foolhardy risk for a man who considered himself the consummate professional. He knew he needed to keep his ego under control and focus on that professionalism; that was what had got him this far, along with a generous slice of luck. He had looked cops in the face and walked away a free man, every time. He says he was caught speeding and happily accepted tickets on three occasions because the identities he used were legitimate. As a teenager, he had been forever having his licence suspended. Now, the most wanted man in the nation could speed with impunity – as long as he kept a polite tongue in his head when those coppers got in his face.

On 29 May 1994, the *Courier Mail* in Brisbane updated the state's Most Wanted list, in which a head shot of Brenden Abbott – from one of the pictures taken with baby James – appeared fourth on the list. He now spent an increasing amount of time in northern Queensland, particularly with the added pressure in Brisbane and the Gold Coast. In addition to the statement from Hardy Brasche mentioning the property up north, another piece of intelligence pointed north – hinting that Abbott employed someone to grow commercial quantities of cannabis in Far North Queensland. It was a region that Abbott, like many locals and visitors, grew to love – a place of true escape, as long as a well-stocked Land Cruiser was handy. He used Cairns as a regular base in early 1994, but was definitely there earlier.

Diane Abbott, now living in the northern city with her five children, Nicole, Crystal, Storme, Teresa and Harley, says,

> He knocked on the door and gave me the fright of my life. He only stayed for about half an hour. I ended up doing some washing and took it outside and thought, If the cops come, I can say I didn't even know he was here. I didn't want to tell him to go, because it was really good to see him. But I was also so frightened.

While in Cairns in June 1994, Abbott replied to a 'masseuse' advertisement in the *Cairns Post*, placed by an attractive blonde named Georgia Smith, whose temper made Louise Laycock look like a Stepford wife. Abbott couldn't get enough of her.

For all the attention Abbott attracted in South Australia, no warrant for his arrest was issued in that state. The declaration of the earlier Salisbury robberies as a major crime allowed the allocation of a lot more resources to the pursuit of Abbott, but this fizzled out. And, after the West Lakes and Modbury robberies in 1993, there were no further robberies with obvious Abbott links. It meant no detectives were actively looking for him in South Australia. Abbott considered it an open invitation.

On Saturday, 23 July 1994, *The Advertiser*'s Andrew Male reported, 'Australia's most notorious bank robber may have added to his total $2 million haul with the proceeds from a Glenelg bank robbery yesterday. Brendan James Abbott is a prime suspect in the robbery, which occurred just before the Commonwealth Bank was due to open ... The robber was described as in his thirties, unshaven, with curly dark hair, black wraparound sunglasses, a Nike jumper, black Puma tracksuit pants, brown leather gloves and a silver watch on his right wrist ... Police suspect [Abbott] flies in and out of a city within hours of a robbery, after booking airline tickets under a false name. National criminal intelligence suggests he spends much of his time between raids on the Gold Coast, in Queensland holiday resorts, or in Outback Australia. A woman who drove the getaway car was described as aged between 28 and 32, medium build, brown loosely curled hair worn below the shoulder line.'

Darlington CIB's Detective Sergeant Sid Thomas considered the robber either supremely confident or an idiot. The robbery modus operandi suggested the former. They escaped with $118,639. Thomas showed pictures of Abbott to staff members, who were virtually unanimous that he was Bandit No. 1.

Finally, there was enough evidence for SA police to secure a warrant for Abbott's arrest and join the hunt. Thomas drew up a plan and launched Operation Passion; he transferred to the organised crime task force at headquarters to oversee the operation.

The experienced detective knew the theories that Abbott did return trips from Queensland; but he thought it just as likely that Abbott rented his own cheap discreet unit somewhere in Adelaide. Either way, Thomas knew he had little chance of finding Abbott unless he knew what went on at the armed robbery squads in other states. He contacted detectives across the country – Glen Potter in Perth, Gerry Costello in Brisbane, Steve Campbell in Melbourne and Angelo Memmolo in Sydney, and, later, Rob King in Launceston – trying to make sense of a jumble of information. At that time, state police departments were haphazard or downright unhelpful in sharing intelligence or co-operating. And, of course, there were always the professional rivalries that developed as Abbott's scalp became more prized.

Despite all that, most detectives directly involved in the investigation saw the bigger picture, so each went off to his respective boss with similar requests to those contained in Sid Thomas's memo to his senior officers: the appointment of a liaison officer in each state police department, part of a national task force to hunt Abbott, co-ordinated through a national body such as the Australian Federal Police or National Crime Authority; the general reward of $10,000 replaced with a specific sum for Abbott's recapture; and the need for detectives to gather for a conference to discuss a national strategy. Thomas's informal poll of the other interstate detectives reached a general agreement that they should meet in Adelaide.

The Thomas memo brought a flurry of activity in Perth, where detectives discovered someone had forgotten to actually issue a warrant for Abbott's arrest after the Fremantle escape. It was an embarrassing oversight and made the detectives there ultra-keen to look assertive and take the lead role in the hunt for Abbott. Glen Potter's submission to his senior officer at the Perth armed robbery squad noted that a National Crime Authority operation in New South Wales reported an Abbott sighting, but, when the information filtered back to Western Australia, it was useless. With no analysis or dissemination between the states, intelligence holdings were poor, he said. And each state and federal body had different priorities. Now it was time to work together for the greater good.

Regular cashflow throughout 1994 allowed Brenden Abbott to return to one of his great passions; he bought a 1972 Holden HQ utility. Like the LC Torana all those years before, it was a shitheap, but he consulted half of Cairns' automotive community on how best to proceed with his new obsession. He kept the vehicle in a storage shed in Hannam Street, Cairns. Around August 1994, he struck up a conversation with a young bloke named David Male, who worked at a nearby shed for a paint and panel business. 'Barry', as he called himself, asked the spray-painter to give the ute a polar-white respray. Georgia Smith, the feisty masseuse, would later tell police,

> While in Cairns, Barry never resided with me on a permanent basis. However, he stayed over with me for about four days at my unit [approximately June 1994]. After those four days, I suggested he move out because I seemed to lose my privacy and him being there interfered with my work and freedom. Barry moved out ... I did not know whether I would see him again. However, he telephoned me a couple of weeks later and we had a pleasant conversation. Our relationship seemed to start again and he called at my unit and asked me if I would like to go on holiday with him to Melbourne. After this, Barry took me again to Melbourne and up to Alice Springs. We flew on both occasions and stayed at the Airport Hotel again in Melbourne and the Vista Motel in Alice Springs.

For all Abbott's hopes to make this relationship different, trouble with Georgia was never far away.

About late July, early August 1994, I convinced Georgia to move down to the Gold Coast with me. We stayed there for a week before I returned to Cairns so I could finish putting the ute back on the road again. I wasn't far off in doing so. Georgia, in the meantime, organised a flat on the Gold Coast. When I finished the ute, I was to drive it down. But after a few weeks, she got lonely and came back up to Cairns to join me on the drive down. We stayed in holiday units together before going back to the Gold Coast. I was getting around in a hire car.

On the first night in a motel room, which I paid for for a week, we were robbed. Georgia, being a smoker, went out on the balcony to have a smoke in the early hours of the morning while I slept. When she came back in, she left the sliding door unlocked.

Wasn't until next morning while searching for my board shorts did I realise we'd been robbed. The fucker had even stolen my small black leather backpack. The keys to the hire car and my gold chain were still on the bedside table. I went out to the car hoping I left my backpack in that overnight but it was wishful thinking. I found out after I came back into the unit that she was also missing her handbag. She then owned up about leaving the sliding door unlocked. I was absolutely furious with her but I didn't have to say anything for her to see that. I then left the motel room and searched the drains around the motel and across the road in case they dumped my wallet or bags after taking out the cash. I had about $10,000 in the backpack, and a few hundred in the wallet that was in my shorts pocket. Georgia had about $2,000 in her handbag. My backpack also contained my mobile phone and a bumbag with my .32 calibre automatic pistol. My major concern was all my driver's licences were in my wallet. My only legit SA licence, one legit NT licence and about three NT licences I used solely for motel booking etc. I was unable to find anything and, getting back to the room, I've told Georgia to get her stuff together because we're booking out. Her response was: 'Why? Let's stay here, they may come back again tonight.'

I thought to myself, Did I just hear her right? The look I gave her quickly had her saying, 'I'll start packing.' I collected the cash from reception (I'd paid a week in advance).

I caught up with someone I knew not far from Cairns and borrowed a few grand. A flight down south had me able to stock up with cash again (that I had in safe keeping). Later, another trip to a storage shed to obtain some more driver's licences, but I didn't have any with names that were legit on the police database, so I later had to set up the camera to make some. I was a little uneasy driving that hire car before then. Georgia never left doors unlocked again either. I never heard about any licences being found by anyone who reported it to the police. I didn't file a complaint either.

There was an earlier incident I had with Georgia, not long after I met her, about July 1994. We went for a trip to a city down south and at the airport we parted company. She took her baggage and a two-way radio to a prearranged hotel in the city. She was to turn the radio on when in her room. I proceeded in a cab to a cheap hire-car company not far from the airport. After filling out the paperwork and putting my bags in the car, I pulled over a few streets away and retrieved my shower bag out of my bag in the boot. Inside the car I assembled my .32 auto pistol and had an inside pants holster for it. I arrived at the motel and found out the room Georgia was in via the two-way that I grabbed out of my bag earlier with the gun. I left the bags in the boot and after a short period in the room with Georgia, I had to catch up with a friend who was also in town staying in another motel. I told Georgia I'd be one to two hours at the most. I took the room key with me. When I returned, she wasn't there, but had left a note to tell me to collect her from a bar at a five-star hotel elsewhere in the city.

She was sitting at the bar with a bloke either side of her and was being chatty with them. I was standing some distance from her hoping to catch her eye and nod to her to go. But she yells out, 'Barry, over here.' Then she introduced me to these two jokers and she was obviously pissed. The look from these two told me I was a spanner in the works. Next thing I'm copping the usual squarehead questions: Where do you live? What do you do for a living? When I said I lived in Alice Springs, you wouldn't read about it, so did one of them. Next I was getting, 'Do you know so-and-so, this place etc?' My knowledge of Alice was limited and he soon picked up on it. Georgia realised she had brought me into a situation in which I needed a quick exit and promptly asked me to take her back to the hotel. Not soon enough, though, as this joker was starting to think I wasn't exactly straight up and down with him. Back at our motel I told her, 'If in future when you see me like tonight, don't call me over. I don't want to talk to people like that.'

She then started to abuse me and fired up about being told what to do. Next thing I'm ducking to avoid copping a shampoo bottle in the head that flew across the room. I've quickly left the room and went to my mate's motel for a while to give the viper time to settle down.

When I returned I knocked on the door. When it opened, SMACK! The fucking bitch punched me straight in the mouth. Didn't see that coming. In an instant reflex, I landed one right on her forehead. She didn't see that coming either. She had a shocked look as she landed backwards on her arse. Then I was the one with the shocked look as she came at me with haymakers. I managed to avoid her connecting again and grabbed her and pushed her back into the room, kicking the door shut with my foot in the process. I was now wrestling a fucking wildcat. We were on the bed and on the floor and she was screaming like a scalded cat to let go of her. This was a situation I'd never experienced before. I managed to get hold of both her hands with my left hand and had her on the floor with her back to me while I was on my knees. My other concern was that someone in another room could be hearing this commotion and calling the cops. I just wanted it to stop, so I've pulled the pistol out of its holster and put it to her head and told her to pull up. Then I've said, 'I'll pull the trigger.' There wasn't a round chambered. But she just kept screaming and got one of her hands loose. I've used my right hand to smack her on the side of the head. Unintentionally, the base of the butt or magazine has opened her head, just back from the hairline, and she had claret coming down her face and she still wanted to go on with it. I've then tossed the gun to another part of the room and then grabbed her around the throat and put her on her back and squeezed. After a short moment, she started to relax and, by the look on her face, I knew it was best to pull up. She knew she wasn't going to win this fight. As I let her go, she slowly sat up and leaned her back to the bed, not saying a word. I've collected the gun and departed the room, grabbing the two-way on the way out.

My mind was set: I would not return and would never see her again. I got to the car and realised that my car keys came out of my pocket during the struggle. I used the lobby phone to ring her room. She answered, calm as ever. I asked her if she was OK and let her know I wanted to come back up, saying nothing of the missing keys. I knocked on the door and, as it opened, I was on guard. I didn't know what to expect from this maniac. She had a towel to her head, cleaning up the claret from her head wound. I found the keys beside the bed, we talked and before long we managed to have a laugh about what just went down. Then she comes out with: 'All you had to do was throw me down and fuck me.'

I couldn't help but think, You sick bitch. You need help.

Sex with Georgia was unlike any I'd had with any other woman, ever. If she wanted sex, she wouldn't ask. She would demand it. And she used language that would have had her mother washing her mouth out with soap. I was somewhat uncomfortable with her at first when it came to sex. She made it clear which buttons I needed to push. From then on, it was great. We never had a similar situation. I just had to throw her down and fuck her as she said, and let her know she's been a bad girl. It worked a treat, but I think I need help now. She also realised that alcohol was an issue for her and she did her best to limit how much she drank.

On 25 October 1994, Abbott bought an electronic pager at Southport, on the Gold Coast. On Saturday, 29 October 1994, burglars hit Gold Coast Shooters Supplies. When the owner returned on Monday morning, he discovered that thieves dodged security grilles and the alarm systems. They cut a hole through the wall and stole a large quantity of high-powered weapons and ammunition. 'Barry Reid' (Glenn Abbott) booked into the Pink Poodle Motel on the Gold Coast Highway, Surfers Paradise, on Sunday, 30 October 1994. He paid cash and gave an Alice Springs address, and then booked out on Tuesday, 1 November – Melbourne Cup day.

Finally, late in 1994, the detectives pursuing Abbott got their national operation, Probe: Flanders, and the Australian Bankers Association issued a reward of $50,000 for information leading to Brenden Abbott's arrest. But the conference that Sid Thomas planned for

Adelaide did not proceed, depriving detectives of the opportunity to meet face to face and 'clear the air' on some issues, as well as formulate a detailed national strategy to catch Abbott, gleaned from the extensive information the detectives collectively held.

Senior police instead opted for Glen Potter's suggestion that the operation be co ordinated through the Australian bureau of criminal intelligence (ABCI) in Canberra. Detectives would continue their informal phone contact, and also contribute intelligence to the ABCI, which, in theory, would compile and analyse the information and then share it between the states. The rivalries in this particular case meant this theory didn't translate well into action, with detectives reluctant to tell others more than they believed necessary. So, whatever the best intentions of Probe: Flanders, at the end of the day, each state's detectives were privately determined they would be the ones to bring down Brenden Abbott.

On 2 November 1994, Glen Potter and other Perth detectives met at CIB headquarters in Perth. Also at the table were their state bureau of criminal intelligence (BCI) analysts to discuss their role in the national strategy. Their main targets: Glenn Abbott, Diane Abbott and Thelma Salmon. Glen Potter also had an ace up his sleeve. While Potter was attached to division 79, Glenn Abbott's de facto wife, Kelly Fisher, had called police and said another ex-con ex-boyfriend was threatening to kill her. In the course of his investigation into this, Kelly's mother told Potter that Kelly told her that Glenn had once disappeared for three weeks. Now that he was familiar with the case, Potter knew that the time frame of this disappearance fitted the Pacific Fair robbery. This was one of several compelling reasons he believed most of their energy needed to go in Glenn Abbott's direction.

While Glen Potter, Steve Drown and other Perth detectives sipped coffee and pondered the challenges of catching crooks, Glenn Abbott headed back to Perth from the Gold Coast. On 4 November 1994, he took a steel trunk and a black sports bag – containing two rifles and a quantity of high-calibre ammunition – to the Honeywell storage units in Charles Street, Maylands, in Perth, where he paid cash for a three-month lease and used the Barry Reid driver's licence as ID.

Meanwhile, on the Gold Coast, around November 1994, Brenden Abbott took part in Operation DRAG, a legal drag race organised by local traffic cops at the old Surfers Paradise Raceway at Carrara.

*I didn't race against the police car. The carby on my ute was
fucked because the secondary jets were blocked. But I did race
other cars, and won one out of three. Georgia was there that day
and thought I had more front than Myer since the police were
running the whole show.*

Glenn Abbott didn't have much luck with traffic cops, either. Pulled
over for a driving offence around this time, he had to face court over
the resulting charge. Glenn used his own ID, which set alarm bells
ringing on the police computer. From the moment he arrived to face
a Mandurah court, outside Perth, on 17 November 1994, he was
under police surveillance. After court, they tailed him to an address in
nearby Halls Head, where everything from the rental agreement and
utilities' accounts to the car in the driveway were in false names.

Glenn's odd behaviour while under surveillance made it clear he
was worried about police, heightening their hopes he was in contact
with his brother. The detectives checked the mail he received at a post
office box at nearby Rockingham, between Perth and Mandurah. He
ordered pepper sprays, listening devices, electronics equipment and
other surveillance devices, mostly from the US. The surveillance
continued for months and it confirmed that Kelly Fisher lived at the
same address.

On the weekend of 19 and 20 November, feature articles on
Brenden Abbott appeared in daily newspapers in Perth, Adelaide and
Brisbane. But the *Courier Mail*'s story – written by an unidentified
AAP reporter – again reinforced the Postcard Bandit myth:
'Australia's most dangerous bank robber has sent pictures of himself
to police from holidays paid for from the millions of dollars he has
stolen.

'Brendan Abbott, 31, sent one picture of himself smiling and
counting money outside a country police station. Another shows
Abbott with friends at Ayers Rock. But police warned yesterday
Abbott was a hardened armed robber who has threatened to kill if
cornered … He may have had plastic surgery since sending his holiday
snaps to police.'

The report did not name its source for the postcard claims, but who
was going to disbelieve it, or indeed disprove it? Abbott, on the Rock,
next to Masao Ayuda, above the headline 'POSTCARDS FROM A
ROBBER'. Anyone seeing the pictures would assume it must be true.
Abbott's pager chirped the next day, flagging a message: 'Read

financial papers yesterday. Had the largest article regarding your company ever written. Congratulations, Greg. Send you a copy soon.'

Three days later the pager chirped again, with another cryptic cheerio: 'Congratulations on Year 5. Regards, Freddy and Myrtle.'

Late in July 1994, Abbott convinced Georgia she should move in with him on the Gold Coast. The following year, in an optimistically titled document, 'Evidence expected to be provided by Georgia Smith', police said, '[She will state that] in about [July/August] 1994, he talked her into moving from Cairns to the Gold Coast, where they stayed at the Pink Poodle Motel before moving into Unit 54, Florida Apartments, just prior to Christmas. She will state that this unit was rented in a false name she was using, Kathy Pearson, and that Abbott used to stay with her on a regular basis. She will also state that Abbott paid the rent, gave her spending money of approximately $5,000 a month, purchased her a car (Datsun station sedan 926CAW) and spent approximately $4,000 on surgery on her nose and breasts.'

Extracts from Queensland police running sheet, 16 December 1994:

'Item 1: Receive phone call from Manager of Westpac, Albert Ave, Broadbeach at 0800 16/12/94 that there are armed men in the branch and they were disturbed doing an armed robbery.

'Item 2: Police Units sent to Westpac Branch at Broadbeach. No vehicles in front of bank. Area cleared and bank secured. Area cordoned off. No movement seen inside bank.

'Item 3: Establish from the accountant that he arrived at 7.30am and commenced his security check. He saw a masked gunman in the bank who was surprised to see him. This person described as 184cm, solid build, slight beer gut, about mid-thirties, wearing navy-blue spray jacket, fawn-coloured trousers, wearing a blue balaclava. Also in possession of a black sports bag. Offender armed with a handgun. [The accountant] was made to carry bag to staff area downstairs where the offender queried him about his security procedures for the morning. The offender had possession of a radio scanner and could hear police channels. The accountant was with the offender for about 25 minutes. At 7.55am, a person was knocking on the front door. The accountant was told to go out there and let him in. The accountant went out and told the manager of the bank what the situation was and ran from the

scene to the Pan Pacific Hotel. A female was seen parked in the brown Galant in front of the bank.

'Item 9: [Witness] stated that she advertised her vehicle, a Brown Galant, in the Gold Coast Bulletin on 10/12/1994 for $1,800. She states that on Sunday 11/12/94 she received a phone call at 10.20am from a male that wanted to buy the car. A male person arrived at 2pm in a grey/blue-coloured Ford XB wagon. He took the car for a test drive by himself for about five minutes. He offered $1,500 for the vehicle and gave a $200 deposit. He left and returned at 6pm on 13/12/94 in a taxi. He stated that the car was for a girlfriend by the name of Judy Thorpe. He signed the transfer papers. Witness viewed photoboard of Brendan James Abbott and positively identified him as the purchaser.'

Item 42 lists the 50 motels and apartments that the detectives doorknocked that day, showing pictures of Abbott to staff. This significant expenditure in shoe leather brought several time-consuming but ultimately unsuccessful leads.

On 22 December, Georgia Smith signed a lease on Unit 54, Florida Apartments, at Surfers Paradise, after replying to an advertisement in the *Gold Coast Bulletin*. Florida Apartments were a postcard-perfect dream. Unit 54 was fully self-contained, with security intercom and parking, accessible only by key using a secure lift, and with views of Surfers, the river and the hinterland. Abbott upgraded the front-door lock, and put the old lock on the bedroom door: a secure private base in the heart of the Gold Coast. The woman calling herself 'Kathy' introduced Abbott to the neighbours in Unit 53 as Barry, her truck-driver boyfriend.

The same day she signed the lease, locksmiths examined damage to an external lock at the Westpac Bank in Biggera Waters. It had a 'centre-punch' believed to be similar to the method used by Abbott. Police surveillance and the special emergency response team (SERT) were moved into place, but, if Abbott was involved, he smelled a rat and never went back. The next day, alarms were activated at the Commonwealth Bank, Broadbeach, at 3.33am and 3.43am. SERT scrambled but found nothing. Someone was running hot to make a dollar. At the same time, Gold Coast detectives crawled out of bed, on their way to prepare a reception committee in nine other banks in the area later that morning. But a single crooked ceiling tile and a missing air-conditioning vent led to nothing.

Georgia checked out of the Pink Poodle that day and moved her belongings into Unit 54. Abbott, meanwhile, visited Rent-a-Shed at Kortum Drive, Burleigh West, and rented shed 351, where he stored his 'back-up' vehicle, a blue Holden HZ station wagon.

Meanwhile, in Perth, at 3.30am on New Year's Day, 1995, Kelly Fisher gave birth to Glenn's first child – a boy named Brenden – in a Perth hospital.

The new baby's uncle and namesake described himself as an earthmoving professional around this time, and it seemed he had secured a new contract. A good thing, too, since the ute was costing a fortune.

At 1pm on 19 January 1995, a man who arrived in a taxi – hailed at a Broadbeach rank – bought an orange Ford Cortina from a couple in Southport who advertised it for sale in the local paper. On 20 January 1995, a man wearing a balaclava and black gloves, with a microphone near his mouth, and a bag and a gun in his hand, dropped through the ceiling of the Commonwealth Bank branch at The Pines shopping centre, Elanora, which had taken delivery of a large sum of cash the previous day. The manager knew something was wrong when he heard a female staff member 'squealing'.

'I turned around and saw a man in a balaclava holding a gun. He said, "Get over here. You know what I'm here for. I'm not going to hurt you. Just do what I say."'

The staff lined up with their backs to the wall. The bandit spoke into the small microphone: 'Can you hear me? Is it all clear? Do you copy?' Some of the female staff sobbed quietly and the bandit let them sit down. He screwed an aerial on to a scanner, placed it on a cupboard and said, 'Do you know what this is?'

The manager nodded. 'We'll do as you say. We'll give you all the cash.'

The bandit said, 'I see you've got the treasury open. I want all the cash. I want one of youse to go around and get the cash.'

'You'll be all right, Victoria,' he said to one of the emotional women. And then to another, the head teller, 'You look the calmest. You take the bag and go and quickly get the money.'

She collected tens of thousands of dollars from the treasury and then sat back down.

'Right, how much is in the ATM?'

'About seventy to eighty thousand.'

'Right, how do we get into that?'

'There's two combinations and an audible alarm.'

These were dealt with and the manager brought back the ATM cartridges.

'After we zipped up the bag, he said, "Is there any security cameras out the back?" We said, "No, the camera is out the front." [He said,] "How do I know it's not running?" [We said,] "There's a display in the BCC room [bank communications centre] that ticks over when it's running."'

He insisted one of the staff show him. He then herded them into an office and said, 'I'm going to wait for my ride now, I don't want youse to come out for five minutes.' Twice, he called out, 'I'm still here.' Twelve minutes after he hit the floor, the bandit took the balaclava off and replaced it with a cap and wraparound sunglasses.

He noticed a bank worker standing at the front door with her teenage daughter, pressing the buzzer and peering in. She says, 'A person I thought was a workman appeared through an internal door. He came over to the side door where I was waiting and opened the door, pushed past us. He said, "There you go, you can go in now."'

Another bank officer says, 'Then we heard the middle door bang and then we heard the buzzer and we knew [the part-time staff member] had arrived. She called out, "Is anyone there?" I opened the door and said to [her], "Where did he go?"'

She looked over to the car park and saw the Cortina driving out. For some reason, she thought it was a Torana. When the car turned, she went out and peered from behind a pillar to try to get the rego. Police later asked her if she could describe the passenger. 'The seat seemed to be far back because he was leaning forward, with his hand hanging out the window. And he was looking at us like ... looking at the commotion that was going on there. In fact, he was smirking and he was looking at us like we were a bunch of bloody idiots.'

'*Item 89: On 20/1/95, the Commonwealth Bank at The Pines shopping centre, Elanora, was held up by an offender dropping through roof, just prior to the bank opening. Offender armed with black semi-auto pistol and had radio contact with the outside helper. Offender stole $354,819. Offender seen to decamp in orange Cortina 895 PIU, located in the car park at the other end of the shopping centre.*'

Detective Senior Constable Glen Prichard arrived at the bank about 10am and got the investigation moving. He spoke to the shocked staff, examined the scene and arranged a photographer. He checked the bank's fire-equipment cupboard where the bandit entered the building, cutting through wire mesh in its ceiling. But the detective found nothing unusual. The bank manager later told a court that, on the afternoon after the robbery, he saw a stain in the cupboard on a besser brick on the southern wall, less than half a metre from the BCC. Senior Constable Andrew Pilotto, a Gold Coast crime-scene unit member, later told a court that there was enough light for him to have seen the stain when he examined the area on the day of the robbery. He checked every negative of every picture he took that day, but the particular area where the stain was found was not pictured; he said it surprised him that he missed it.

On 23 January 1994 – the same day the Elanora bank manager decided he should probably tell someone about the stain in the fire-equipment cupboard – Brenden Abbott headed back to Cairns, where brother Glenn joined him the following day.

'Congratulations on business transaction. Fred.'
Brenden Abbott's pager, 8am, 23 January 1995

'William Harris' and 'Barry Reid' met up at the appropriately named Balaclava Hotel in Cairns the next day to toast the latest success, which was all over the papers: 'POSTCARD BANDIT IN HUGE ROBBERY'; 'HAPPY SNAP BANDIT BACK'; 'BANK ROBBERY BLAMED ON POSTCARD BANDIT'.

Abbott, Glenn and a third man Abbott will not name adjourned to a room at the Balaclava to dissect the operation. Abbott sat on a bench next to the room's TV, examining a 9mm Glock pistol that Glenn had brought with him. He ejected the magazine and the round in the chamber and placed them on the bench, and, as he sat chatting to the others, pulled the slide back, and pulled the trigger, idly repeating the process several times. 'After a while, I put the magazine back into the pistol and pulled the slide back and chambered a round. It wasn't until the pistol went off that I realised what I'd just done. It totally frightened the shit out of me. Glenn couldn't contain himself. He was pissing himself with laughter so much he had tears in his eyes.'

While Glenn rolled helplessly on the bed, Abbott checked the door and windows to make sure the shot hadn't attracted attention from housekeeping or other guests; but the cleaners were going about their business, oblivious. The bullet went through the room's window and through an adjacent vacant block, and did not appear to have claimed any victims. The only worry was the bullet hole in the glass, so Abbott went outside and smashed it, and they checked out soon afterwards.

They all saw the funny side of the incident, but Glenn remained tickled for days. He eventually admitted to his brother that it was because he'd done virtually the same thing himself only months earlier at the Pink Poodle Motel on the Gold Coast. Glenn had been lying on a bed watching TV and playing with a .22 automatic pistol. Unaware that he had chambered a round, he took aim at a TV character and scored a direct hit, putting an end to his evening's viewing. The silencer on the pistol subdued the noise, but Glenn was forced to smash the screen in and dig around inside the set until he found the slug. He told management that he had knocked it over and broken it, but, when he offered to pay, they refused, saying insurance would cover it. The embarrassed Glenn had then hung a towel over the TV to hide the damage from his brother, who looked at it oddly when he arrived to pick him up the next day.

Wayne Brown, of Southside Automotive in Cairns, was helping Abbott restore his new ute. He says,

> *He disappeared and we didn't see him for a little while and then two or three weeks later he turned up [approximately 24 January 1994]. He came back with the ute and said, 'Oh, it's goin' really good, but I took it out the other night.' I think he was out racing one of the guys, Nipper, from the panel shop, out at Yarrabah. He said, 'The buggers beat me. I can't understand it, because they shouldn't be, this ute should go quicker than that.'*
>
> *And I said, 'It won't with the gear you've got on it. We need to change some of the things. You should have better cylinder heads and this and that.'*
>
> *So Bill [Abbott] said, 'All right, well, we'll do it. What do I need?'*

In less than a week, the motor was transformed. Getting beaten by a kid brought out Abbott's competitive streak. After Elanora, money was no object. He couldn't leave town until Nipper ate his dust. The result became local legend.

Wayne Brown says,

> *He went out on the Sunday [29 January 1994] and raced this guy and he had three races with him and he beat him three times, just*

annihilated this bloke. He went from being four car lengths behind him to being ten the other side. Ah, it went well. He was impressed. He had three races with the guy and then, on the fourth race, he broke the car. Because it was making that much power that it actually broke the drive shaft. And it snapped it and it got tangled up under the back axle and tore a hole in the fuel tank, tore the exhaust off and smashed the transmission in half. Tore the gearbox off the back of the engine. And he said, 'Ah, it goes good, but I whacked it.'

He called me a few days later and I'd had a look at it and had a laugh at all the damage that he'd done to it. And he said, 'What am I going to do?' and I said, 'Yeah, we can fix it.' So we left it at the shop and he was away something like three weeks. A couple of times, he'd ring up and say, 'How you doing?' You could hear all this noise in the background. A few times I asked him what he did. He said, 'I'm into earthmoving and I travel around and do contracts and stuff like that.' He'd call and it would be: 'I'm in Darwin', and then he'd be on the Gold Coast or in Melbourne. So I was getting a phone call every couple of days to see how it's going, because I'd had to order a new gearbox for it and he'd popped in and I think he came back halfway through his stay away for a few days, just to see how it was going.

We got to be good mates. Lizzy and I would have to go off into town to do the banking and things like that. He'd stay there and customers would come in and pick up their cars and he'd take their money off them and answer the phones and all that stuff. He was brilliant. And he said, 'You know, when I get around to retiring, I'll come and work with you. Yeah, I'd like to do that.' We got on really well and he used to learn so much, you know, and he'd watch and ask questions. He was very, very particular with everything that he did and, you know, I've employed tradesmen over the years and it's very rare that you find that quality in anybody that you employ in the automotive industry. I think that's why we got on pretty well, 'cause we're much the same in that respect. I think he gave me a hand to put the gearbox into the car, then he disappeared again. He said, 'I'm off, I'll leave it here for a few days', 'cause there was stuff we had to finish off and there was a few things we wanted to do. He said, 'If you get it going, I'll be away for another few weeks. Just leave it there and I'll fix you up when I get back.'

And then he came back [in the first week of March] and he was around for about a week … people geed up and he went out and had a bit of a play and raced a couple of the local fellas. He used to have to put a couple bags of sand in the back next to the tailgate so he could get traction. 'Cause it was a real animal after he sorted it out. [Its specifications read like an ad from a custom-car magazine: 400 cubic inch Chevy motor, nine-inch differential, turbo 400 gearbox, 16-inch tyres and modified suspension.] It earned a fair reputation. It was a 1972 HJ/HQ ute. Bill had probably spent 20 to 25 grand on it. It just looked like a dead-standard brand-new Holden ute, but inside it had a nice stereo and nice interior, it had the lowered suspension, it used to handle like a race car and it was a very, very nice car. But it was painted plain white with black tinted windows on it …

This guy dropped him off and Bill picked his ute up and he was all sunburned. I said, 'You don't work for the cops, do ya? For the Ds?'

He said, 'Nah, nah, that's a mate of mine, he just looks like that.'

I thought, Oh yeah, OK. Because he was so meticulous and very protective of what he did. You got the impression he could have been a copper, like an undercover dude. Because he always dressed really well. I thought, Oh, something's a bit funny, but I don't want to know about it.

And I guess he made a lot of other friends along the way, too. And there are policemen who have met him. And they've sat down and had beers with him. There's one policeman in particular who sat down and spent a lot of time with Bill, because the policeman used to hang out in my workshop all the time. They were good mates. They would sit down and they'd talk about all sorts of things, and society, and how it was going, and laws, and guns, and all sorts of stuff like that. They'd have great old raves, you know? And the copper used to go out and watch them all drag race. He used to say, 'Don't tell anybody, I'd be in the shit if I got caught out here.' The cops would turn up all the time, see.

Abbott:

A cop I met numerous times, he even took the ute for a test drive. If only he knew what was between the seats – a black leather backpack full of cash with a pistol on top. I had to smile to myself at that one.

Wayne Brown:

One day, I remember [approximately February 1995] the policeman came in and he said, 'Do you know who he is?'

I said, 'No, why?'

He said, 'Have a look at this.' And he showed me a reward poster for him. And it was Bill. It was a really early photo of him. It must have been taken when he was in Perth. And the policeman hung it up and said, 'Does that look familiar?'

I laughed. 'Oh yeah, OK.'

He said, 'Nah, he's too nice a bloke. Can't be.'

But, deep down inside, he knew bloody well it was him. So it was just left at that. I suppose at any time he could have rung up and said, 'Here he is, come and grab him.' But he didn't, purely, I think, out of respect for him. He liked him as a person. Bill wasn't nasty and there wasn't a mean streak in him. And they had spent enough time around him, and you can pick it with blokes, you know. He was a real gentleman and very smart and very intelligent. So he got a lot of respect from me and a lot of other people that he came into contact with.

On 3 March 1995, Abbott got a message on his pager to contact his brother Glenn.

On contacting him, he advises me of some items for sale, the asking price $4,000 (handguns). The afternoon of 7 March 1995 (a Tuesday, I think) I forwarded $4,000 by wire to Glenn to be picked up at the Cloverdale post office [near Belmont, Perth], unaware that the post office was no longer operating. It wasn't a problem, Glenn just needed to go to another post office to collect near by. But, unknown to him, he was under surveillance.

Glen Potter and his team did their best to watch Glenn Abbott's every move after picking up his trail in Perth the previous year; but he was a slippery customer, adept at employing anti-surveillance techniques, so they didn't get close enough to find out anything of real value. West Australian laws didn't allow police to place listening devices in the premises that interested them most – Glenn and Kelly's Halls Head rental home and Thelma Salmon's modest Carlisle unit. But Potter thought it through and came up with a viable alternative. It was tricky, but it could work.

Senior Constable Graham Randall and Detective Constable Doug Nelson partnered for the Division 79 morning-shift patrol on 7 March 1995. Glenn Potter summoned them to the armed robbery squad offices, where he explained his plan to hide listening and tracking devices in Glenn's Land Cruiser. The trick was to do it without raising suspicion. Glenn was driving without a licence after his court appearance the previous year. If they pulled him over and took him back to be charged and processed in the city, the surveillance team would have sufficient time to get the vehicle wired up.

The officers pulled Glenn Abbott to the side of the road and things immediately started to go wrong – a perfectly calm Glenn Abbott presented a Barry Reid Northern Territory driver's licence. Randall spotted ammunition inside the vehicle, then Nelson picked up a metal cylinder from the vehicle tray. 'It's a muffler for a go-kart,' Glenn insisted.

The next find was an instruction book for a Ruger Mini-14 – a semi-automatic assault rifle. And it was fitted with a silencer.

'They look pretty similar, don't they? You're under arrest.'

'Do I have to go with you?'

'Yes.'

'So I'm under arrest?'

'Yes.'

Glenn tightened his grip on the small CS gas spray in his hand, a highly concentrated form of pepper spray. Perth *Sunday Times* police reporter Nick Taylor described the ensuing battle in 'BANDIT'S BROTHER IN VIOLENT ESCAPE BID', on 13 March 1995:

The brother of notorious on-the-run bank bandit Brendan Abbott stuck a policeman's own gun in the officer's ribs in a bid to escape arrest this week, it is claimed. Glenn Norman Salmon is alleged to have ripped the gun from its holster after blinding the officer with pepper gas. Senior Constable Graham Randall had rugby tackled Salmon as he tried to run off and was struggling with him when the gun was taken. Luckily, Constable Randall managed to smash the gun out of Salmon's hand ...

Salmon, 26, who has changed his name by deed poll, was spotted driving erratically and stopped by the Division 79 officers in Orrong Rd, Carlisle, early on Tuesday ... The two policemen were treated at Royal Perth Hospital for eye injuries caused by the spray. Salmon appeared in court on Friday charged with possession of unlicensed firearms, using a noxious gas to debilitate to prevent arrest and producing false identification.

Glenn's attack on the officers made Potter cringe; he had warned them to be careful, but they couldn't be prepared for such a vicious reaction. Potter and other detectives raided the Halls Head home, where a defiant Kelly Fisher didn't blink when the tactical-response group stormed the house. She followed Potter around the house with her son Brenden on her shoulder, spitting venom: 'You'll never get my man. He's smarter than you guys. They're professionals. You guys are amateurs.'

Around the house, the police found ammunition for a .22 semi-automatic pistol; eleven .22 silencers; electronic lock picks; pepper sprays; listening devices; night-vision equipment; an 18-inch sniper's rifle silencer, a homemade rocket-launcher capable of firing incendiary devices up to 150 metres; and a 120,000-volt stun-gun (which Glenn admitted testing on himself – an incident later recreated for a movie). A West Australian driver's licence copy covered a wall, with a gap where a person stood for their headshot to be taken exactly to scale. On a computer, endless forms of false identification and documents could be produced in order to obtain 'genuine' false identities. The house itself was also loaded up with listening devices and cameras. And then Glenn's pager started beeping. Potter's face lit up.

Abbott:

Over a half-hour went by and I had no response from Glenn and contacted his pager, again advising him of the money order sent. Still there was no response from Glenn and I sensed something was amiss and I thought the worst scenario: he'd been busted, they've got his pager and the message of the money order. If so, they could soon track where it was sent from. If they assume I'd sent it, the heat would be on. I decided it was time to depart Cairns ASAP.

He was driving around Cairns with Wayne Brown at the time and immediately dropped the mechanic back at his workshop.

Wayne Brown:

[On 7 March 1995] he had been playing around with his car for a while. He jumped in the ute and was sitting in it, warming it up. Lizzy and I were standing there talking to him and he was off down the Gold Coast. And I said, 'Yeah, all right, Bill, see ya.'

And he said, 'I'll give you a call in a few days. I'll take my time going down there and I'll give you a holler when I get there.' And he drove out of the shed and off he went.

Lizzy and I just felt really weird. We just looked at each other and I think Lizzy said it first: 'I don't think we're going to see him again.'

I knew that he had a few cars around the countryside. I know that he had one on the Gold Coast and one in Sydney. He rang me from the Gold Coast several days later and he was telling me about this Toyota Land Cruiser he was playing around with [bought in Brisbane on 12 March 1995]. And then he said, 'I know what I'll do. I'm gonna come up in the ute and bring the engine up for this Land Cruiser and I want you to build it so I can take it back down and put it in and bring the Land Cruiser up.'

Abbott:

I considered driving the ute back down to the Gold Coast, but, thinking of the possibility of the police becoming aware of it, I decided to put it into a storage shed instead and take my chances in flying out. I paid a month in advance for a storage shed and left some cash in the car, around the ten-grand mark.

On 7 March 1995, a 'Peter Allen' rented a shed at the Airport Mini Warehouse, 6 Greenbank Rd, Strathfield, in Cairns, for $30 a week, paid up until 27 May. This Peter Allen might have called Australia home but he couldn't sing. He could, however, fly. He went to the airport – he had already booked a ticket after deciding to leave town – and flew to Brisbane. As he would say later, when a fugitive sees so many people standing around at an airport looking at passengers arriving, it 'has its moments'. Any of them could be police.

Not long after arriving in Brisbane, I phoned my pager service using the phone at the top of the stairs at the airport. I was checking if Glenn had sent me a message during my flight. I landed in Brisbane around 6pm (Queensland time) and left another message on Glenn's pager to contact me ASAP. I then proceeded to the airport monitors to see what flights were due to depart Brisbane in the next hour or so and noticed one to Melbourne. I then collected my baggage, got into the Datsun I'd parked in the car park prior to flying to Cairns and headed to the Gold Coast. Part of the way home, I stopped at a phone box and sent Glenn another message advising him I was in Brisbane and due to fly to Melbourne soon and to ring me urgently. After sending that message, I contacted a friend whose codename was Sam to make enquiries about Glenn, because I was of the belief he'd been pinched.

Sam contacted me on the pager at about 11pm, advising me he hadn't been able to contact Glenn as yet and would contact me as soon as he does. [Later,] I sent Glenn's pager another message, advising him I was in Melbourne and to call me at home. If I was correct in thinking that Glenn was pinched, the bogus messages would keep the boys in blue busy and rubbing their hands with glee, thinking they were on to a good thing. I sent these messages in an effort to distract attention from the Cairns area. As it turns out, Glenn had been pinched and the cops were kept busy for the next few hours sitting on the edges of their seats.

Abbott's every nerve jangled. But he thrived on the pressure and the need to think ten moves ahead. Now that the cops were chasing their tails, he could establish exactly what had happened to his brother, and whether or not his life as a fugitive was on the line.

Chapter Twelve

March 1995

The Metropolitan Security Unit brought a grim-faced Glenn Abbott from Casuarina Prison to the offices of the Perth armed robbery squad on 9 March 1995. Detectives Glenn Potter and Steve Drown sat in front of him in one of the squad's claustrophobic interview rooms and, after several hours of good cop–bad cop, finally extracted a single vital piece of information.

Brother Brenden takes up the story:

On 9 March 1995, I got the message that confirmed my belief [that Glenn had been arrested] and had me questioning how the fuck the cops got my post-box details. I told Georgia not to send any further messages to my pager and spent the next half-hour or so advising others the same thing. I couldn't help myself after hearing of Glenn's plight and sent one last message to the cops: 'Sorry, guys, but your little plan failed, maybe better luck next time, from BJ.'

On hearing of the post box now exposed, I had two concerns. One, Georgia had a few days earlier arranged to have something sent to that post box. After a phone call, she discovers it hadn't been sent as yet and gives another address to have it sent to.

The second concern was the one time she had sent me her mobile number. This phone bill was addressed to the unit we lived in. The big question on my mind was do they [Telecom] keep a record of that. In hindsight, it was stupid of me to think otherwise, but, at the time, I was led to believe that they didn't. On getting the pager, as with the others I had over the years, I was told they only keep records of messages for 48 hours. I actually rang the pager-service operator to see if the message of Georgia's phone number could be recorded in any way. The operator referred me to the supervisor, who told me the same thing I'd been told in the past: messages are only stored for 48 hours. I hung up feeling the message sent some months ago was no longer a concern.

How the WA CIB gained knowledge of my post-box number, I'm not quite sure about, but it was obvious it was through Glenn. I've heard he willingly gave it to them and I've heard it was found on a piece of paper, either from his car or in his house. However it came about, I don't for one moment believe that Glenn would've sold me out intentionally. He maybe thought he was using the opportunity for his own gain, thinking it would take them no further than the post box itself. He was unaware of the link that would lead to my arrest, just as I was unaware. He knew the rules with using the pagers and followed them better than I did: he didn't give his girlfriend the number. I feel his tactics in the attempt to get bail backfired. He did his best to get word out and a message to advise me in the following days that my post-office box 'stinks'. At the end of the day, he fucked up in more ways than one and he regrets it.

On about 14 March 1995, a Telecom pager bill arrived at my post box and was then taken by Detective Costello. The following day, a printout of all pager messages sent to that pager service was obtained. In the following days, a phone number within a message sent to the pager is found to be that of an Optus mobile service and the user's name was Kathy Pearson of Apartment 54, Florida Apartments. I made a false NT driver's licence for Georgia with the same alias. With that, she obtained the phone through Optus and the apartment was rented in the same name.

I rented two storage sheds at Rent-a-Shed on Kortum Drive, Burleigh West. I started renting shed 351 from 23 December 1994, under the alias of P. Allen. The second shed, 283, I started renting from 27 December 1994, under the alias of Gary Forster. Using different names was deliberate. In shed 351, I kept a blue

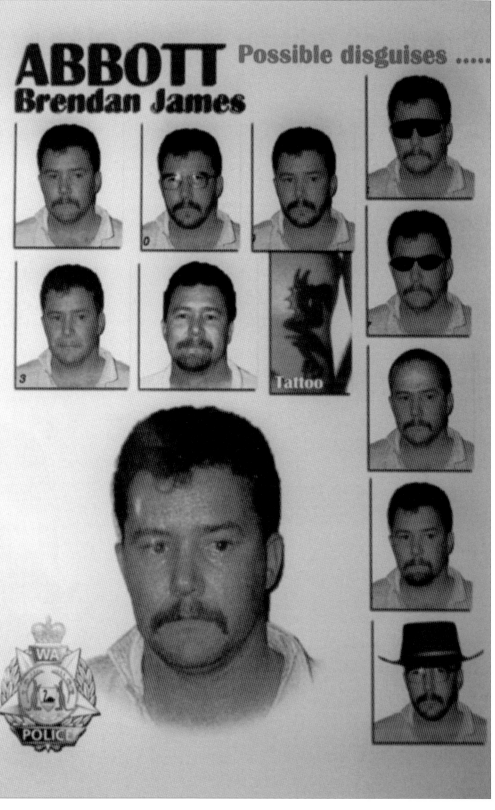

A poster showing variations in Abbott's appearance, created by the police.

Special Circular

Central Records Branch
Issue No: 7/97
Date: 05/12/97

VICTORIA POLICE   Published by the authority of the Chief Commissioner of Police

CONFIDENTIAL - FOR POLICE ONLY - NOT FOR PUBLICATION

ATTENTION ALL MEMBERS
ESCAPE FROM SIR DAVID LONGLAND CORRECTIONAL CENTRE
QUEENSLAND

ABBOTT

BERICHON

On 3 November, 1997, at 0050 hours five prisoners escaped from the Sir David Longland Correctional Centre, Queensland, with assistance from other persons. During the escape shots were fired at Prison Guards.

Since this time four of the escapees have been apprehended. One of the escapees, Andrew John JEFFREY (16/12/1976) was apprehended in Footscray, Victoria, on 30 November, 1997. A search of a motel room occupied by JEFFREY located a sawn off .22 rifle and loaded magazine.

At present, the whereabouts of the remaining escapee, Brendan James ABBOT (08/05/1962) are not known. ABBOTT is believed to be armed and is considered dangerous.

DESCRIPTION:

Brendan James ABBOTT (08/05/1962)
180 cm tall, fair complexion, hazel eyes, brown short hair and moustache, heavy build, 5 cm scar on left side cheek. Tattoos: Left Upper Arm - Large winged serpent/dragon.
Photograph of ABBOTT herewith reproduced.

Couldn't do at least

let me finish my washing R.J. Abbott

Above left: The high life – the Abbott brothers at Thredbo in the winter of 1993.

Above right: Michelle.

Below: Berichon being driven from the Luma Luma apartments in Darwin.

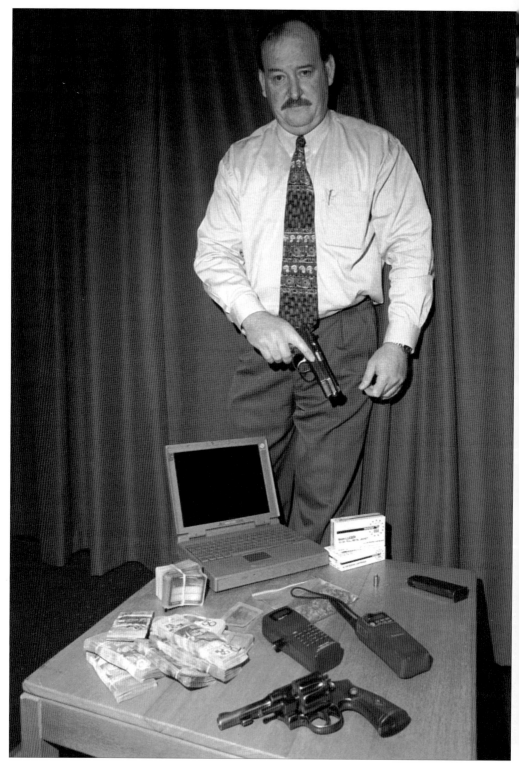

Very pleased! NT police commander Gary Manison shows off Abbott's stash: two pistols, ammunition, a laptop computer, 'walkie talkie' radios, forged drivers' licences and $22,000 cash.

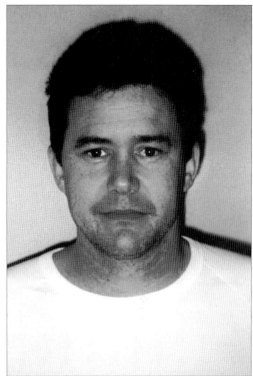

Above left: Nicked – Abbott pictured on arrival at Woodford Prison, May 1998.

© *Anthony Weate/Newspix*

Above right: Doing time in 1997.

Below: Escape from it all – Abbott's Toyota seized by police in Darwin.   © *Dennis Brooks*

Above: Photo opportunity – 'They deliberately didn't open the main gates at Woodford for a few minutes to allow the media plenty of photos of "Queensland's Monster."'

© *Anthony Weate/Newspix*

Below: Outgunned – Abbott enters Woodford in 1998.   © *Anthony Weate/Newspix*

Framed – criminal lawyer Chris Nyst with Abbott's Archibald Portrait Prize entry of him.

Above left: Tilly Needham, who paid Abbott a memorable visit in prison.

© *Patrina Malone/Newspix*

Above right: Father and son – Abbott and James in 2002.

Below: Setting the scene – director Tony Tilse, actor Tom Long and producer Matt Carroll on location filming *Postcard Bandit* in December 2002.

*Holden station wagon. This I used as a back-up vehicle in case
of an emergency. In shed 283, I kept much of my personal
property such as clothing, some household stuff, tools of the
trade such as firearms, lock equipment, driver's licence-making
equipment and back-up licences.*

*On Friday, 24 March 1995, I went to finalise shed 351. I
collected the receipt from shed 283 and drove to the office where
I noticed the staff member on was the one who I dealt with in
getting shed 283. I actually thought about returning the receipt to
the shed but decided against it. I drove off with all intentions to
return that afternoon when the other staff member was on. I then
went home to the apartment and planned to stay there until that
afternoon. When I got home, Georgia wasn't there and she arrived
home an hour or so later with a new digital phone. Due to some
drama with the paperwork relating to the phone, I spent the
afternoon running about to sort that out with her. By the time that
was done, it was too late to sort out the storage shed. I decided I'd
sort that out after I returned from Cairns. On Sunday, 26 March
1995, I was to fly to Cairns to pick up the ute. Just after 11am, I
left the unit to go to the four-wheel drive Land Cruiser I had in the
car park of Aquarius Apartments on Old Burleigh Road.*

Abbott had bought the 1984 short-wheel base Toyota Land Cruiser
from a Brisbane man on 12 March 1995, and planned to have Wayne
Brown put a new engine in it.

*The walk (to the car park) was only minutes from where I lived. I
was carrying a leather overnight bag, a plastic bag with a number
of rental videos I was returning before heading off to Brisbane
Airport, and around my waist was the usual bumbag, containing
my .32 automatic pistol and cash, around four to five grand.*

It was the fugitive's 1948th day on the run.

Operation Braille running sheet:

*'Item 1: At 1033hrs Abbott observed from Observation Post to
be folding clothes and ironing a shirt. He then gets dressed and
moves to lounge room and kisses female and disappears from
view. Abbott then seen exiting the car park. (Approval obtained
Platz via Costello to intercept Abbott ...) Abbott carrying a*

black bag and a white shopping bag. Abbott crosses the highway and walks to Fern Street.'

Abbott:

I made my way to Old Burleigh Road and was almost to the driveway into Aquarius Apartments. I noticed what I think was a Magna-type car drive past me going south do a U-turn and stop on the other side of the road. The driver got out of the car and crossed the road, walking towards me. He didn't look suspicious in any way until almost near me, when he pulls a stainless-steel revolver out from under his shirt and points it at me and tells me he's the police, and to get on the ground. At first I didn't believe him. I thought, This cunt is trying to rob me. I looked around and hesitated, but hit the deck when he repeated the demand. When I was on the ground, I spotted this other joker running to where we were and then there were cunts everywhere.

The bumbag was taken from around my waist and I was handcuffed. I was asked my name and I gave the alias that matched the driver's licence; all in vain, though. I was soon rolled over and a photograph was taken by a female plain clothes; I guess the shot was for someone's album – haven't seen that picture in any papers. It was reported I said the words: 'I had you cunts shitting.' I don't recall saying that, but anything is possible. It was a sinking feeling, especially after five and a half years. I thought I had it covered and getting caught like that I never expected.

In about a minute or so, I was put in a police vehicle and driven to Broadbeach police station. I was placed into an interview room that had tape-recording devices and video cameras in it. My hands were handcuffed behind my back and next to me sat two uniform coppers. After about 30 minutes to one hour, a Detective Costello introduces himself. His first words were: 'Good to finally see you in the flesh.'

I basically said I couldn't help him with his questions, but it appears he and Platz (who I met soon after Costello) made statements later claiming I said a number of things to suit their investigation, as many of these [officers] tend to when you don't give statements yourself.

The classic verbals are still allowed in courts to this day and age, despite the technology of tape recorders and video, as were in the room where I was being interviewed. But I guess they were broken? Not only that, Platz and Costello, with their years of experience, carry these recording devices in their pockets.

Detective Inspector Ray Platz later told a committal hearing in Southport in June 1995, his version of the interview with Abbott. The court transcript states,

> PLATZ: *'We are investigating a series of armed robbery offences here on the Gold Coast.'*
> ABBOTT: *'I don't do armed robberies.'*
> Platz's notes say that: *'Abbott smirks.'*
> PLATZ: *'Do you travel overseas?'*
> ABBOTT: *'I've been overseas.'*
> Platz claims Abbott said: *'I'll fight each one of [the charges] in separate trials in front of 12 members of a jury. I have plenty of money. Lawyers will be fighting to use it. I don't care if I spend everything I have stashed away. I'll fight you trial by trial, that's the system – trial by judge and jury.'*
> Abbott's lawyer, Chris Nyst: *'It's a nice little speech.'*
> PLATZ: *'It was.'*
> NYST: *'Where did it come from?'*
> PLATZ: *'Your client.'*

Detective Senior Constable Glen Prichard arrived in Old Burleigh Road to find Abbott already in custody. He, like many of the other detectives on this case for so long, wanted a close look at his quarry. He followed the van from Old Burleigh Road back to the Broadbeach police station. He then seized Abbott's expensive Tag Heuer watch and gold neck chain and logged them in as evidence. On Abbott's person, they found $4,535 in a leather wallet; $1,635 in the belt bag; $260 in wallet in his pocket; Chubb keys; radio scanner; and various false documents and ID.

Late that night, Prichard went to the Rent-a-Shed complex with the Chubb keys found on Abbott. Shed 351 was empty. But Detectives Durre, Morris, Jory and others gained entry to shed 283 at 11.30pm. They were itemising the contents until 3.30am; there were travel guides for Chile and Argentina; a blue balaclava, two-way radio, microphone and headset; listening devices; binoculars; a Pink Floyd CD; Best of the Eagles CD; and a West Australian police ID in the name of BJ Tucker. It was a treasure chest of evidence.

Abbott:

After some time, I was escorted to Southport watch-house and placed into a cell. I refused to give my fingerprints at first, wasn't feeling in the mood to co-operate at the time. Eventually, I gave my prints and Costello was present as well as Platz, I think. Costello asked me how it was that I made an income for all those years. I said I'd been selling my arse. That, I did say to him, and, during the trial, a number of the jury found it amusing.

Prichard claims I opened up to him. He felt it was the first opportunity for me to speak as Brenden Abbott and he was at a loss as to how I knew they'd discovered shed 283. Well, it was because he slipped up when he thought I was opening up to him. Truth is, I was interrogating him for info and it worked. Got to remember he was still a young detective [in 2004 he'd become a senior investigator with the Australian Crime Commission] and thought he'd get brownie points if I gave him anything to help their case. It's no secret many of the jobs I did were with others. After my arrest, they found nothing in regards to who these people are. They believe Glenn may have been involved in one or two after mid-'93, but that's as far as it goes with them.

It was [the investigator's] slip-up about the driver's licences I made for myself. I asked him as to what he thought about the photo licences that were in my wallet when arrested. He then said, 'It must've taken you ages sticking the letters on the board.' Bingo! I knew they'd found shed 283.

After my arrest I knew they'd find the receipt for shed 351 in the apartment, after hearing questions about Georgia. I jerried that I had four keys of the same make among the keys I had with me. I'd still left the lock on shed 351. Will they check the same locks found on other storage sheds? I guess they would've spent hours trying every shed. My goal while at Southport watch-house was to get word out to friends to clear out shed 283. I couldn't start drilling a tooth of one of the detectives, so I had to resort to other tactics, hence targeting [the investigator]. Of course he won't admit I got it out of him. Who can blame him?

After realising that shed 283 had been discovered, I thought,

Not good, it's full of evidence, but only to do me harm. I was very careful not to have anything that would lead police to any of my criminal associates. Even after using their photographs when making the false driver's licences, I destroyed them. I put all contact details in a code if they had to be recorded. Otherwise, I'd try to rely on memory. After I was arrested, there would have been panic going on with a number of people.

The loss of his battered address book upset Abbott more than anything else they took from him that day. A polaroid photograph taken at the police station shows him in a belligerent stance with a deep scowl. He continues,

Surprisingly, the first night's sleep after my arrest wasn't as restless as I thought it would've been. I guess the adrenalin from the time of the arrest and hours after and the mind working overtime drained me. I had so much on my mind, the main thing I needed an answer for was: 'How the fuck did they get on to me?' It eventually took months to work it out. Receiving the brief brought it to light and had me kicking myself for not knowing better. The next morning, the reality of my surroundings hit home. Georgia had started the habit in the last month or so of bringing me breakfast in bed. I believe she had started having feelings for me after all and was not just after my money. After I'd woken up in the cell, a copper brought me my breakfast and, as he handed it to me, I envisaged Georgia handing me my breakfast. That was a sinking feeling that I'll never forget; the old saying is you only miss it when it's gone. I only saw Georgia one more time after my arrest and that was in court the morning after. We didn't say anything to each other, but I thought I'd see her in the following days.

She did try to visit me at the prison some days later, but, due to the police taking all of her ID, she had nothing to show at the front gate. She had caught a cab to the prison from the Gold Coast, about $80 one way. I've no doubt that, after being denied the visit, she would've played up, big time, at the front gate. Something that I admired about this girl – but at times it did cause me some concern – was the fire within her. I've often thought about Georgia and the times we had together. I wonder what she's doing now. So, Georgia, if you read this, be a good girl.

Chapter Thirteen

1995–1996

The news of Brenden Abbott's arrest surprised no one more than Wayne Brown, premonition notwithstanding. He got a call from a mate who saw the story of Abbott's demise on the TV news, which showed a picture of 'Bill' the car fancier. Within a few days, Wayne received another call he would later recall this way:

*One of the cops rang me when they got Bill on the Gold Coast …
this particular policeman said that he held him in high regard and
he's been chasing him for years, but could never get his hands on
him. But he quite liked him 'cause he was smart and he's not like
the other shitbags they have to deal with. He said, 'He's not taken
money for drugs and all that sort of stuff. He just likes to enjoy
life and have a good time and that's all he was doing.'*

*One of the arresting officers flew up and interviewed me. They
wanted to know did he steal anything and did he do this and did
he do that? Probably expecting negative things from me about
him. But I didn't. He said, 'I can understand that. And, between
you and me, and off the record,' and he switches his tape
recorder off, 'I've got a lot of respect for him.'*

*'Item 56: Abbott received visit from mother Thelma Salmon,
brother David Abbott, and Glenn Abbott's girlfriend Kelly
Fisher at Wacol R&R. Surveillance followed same after visit and*

David Abbott was seen boarding an Ansett flight to Cairns arriving at 3.25pm [30 March 1995]. David Abbott supplied Alice Springs address. Det Craig Durran of Cairns CIB contacted with regard to brother David Abbott's visit.'

'Item 61: David Brian Abbott 25/12/58 located at Cairns airport by Det Sgt David Austin (Mount Isa CIB) and Det S/Const. Jason Gough (Cairns CIB) in possession of $9,000 on 31 March 1995. Abbott stated that he had spoken to his brother Brenden at Arthur Gorrie Correctional Centre and as a result he had gone to Cairns storage shed number five (rented in name P. Allen) where he had located the money behind the seat of a 1973 Holden Utility 412ZB (Qld rego in the name of William Harris of 6/283 Lake St, Cairns). He flew to Cairns and was to proceed to Alice Springs under the alias D. Lewis. He stated he assumed the money had come from bank robberies by his brother. David Abbott was charged with possession of money reasonably suspected of being tainted.'

The ute – and many other items seized from Abbott – would eventually be auctioned off, after he found himself in a position familiar to many law-abiding Australians: owing too much money to too many banks.

After fronting court on the Monday after my arrest, I was returned to the cell and then transferred to the Arthur Gorrie Correctional Centre at Wacol, west of Brisbane. This was my first stay in a Queensland prison and they dished out treatment I'd never experienced before in prison. I was placed into a punishment cell and remained in that type of cell for the next three months. To say it was a shock to the system would be an understatement. For the past five years, I had been living a lifestyle that few would experience in their lives and I can say the same again as to how it's been since. Some days after arriving at Arthur Gorrie, the jacks from Queensland, SA and WA paid me a visit. That was good of them.

'Item 59: [Costello attends] Wacol R&R in company of Det Sgt McAllister of CSU, Det Sgt Sid Thomas, of Adelaide Armed Robbery Squad, Det Sgt Glen Potter of Perth Armed Robbery Squad. Abbott happy to speak to police in general conversation although refused to be interviewed regarding allegations of

*armed robbery offences in Adelaide. Abbott told of how he used
Sabre police radio to call up police channels and do Main Roads
checks on vehicles he suspected of surveying him. Abbott told of
Holden S/Wagon in Cairns and conversation had to be stopped
as Abbott was happy to talk all day [about cars].'*

Glen Potter says, 'He sat in the corner and wouldn't talk to us. He let
a few things out, but made no admissions. It was like talking to a
copper. He was gleeful about the way he had beaten the cops. He had
a lot of the same attitudes and views on crime, but on the wrong side
of the fence.'

> *'Item 62: Attend Arthur Gorrie Correctional Centre and arrange
> for GMO to take sample of blood and hair from Brendan Abbott
> … Blood sample obtained, delivered to Leo Freeney at forensic
> section, John Tonge Centre. Sgt Simon Baker, Southport Scenes of
> Crime, who obtained the sample of blood from The Pines AHU,
> is delivering the blood to John Tonge Centre, to be compared.'*

On 5 April 1995, Georgia Smith moved out of Florida Apartments
and left a forwarding address of a Southport motel. She told the cops
to stick their indemnity up their arses. They had nothing on her apart
from three cannabis plants. Abbott had taught her well: 'Tell them
nothing.' A week later, Smith faced court over charges arising from
the cannabis plants and was fined $600. She moved back to Cairns
and vanished from Abbott's life, the failed attempt to visit and their
courtroom stares the only footnotes to their fiery affair.

Detective Platz went to Arthur Gorrie Prison to interview Abbott
again on 7 April 1995, also handing him a receipt for the $76,000
found in the unit and in his bumbag.

On 9 April 1995, after earlier complaints by Abbott were brushed
aside, Chris Nyst announced Supreme Court proceedings to force
Arthur Gorrie management to remove Abbott from solitary
confinement.

The luxury unit next to Unit 54 that police used as an observation
post remained in 'police custody' for a few days. As a result,
detectives Thomas and Potter found themselves in five-star
accommodation with a bird's eye view of the hiding place of the man
they had hunted for so long. But, like the Queensland officers, they

uncovered little – nothing on the still missing Trevor Bailey and certainly not enough for more bank-robbery charges. This was a moot point anyway, since Queensland made it very clear it was a case of finders keepers. With shed 283 and all its booty, they were clearly best placed to take first shot at him.

Those jacks from the other states suspected me of robberies in their states and [thought that] doing their jobs and getting a holiday to Queensland justified the costs in sending them here. I wasn't able to assist them with their enquiries. I chatted away with them on topics totally unrelated to the purpose for their visit. I was also trying to find things out myself, but, in the end, neither of us gained the info we were all searching for.

A week or so later, the Queensland jacks were out there to see me again. It was obvious they'd come to a dead end with their enquiries to find out who my associates were. After pinching me and finding the storage shed, they thought they were on a roll. They soon realised that was as far as it went.

During their next visit, they even had the nerve to ask what the remaining keys on my key ring were for. It was put to me in a roundabout way that I didn't have to do my time as it was then. The offer basically meant 'help us and we can help you'. I remained within the detention unit of two prisons for the next 18 months. Locked in my cell for 22 to 23 hours a day.

I'm not ashamed to admit it: there were some hard times in that period. I've done some lock-up in the past (I'm talking solitary) but not to this extent. It hardens you up, but it does fuck the head around and, for some, on a permanent basis. I had very little association with others, many who would have no problem in getting into the witness box to say I told them I did this or that. For the first few months at AGCC [Arthur Gorrie Correctional Unit], even some of the screws had it in for me. A number gave some grief, for reasons I'm unsure of. Maybe an element of jealousy and some to do with many rumours floating about relating to the treatment dished out to the screws from the Fremantle riot, of all things. One that the prison counsellor told me was we had ripped out the fingernails of a screw. I found it difficult to believe that such crap can fly about and people believe it.

But, as time went by, the fact from fiction was soon sorted out. Certain individuals started to ease up. One fictional yarn that people still believe relates to me sending postcards to the cops while on the run. Even to this day, people disbelieve me. It was in the papers, so it must be true. Not long after my arrest, some imbeciles couldn't help themselves and I was receiving postcards. Even some screws got in on the act. The Perth armed robbery squad thought there was no better opportunity to give me the payback over the last message I sent Glenn's pager. Paybacks are a bitch. I guess I had that one coming.

The postcard from Perth read,

'Brenden Baby! How are ya!!
Only one thing to say: GOTCHA!!
Perth CIB'

Abbott enjoyed the one-star luxury of the Southport watch-house during the week, before returning to Arthur Gorrie on the Fridays. Another postcard later came from Brisbane, dated 10 July 1995, the start of the Southport committal hearings:

Brennie baby – thanks for all your postcards. Your mates on the good side of the wire at Arthur Gorrie look forward to your return. A little surprise package awaits you – after all, you do claim to have the tightest and cutest set of buns around. See you around, babe! (PS Bring some baby oil, you will need it.)
Signed Night Shift AGC.

Abbott:

One particular Arthur Gorrie screw gave me a hard time at first. Come a chance to breach me, he jumped at the opportunity. Most who are housed within the detention unit are in for punishment for up to seven days. They are allowed nothing but their bedding.
Since I wasn't on punishment, I could purchase items from the prison canteen. I didn't smoke, but many on punishment did and, as I know personally the craving for tobacco is the worst part of doing lock-up, I bought a packet of weed and papers and, when possible, would slide a cigarette under my door and across under the door to the cell opposite me. At other times, the DU

[detention unit] cleaner was doing the floor and he'd pass it to the cell I couldn't get it to. One day, this screw (Merv was his nickname, due to the moustache similar to a well-known Aussie cricketer) spots the cigarette coming out. It only made it halfway across the corridor. Well, he couldn't help himself, he was out of the fishbowl (that's the name for their secure area) and down to get the cigarette and coming to my cell-door window and advising me I was breached. Yeah, a major bust for him.

Come time to front the breach, about a week later, and I beat it. I said I was putting the cigarette outside my door for the cleaner to take to another inmate who was also in the DU, but not on punishment. The senior ranking officer hearing the breach goes and confronts the cleaner to see if I've been getting him to do this. He returned and the matter was dismissed. A week or so later and I was transferred to the other DU – swapping DUs was a common practice with me (a security matter, they'd say) – and Merv was the screw working in there. Making eye contact and smiling at him, he knew I was lapping it up and he was really happy about it as I was going through the main door of the DU. I said to him, 'Hey, did you know I beat that breach?'

The screws escorting me saw the funny side of it more than Merv did. But it got even better. Whenever my cell door was opened, I had to stand and face the wall next to my sink and shit bowl with my hands on the back of my head and feet apart and wasn't allowed to move until told to do so. Some days after the breach incident, Merv and some other screw bring my breakfast and want to look around my cell while they're at it. Merv has the bunch of cell keys and they're only half in his pocket. He comes close to where I'm against the wall and they come out of his pocket and land inside my shit bowl. Made my fucking day, that did. I've quickly taken a glance when hearing them hit the stainless-steel bowl and spot the bunch of keys taking a swim. A quick look at Merv and a smile of satisfaction and the words: 'In ya go.' I couldn't resist. He had no choice but to stick his hand down and grab them.

Come lunchtime and the senior officer is in the DU to help dish up lunch. I could see him and Merv from my cell door and I bang up to get their attention.

'Yes, Abbott?' asks the senior.

Merv has also stopped what he's doing and he's looking at me.

'Yeah, can you just make sure Merv washes his hands before touching the meals? He's been sticking them down shit bowls earlier.' From then on, I never really had any problems with that screw.

The security for the first day – and every day – of Abbott's committal hearing was adequate for the Fremantle Prison riot trial. But back in 1988 there were a couple of dozen villains in the dock. In the Southport Magistrates Court on 10 July 1995, there was only one overweight bank robber.

Prosecutor Bernard Reilly spelled out the extraordinary security measures to Magistrate Marshall Davies, and the reasons for them, including the nature of the alleged offences; their commission while on the run; Abbott's five-plus years of avoiding police; the large quantity of weapons and ammunition seized; and the accused's reference to escape attempts in conversations with police. The magistrate looked over to Abbott's lawyer, Chris Nyst, and asked, 'Do you wish to be heard on that?'

Nyst stood up and immediately started earning headlines:

I certainly do, your worship. You will have seen that Mr Abbott appears before your worship shackled hand and feet, two sets of handcuffs on his hands and one set of handcuffs or leg irons on his feet. I would ask that those restraints be removed immediately and that he be allowed to sit here at the Bar table to give me some instructions.

An unwarranted dignity ... an affront to our system of justice ... trussed up like Hannibal Lecter ... I have never witnessed such a to-do with any prisoner in the 18 years I have been practising as a solicitor.

I make it clear that I know that these are instructions that come to my learned friend and I know that they don't initiate from him and, indeed, I would ask who they do initiate from. Nobody seems to want to own up to ownership of these instructions. [Abbott] has effectively been written up [in the media] as the biggest criminal – the biggest bushranger since Ned Kelly. And generally there's been a campaign to have the public accept and believe that he is public enemy No. 1 and that he has been thumbing his nose at police by sending them postcards. On my instructions, Mr Abbott has never, ever sent any postcard to any police officer and I challenge the police through my learned friend to put any postcard from Brenden Abbott to police before the court ...

And on he went. But the security measures remained. The six counts of armed robbery and one count of attempted armed robbery that Abbott faced, related to the robberies at: Elanora on 20 January 1995; the attempted robbery at Broadbeach on 16 December 1994; Pacific Fair, Broadbeach on 24 December 1993; Tugun on 21 May 1993; Palm Beach on 1 February 1993; Coolangatta on 24 December 1992; and Springwood on 16 April 1992. Reilly wanted all charges heard together at trial based on similar fact evidence, but Abbott and Nyst weren't having a bar of it. Abbott thought they wanted to nail him on anything and everything and he wanted to fight every charge, all the way.

On the way to the first day of my committal hearing, escorted by the state's SERT, my notes for Chris Nyst were read by one of them. I wasn't allowed to have them in the van. Platz and Costello's statements regarding the so-called comments I'd made [at the Southport police station on the day of the arrest] also claim that I had lifted my sleeve to show my tattoo. They forgot I was cuffed behind my back. My notes for Nyst pointed that out and the two plainclothes cops were also aware of me being cuffed.

Just prior to the committal starting, Nyst is handed amended statements by Platz and Costello claiming they'd made a mistake and one of them lifted my sleeve. This incident was raised while Nyst drilled Costello on cross-examination. And what about the evidence relating to the key found for the Cortina on the Elanora robbery? Platz finds it in a bag that was recovered from shed 283, weeks after everything was itemised that was in the storage shed. No record of any key. Platz rocks up to where it was all held at the Broadbeach police station, goes through a bag and finds himself a car key. Forensics go through their paperwork and find nothing listed relating to that. Guess they missed it?

Platz, I believe, was the first to the car used on the Elanora job. I can tell you, that key was on the driver's side floor. Platz also collects the blood sample [from Abbott] to take to the John Tonge Centre. Afterwards, he takes the sample of blood found at the [Elanora] crime scene to John Tonge Centre. This was in the fridge at Southport police station. It's no wonder their credibility was attacked during evidence at the committal and the trial over that robbery. They had to get a conviction; can you imagine how it would look if I beat it?

I remained in the DU for the whole time I spent at Arthur Gorrie. I went through the committal and the trial on the Elanora robbery while at AGCC. The committal went for almost four weeks, broken up over a number of months. There were numerous helicopter trips to and from the Gold Coast. The first day of the committal drew numerous reporters and I couldn't understand the big deal. During the week of the committal, I stayed in the cells at the watch-house and, after the weekend back at AGCC, returned on the Monday morning.

I spent many hours in the presence of the SERT and they gave me no grief whatsoever, other than the one who told Platz and Costello about the sleeve incident. They treated me civilly, as I did with them. To do otherwise, I can't see the point. The same goes with any copper or screw. I may have been a dickhead years ago, where I ran with most in hating those on the other side of the fence. What a waste of energy and a pathetic way to carry on. I chose the way of life I took and it's not as if I didn't know the outcome if I got caught. Better off just playing the game; to do otherwise means making matters harder on yourself, it's as simple as that in my view; although you do get those on the other side of the fence who get some satisfaction in making one's life difficult and feel their job includes being judge, jury and executioner. But, in all walks, there's always some cunt who wants to fuck your day.

Some of the SERT would even shout me a meal when seeing the watch-house meals that came to me. One made the comment once that I should be shouting them lunch. A couple actually asked me to send them a postcard the next time I took a runner. They were even predicting among themselves how long it'd be before I'd fuck off again – five years was the minimum prediction.

Jeff Beaman probably agreed with their idle musings. He came to the Gold Coast for the committal to be on hand to provide positive identification of Abbott. When the old foes came face to face at the Southport watch-house several days later – at Beaman's request –

Abbott told the detective, 'You owe me a holiday.' And Detectives Prichard, Potter and Beaman used the happy coincidence of the committal to finally raise their glasses and toast the defeat of a common enemy. The local XXXX brew took a savage toll on the West Australians. The story goes that Potter ended up taking custody of a potted fern, waking to find it in his hotel room.

Abbott recalls bitterly his experience with another inmate at Arthur Gorrie:

By what he claims I told him, I must've all of a sudden become religious and mistaken him for the parish priest. This turd has been all over the country in different prisons and then been a Crown witness against other inmates. Another turd made a statement that I'd offered him $75,000 to make a phone call for me. The turd who gave evidence against me at my committal was doing his best to befriend me. It was obvious from the start what this piece of shit was up to. He was even slipping notes under my door, giving me details on the security set-up of the prison, claiming he could arrange flying me out of the country etc. After giving me a note, he'd return later, enquiring about the whereabouts of the notes he was giving. I told him I tore them up and flushed them down the toilet, one time saying, if the screws found it, there'd be dramas.

When I was at the exercise yard, he'd be at the bars that divided us, talking away and I'd fill him with so much crap and then he'd be off to his cell writing down much of what I said. He must've really thought I came down in the last shower. When I got a visit from my solicitor, I told him about this turd and gave him the notes he'd been slipping under my door. Eventually, I was moved to another detention unit and, sure enough, come the committal hearing, the turd was called to give evidence. He denied ever giving me the notes under the door and, when that was raised, you could see him shitting himself, wondering if I had kept them. After some hours getting roasted in the witness box and denying the notes, he'd dug himself a hole so deep he would no doubt have been charged for perjury if the notes were produced there and then. My solicitor felt it best to leave it for a jury at the future trial.

Come the trial and the Crown felt it might be damaging for their case in calling the turd to give evidence. Maybe it would've been best to just pull the notes out at the committal. Seeing this turd come undone for perjury wasn't the aim, more so to putting a stop to him doing damage to the lives of others awaiting trial elsewhere. To protect the identity of this turd, the magistrate directed that his name be suppressed.

Due to the strict regime I was held under, I thought it was worth a try in getting it relaxed through the courts. Corrective Services weren't coming to the party in giving me the same privileges as other high-security inmates.

Abbott's successful appeal to the Supreme Court resulted in a Judicial Review in July 1995, after the committal was adjourned until the following month. On 20 July, the *Courier Mail*'s Matthew Horan reported, '[Arthur Gorrie's] general manager, Gregory Howden, told the court yesterday the jail was not secure enough to hold a prisoner as dangerous as he considered Abbott to be. The heavy-set Abbott sat in the witness box, manacled with two pairs of handcuffs around his wrists and shackles around his ankles, chained to a body belt. Justice Paul de Jersey ruled he had the right to be present, despite the fear that he could take hostages ...

'Justice de Jersey asked Mr Howden if his concerns were with the ability of the detention unit or the centre to hold high-security prisoners.

'"Both," replied Mr Howden. "It is not sufficient to hold a prisoner, in my belief, of the calibre of this inmate."'

Abbott was not flattered by this backhanded compliment:

To this day, I feel the strict regime is unjustified. There are people within the prison system who are responsible for some of the most horrendous crimes and who never set foot inside the MSUs [maximum-security units]. Jails are full of armed robbers, so my crimes aren't anything outstanding, except I may have gained more money than some. The difference with me is I robbed the banks and hit them hard, and, because I used my wits a little more than some in avoiding capture, I have to endure the harshest prison regime for much of my time while in custody. Fuckin' just not cricket.

The first Judicial Review caused some grief, especially when I requested to be in court to hear it. What surprised me was the extent of their paranoia with me, what a complete waste of money. After the hearing, I was driven out of the court complex to the Brisbane River to a helipad and taken to a helicopter. I asked where I was being taken, without a response. The last thing I expected was landing inside the prison in a helicopter. Being escorted from the oval to the DU, I had to pass a number of units where blokes were giving the screws escorting me a payout. Some smarty yells out that I was supposed to use the chopper to fly out, not in. As for the Judicial Review, well, the lawyers won out – but it didn't get me released from the DU.

Chris Nyst arranged for a psychiatrist to visit Abbott to gauge the effect of solitary confinement, provide insight into Abbott's situation and, hopefully, produce ammunition for the Judicial Review. Dr Peter Mulholland reported,

1. I interviewed and examined Brendon Abbott in the detention unit at Arthur Gorrie Correctional Centre on 12 June 1995.
2. He is in a cell which is about 3m by 3m or a little larger. The cell is adjacent to a room of the same diameter. The room is bare except for a plastic chair. He now has a television set, radio and reading material.
3. On a typical day, he is woken at 7 to 7.30am, given breakfast and his cell is searched. He then remains in his cell area until lunch at about midday. He is then let out into the exercise yard alone for about two hours. The exercise yard is about 15m by 7m. He is then locked in his cell in the middle or late afternoon. He then has his evening meal between 5.00 and 5.30pm. He then stays in his cell overnight. He can now control his own lights, thus he can decide whether he can have his light on or off overnight. He is in his cell, or the room next to his cell, for about 22 hours per day.
4. He reports he is not allowed any contact visits or gym activities and he is strictly not allowed to have any contact with other inmates.
5. In terms of his past medical history, he had a skin graft over his left eardrum when he was about 12 or 13. Hypertension was first diagnosed in 1994, but he has not been on treatment. He is complaining of a visual disorder in terms of 'spots before his eyes' and is dreaming a lot.
6. A few weeks ago, his cell was searched and the officers left a

major mess. This resulted in an acute emotional decompensation. [The inability to maintain defence mechanisms in response to stress, resulting in personality disturbance or psychological imbalance.] He went on a hunger strike and had suicidal thoughts for a few days. He saw the prison psychiatrist on a few occasions. That issue is now past.

7. He has no previous psychiatric history.

8. It does not sound as though drugs or alcohol have been a major problem with him. He has occasionally used cannabis, but does not like same because it tends to cause paranoia.

9. He has a four-year-old son who lives in Sydney with his mother. Brendon alleges that his former partner is being harassed by police. He told me that a contact visit with his son has been approved but, out of concern that the boy's mother would be apprehended or pressured by police, he has put this contact visit off indefinitely.

10. He described his emotional state as being 'not too good' and described generally feeling pessimistic and having vague suicidal thoughts, although there is nothing particularly active or definite. He described a general sense of depression, which is gradually becoming more pronounced. He described having a distinct sense that the authorities are trying to drive him 'crazy' or are trying to make him 'snap'.

11. He is only allowed to talk with the officers, some of whom treat him reasonably well and some whom he regards as 'having a go' at him, others as trying to goad him and he regards others as 'playing games' with him.

12. He described frequent wakings with disturbing dreams and reported that he is convinced that his cell is 'bugged'. He is also concerned, to the point of being convinced, that the cleaner (i.e. prisoners who are engaged in cleaning duties) is being sent to spy on him. He also described having a sense that everything he says is likely to be misinterpreted ...

15. Brendon Abbott has a high degree of suspiciousness of a paranoid nature. As previously discussed, it is difficult to ascertain to what extent his concerns are reality based, fantasised or a combination of both. A problem with this man is that, as he is living in a relatively isolated situation without contact with fellow prisoners, the only contact he has with fellow human beings is the somewhat stilted contact with prison officers. Thus, he has the problem of sitting around all day ruminating over his suspicions and it is likely that such suspiciousness will grow, be exaggerated, magnified and distorted, such that there is a likelihood of his developing a full-blooded paranoia ...

19. It is noted that the situation in which Brendon Abbott is being held – and I understand it is the authorities' intention that he continue to be held in this way – is restrictive and one cannot help but note that there is a somewhat threatening and punitive quality to it. He informs me that it has been clearly indicated to him that, if he confesses to various alleged offences, he would not be in his present environment. It would appear that it is likely that there is a measure of coercion or implied threat involved in his management, thus resulting in encouragement or inducement to him to confess to offences he may, or may not, have committed.

Essentially, Brenden Abbott's life was now a long, long way from Surfers Paradise. And the only thing he could change was the channel.

On 19 August 1995, Magistrate Marshall Davies suffered a heart attack and the committal hearing was adjourned again. When it recommenced in September, Hardy Brasche took the stand to give evidence about Louise's boyfriend, Pedro the merchant seaman.

'Can you see the person you know as Pedro in this courtroom?'
'Yeah ...'
'And where is he?'
'In the dock. He looks a bit different now. I don't know what youse have been doing to him. Are you starving him or something?'

The detention-unit cleaner turned 'parish priest' – whose constant visits irked Abbott so much – took the stand on 24 October 1995. Chris Nyst didn't think much of 'the turd' either, labelling him a tall-tale teller, a liar and a dog. He clearly enjoyed making the notorious informer squirm on the stand, bringing up plenty from the past. Between them, the lawyer and the turd manage to drop the famous Australian criminal names Christopher Dale Flannery, Tom Domican, Lennie McPherson and Louis Bayeh in the space of just a few minutes. And, among his many claims, he told the court that Abbott said he did 'many other robberies not contributed to him'. Nyst toyed with the turd like a cat with an insect – just enough to let the prosecution know that, if they put this man on the stand in a trial, he would make even Brenden Abbott look like a pretty good bloke.

On 16 January 1996, Abbott was finally committed for trial in the Brisbane District Court on six counts of armed robbery and one count of attempted armed robbery. 'I was trying to negotiate with the Crown in getting an interstate transfer by pleading to charges, but they didn't come to the party, so it was: "Get fucked, I'll fight them all."'

It could potentially have taken years of trials before all the charges were resolved. Court was boring, but no worse than sitting in a detention-unit shoebox. The most recent alleged robbery, of $354,000 from the Commonwealth Bank at The Pines shopping centre, Elanora, was first. After protracted argument over the security arrangements, Judge Brian Hoath ruled that the leg irons stayed and that two correctional officers and three plainclothes officers could remain in the court. Abbott personally handled jury selection, eventually exhausting his challenges.

There was much debate over the admissibility of items from Unit 54, Florida Apartments, particularly the $9 in old notes that were consistent with the $9 in damaged notes from the Elanora robbery. Throughout the trial, the jury bounced back and forth between the court and the jury room, with constant worries about them finding out about evidence connected to other robberies. Shed 283 was a treasure-trove, but also a legal minefield. Trying to excise only the items relevant to this specific case, and presenting them to the jury, was no easy task. Barrister Denis Lynch, acting for Abbott, leaped to his feet each time he felt the prosecution strayed into dangerous territory. And Abbott covered up his many chains to prevent them rattling, to try to convince the jury that this was just a routine bank-robbery case.

Abbott made sure his counsel focused on his allegations about the blood found in the Elanora fire-equipment cupboard and his allegation that the police tampered with the blood samples. Senior Constable Andrew Pilotto, from the Gold Coast scenes of crime unit, was one of the key players. He told the court there was enough light for him to have seen the stain when he examined the area on the day of the robbery. He was 'surprised I missed it'. Every negative from that day was carefully checked. But the blood stain the bank manager said he found was nowhere to be seen; that specific section of wall was not photographed that day.

In his summation to the jury, Judge Hoath addressed the crucial issue of the blood in the cupboard, saying,

What is alleged, there can be no doubt about it, ladies and gentlemen, is a serious criminal offence. It is alleged that either Inspector Platz or Constable Durre or both, committed a serious criminal offence – that offence being the fabricating of evidence. In this day and age, ladies and gentlemen, we cannot shy away from the fact that there are numerous reported instances of police fabricating evidence. It is a fact of life ... It is obvious that it would not have been impossible to open the sealed envelope, extract part of the blood sample, seal the envelope up again and then go down to Southport, get into the office of the scientific section, go to the refrigerator, remove the sealed bag, cut the sealed bag, swap over the swabs, seal the bag up again. That is not impossible. It is a question, ladies and gentlemen, however, whether it was done in this particular case.

On 6 June 1996, the jury found Brenden Abbott guilty of the robbery after 10 hours of deliberations, punctuated by a night in a hotel. Reporting the result of the trial the next day, the *Courier Mail* noted how crucial the DNA evidence was in convicting Abbott.

The following day, he was sentenced to nine years in jail, with Judge Hoath declaring the 439 days since his arrest as time served. Now Abbott was a sentenced prisoner and, in September 1996, he was transferred to Sir David Longland Correctional Centre in Brisbane.

Chapter Fourteen

1996–1997

L ike the powerful cars that his brother built, Glenn Abbott could
sometimes run dangerously out of control. While Brenden was
mostly calm and controlled in a pressure situation, Glenn was often
the opposite, and his last stint in jail – for his extraordinary 1995
roadside attack on the two Perth police officers – taught him little.

On 6 September 1996, the newly paroled Abbott drove at high
speed on Guildford Road near Tonkin Highway in Perth, on a stretch
known to locals as the mad mile. Senior Constable Lee Watson, en
route for a leather-jacket fitting, didn't know the driver's background
and had no idea what happened the last time this man pulled over at
the direction of police. He wanted to keep moving, but couldn't
overlook 160km/ph in a 60 zone. Glenn got out and faced the officer,
who looked him up and down. Two men working on a road sweeper
just metres away watched the situation unfold.

Watson ordered Glenn to empty his pockets. Glenn had 14 rounds
of ammunition in his pocket, as well as a magazine with 15 cartridges
and a badly maintained Glock semi-automatic pistol that once saw
active duty in a Cairns motel. Then things started happening very
quickly. He fired a shot that lodged in the policeman's left leg. Glenn's
gun jammed. Lee Watson emptied his gun chamber in Abbott's
direction. Three of the bullets found their mark. Road worker Ian
Robinson remembers, 'The cop was lying on the ground and we seen
the bloke taking off like a startled rabbit. I took off after the joker,

who ran across Guildford Road ... but he'd disappeared, so I went back to the cop.' The workers went to the officer's aid, but then noticed Glenn Abbott's return. Robinson continues, 'He fell down and that's when we noticed his shirt was covered in blood. When I opened it up, he was full of holes.'

Lee Watson radioed for back-up. Police swarmed over the area.

Glenn sobbed quietly. 'I didn't mean it – tell him. Is he going to be all right? I'm sorry. I'm a criminal, mate, not a killer.'

He reached for his mobile phone and rang Kelly, 'I love you, doll, love the kids; I don't think I'm going to make it this time.' They sounded like last words, well practised. He survived the ride to hospital, insisting all the way that the cop fired the first shot. On arrival, he went in for emergency surgery. He needed a miracle to survive.

On 11 October 1996, the Court of Criminal Appeal dismissed Brenden Abbott's lengthy list of grounds for appeal on the Elanora conviction. But six more charges needed to be dealt with, and Detective Senior Constable Glen Prichard was the man with the lion's share of the work, preparing the brief for trial. During his enquiries, he interviewed Abbott's sister Janet, who made her first and only visit to see her brother in prison in November 1995. Their relationship, always distant, never improved. Janet didn't know it, but she literally ran into her brother while he was the nation's most wanted man. The author interviewed Diane Abbott in 2002 for an article in the *West Australian*'s 'Big Weekend' section. She said,

> *My sister [Janet] and I went to a shopping centre in Cairns one day. I was looking at her because she was talking to me as we walked in, and she ran into somebody. I looked up, and it was Brenden. He was looking at photos and wasn't watching where he was going. He looked her in the eye and she looked at him and my mouth just dropped. I thought, What am I going to do if she goes to a phone, because she would have rung the police straight away [if she'd recognised Brenden]. He stepped to the side and kept walking and so did she. My heart was pounding. I didn't tell her for three or four years. Afterwards, he saw me and said, 'You bloody nearly gave me away.'*

Brenden Abbott appeared in court on 2 February 1997, for a routine appearance over the yet-to-be-heard bank-robbery charges. But, before he made it into court, an incident in the court cells occurred that a psychiatrist might describe as 'acute decompensation'. Abbott's court clothes were not there as requested and he protested loudly. His lawyer for that day, Dennis Lynch, was told of a problem with his client. He went to the cells to investigate and found a defiant and naked Abbott, who was eventually forced to appear barefoot, in clothes scrounged from the cells – and not exactly Versace cast-offs.

On 6 March 1997, Abbott's defence team made an application for the remaining robbery charges to be heard separately. The application was refused and things didn't look good. The prosecution wouldn't have the difficulties encountered with Elanora – there was no other DNA evidence, but the entire contents of shed 283 were admissible, probably along with details of his fugitive lifestyle.

The prosecution wanted the six counts to be heard at a single trial, on the basis of similar fact evidence. On 29 April 1997, Judge Eric Pratt ruled that five charges could be tried together, and that one be tried separately. Abbott's legal team sought an adjournment and, 53 minutes later, Brenden Abbott took his medicine – the prosecution offer of guilty pleas on counts one and five (Springwood and Pacific Fair, totalling more than $1 million) in exchange for dropping the remaining charges.

On 2 May 1997, the judge handed down sentences on the Springwood and Pacific Fair robberies of ten and nine years, respectively, noting that 'unless my arithmetic is completely shredded, I think it's 60 we're looking at by the time he walks about a free man again'. But he 'must take into account the real probability that this particular prisoner's ultimate release will be cushioned by access to large sums of stolen money'. For all of this, Abbott clearly impressed a man who saw all manner of villains in his many years on the bench:

Despite the trauma that the accused himself has undergone in the period in which he has been in custody here in Queensland, it has to be acknowledged that he is a studied, disciplined, intelligent bank robber. The ingenuity which he has displayed is remarkable and, as Mr Reilly from the Crown acknowledges, it is still not understood precisely how he pulled it off.

Glen Prichard went to see Abbott on 22 May 1997 about one outstanding detail. The banks wanted their money back, and they wanted a lot more than Abbott had left behind in Unit 54. A pecuniary order for $1.24 million was later issued and that essentially meant that the banks took ownership of Brenden Abbott. He lost his cars, contents of the storage sheds and Unit 54, including all the cash, and anything else of value that could be sold off. Prichard's 45-minute interview was relaxed and Abbott was reasonably expansive, but giving nothing away. He kept needling the detective about his desire to go back into business.

Prichard: 'Sounds like you're just trying to improve for next time.'
Abbott: 'You can never give up trying, can you?'

To Abbott's great surprise, he was finally released from the Sir David Longland (SDL) detention unit in August 1997, the same month he dispatched a birthday card to Jackie Lord ('Love always, Brenden xxx'). She was living in Perth and writing regularly to Brenden. SDL management sent Abbott to unit 4B in B block, and suddenly Abbott had company for the first time in over two years. His new management plan allowed for 11 hours a day out of his cell; access to contact visits, sports, the gym and the health centre; a job as a clerk in the library; and the standard ten callers on his approved telephone list. The plan's stated intention was to: 'Reduce the risk of escape of Brendan James Abbott from Sir David Longland Correctional Centre and to maximise Brendan James Abbott's personal programme objectives within a secure environment.' But these were conflicting aims; Abbott's objective was escape.

The court cases were draining and I think everyone was glad when it came to an end. I was convicted on one and pleaded guilty on two others, with the agreement the remaining charges be dropped. Eventually, a conviction was recorded on three out of the seven. The sentences may've seemed light on their own, but, with the total time I'll spend in jail, it will exceed most sentences imposed for murder. By the time the final guilty pleas were entered, I had been placed in the mainstream unit, but still they kept a close eye on me. I was confined to the unit, but, after a few months, they relaxed a bit and I was getting access to the oval and then gained employment within the library of B block ...

When I was finally let out of the DU after 18 months, I was placed into a unit that housed mainly new arrivals to SDL. After a number of weeks, they were moved to other units within SDL. I think [future associate] Brendan Berichon was in there as well at the time. There was this one bloke in there who I was sure was a spy and kept an eye on my moves. I expect this whenever I go in the prison system. This particular person was nicknamed 'Thirteen' in honour of Agent Thirteen in Get Smart. Maxwell Smart would find Thirteen in hundreds of places and give him the mail on what's new.

After a week or so, the unit was emptied out – except for myself – and, that same evening, they put about another nine inmates into it. It was turned into a high-security unit and those within it were of a high risk of escape and considered a management problem. After a day or two, I wasn't comfortable with them at all. There was only one or two that I really had anything to do with. The others got around with the 'hate the world' attitude and, if you weren't with them in their way of thinking, you were a stiff, as they'd say.

They soon realised I didn't want to be any part of their knuckle-dragging world and sensed with a few that I could be in with some barney down the track. I kept much to myself in my cell or with one of the other two I got on with. After a few weeks, one of the blokes who, like myself, kept pretty much to himself was found hanging from his cell bars. The sight of that I found distressing and couldn't comprehend why he would kill himself. This bloke would close his door and put a towel up over his cell-door window if he didn't wish to be disturbed. This practice we all did if you wanted to do the same.

I was in the day room playing a game on the Sony PlayStation when the two screws came in to do a head count, as they did many times during the day and night. One of the screws then runs past where I was sitting and heads for the fishbowl where another screw was sitting and made a throat-cutting gesture. He was after a knife to cut the noose from the bloke's neck. I've gone down to see what the commotion was at his cell. One of the other inmates had hold of his legs, pushing this bloke up to take the weight off the noose from the bloke's neck, while a screw was trying to get the noose off. It was a sickening feeling seeing this and the reality of it took some getting over. Some weeks later, the unit ceased operating as a high-security unit and we were broken up and placed into different units and some into the DU.

Days after the event, rumours were getting around that it wasn't a suicide. But, without the evidence to prove otherwise, it *was listed as a suspicious death in custody, as with the cases of two others who were found hanging in their cells months later. I was confronted months later by a prison manager in relation to the earlier hanging, in an attempt to see if I'd help with the investigation and was told that, by assisting, it would see my transfer back to WA. I wasn't able to help with it and just the fact it was put to me caused me some concern for my safety. I saw nothing and know nothing, other than the jailhouse rumours. A lot of the shit that goes on in jail, I don't agree with and I don't think too highly of those who do certain things. Corrective Services have a lot to answer for over some of the incidents that have gone down, but this will never be brought to light.*

After being moved to four different units after my release from the DU, I ended up within 4B of B block. I was the unit cook, before getting the position in the library – a job that got me out of the unit much of the day Monday to Friday and away from the bullshit that goes on. As well as that, I was using a computer most of the day and doing the computer courses available. On discovering the many uses for them, I only wished I'd done so years earlier. The hours flew by while messing around with them. Some weeks earlier, there was talk of a maximum-security unit opening up within the new prison built at Woodford and my name was on the list to be placed there. Even the Sunday paper ran a front-page story on it and my name as a candidate for the joint. The same day the story ran, I was confronted by management (as were the others who were mentioned to be placed into it) to assure me it's not so and to pay no attention to it.

On 25 May 1997, Darren Giles's front-page story in the Brisbane *Sunday Mail*, headed 'SCREWS TURN ON TOP CRIMS', reported, 'Prisoners considered the highest escape risks in Queensland's jail system will soon be moved to a special unit at the Woodford Correctional Centre. At least ten inmates – including the infamous "Postcard Bandit" Brendan James Abbott and convicted killer Adam Vickers – have been identified as candidates likely to go over the wall. They will be the first residents of the escape-proof lock-up.'

Prison officers told their union there were teething problems with the hi-tech security system at Woodford. Doors to secure areas kept flinging open when they shouldn't. Wisely, Woodford management refused the request for Abbott's transfer.

But I soon learned it was to be otherwise. One way or another, I was destined for the place. After 18 months already inside the detention units, I wasn't looking forward to returning to one. An escape plan was already in the making when I got the word I was to be transferred to Woodford, but that plan was still months away from being pulled off. I thought there wouldn't be enough time to get it done, but due to a conversation among a number of blokes while we sat out in the exercise yard of 4B, a new plan was soon to emerge.

Glenn Abbott, aka Glenn Salmon, got his miracle. After being resuscitated several times on the way to Royal Perth Hospital on 6 September 1996, he seriously tested the skills of the surgeons. Two of his wounds went vertically through his body. One bullet entered near his right nipple and passed through his liver and bowel before lodging on the left side of his pelvis. The second travelled from his abdomen down into the right side of his pelvis. And a third bullet passed through his left leg.

Abbott:

The ballistics showed that Glenn was on the ground when he got hit a couple of times. I don't know the story properly, but I know Glenn. He's my brother and I know there's no way in the world he'd just pull a gun out and just shoot a copper. There's no way he'd do that. It's just not him.

At Glenn Abbott's trial for attempted murder in the Perth Supreme Court in August 1998, the jury settled on the alternative charge of causing grievous bodily harm to prevent arrest. Senior Constable Lee Watson was fortunate that Abbott's poorly maintained Glock pistol jammed after a single shot, which tore through his groin and exited via a buttock, after passing one centimetre from the main artery in his left leg.

News Ltd's Mark Russell reported, '[Justice Heenan said] Salmon had a history of assaulting police and prison officers, but was still young and there was some hope he might some day become a useful member of society, if only for the sake of his de facto wife and two children. "It is quite clear you are now a dangerous criminal," Justice Heenan said. Salmon showed little emotion when he was jailed for eight years with no parole.'

His troubles didn't end there. In July 1997, Glenn, now aged 29, stabbed fellow Casuarina inmate Bradley Novac in the neck and face with a homemade knife, landing him four months of solitary. The following month, he pleaded guilty to receiving two rifles – a US Army Springfield and a Ruger – stolen on Saturday, 29 October 1994, during the burglary on Gold Coast Shooters Supplies. During his crucial interview with Detectives Potter and Drown in Perth in March 1995, Glenn revealed details of his lease on the Honeywell storage unit in Maylands, and the detectives seized the weapons from it. Another charge, of being party to the theft, was dropped. His lawyer, Richard Bayley, said Brenden Abbott sent the rifles to his brother for storage. Glenn was sentenced to an additional six months' jail, and then, in December 1998, received a further three years' jail for unlawful wounding, over the prison stabbing.

If he ever hoped to be a free man again, he needed to control his temper and start thinking about giving away crime. But Glenn faced many more months of solitude in Casuarina Prison's special handling unit as a direct result of more violent and outrageous behaviour – his brother's, on the other side of the country.

Chapter Fifteen

August 1997 –
6 November 1997

I n the lead-up to a surreal night that made international headlines, Brenden Abbott's long-lost love Jackie Lord was thrilled to be corresponding with him again. She says:

Brenden and I started writing again in 1997. We used to write a lot and he would call every weekend. He was supposed to go to Woodford. That was why he wanted to break out. He said, 'I'm getting a transfer to Woodford and I don't want to go there. So, if you don't hear from me for a while, don't panic.' He kind of even hinted to me that he was going [to escape]. He said something about someone having organised him passports.

I said, 'What are you talking like this for? You're locked up.'
He said, 'Yeah, but that can change.'
And I thought, What is he up to now?

Abbott:

There wouldn't be a day that goes by in maximum-security prisons where escape is not talked about. On this day, in the 4B exercise yard, someone raised the possibility of an escape being pulled off by getting outside assistance. It was an idea that had been raised by many – and, on one occasion, even tried, with those involved coming undone at the fence. I spoke up with an idea, saying something like: 'It'd be easy to do, but the biggest hurdle is finding someone who'd be prepared to help from the outside and be prepared to shoot at the perimeter vehicle.'

A bloke speaks up, saying he'd do something like that. You hear people talk shit all the time in prison and, on hearing that, I didn't think any different. Someone else told him what I was just thinking and the bloke who claimed he'd do it again speaks up: 'What's so hard about that? As long as you've got the right gun, you could take the vehicle out.'

I was already aware that he was due out in a few weeks and, after what he said, I thought I'd have a quiet word with him later. I pulled him aside and asked him if he was serious. Without hesitation, he says, 'Fucking oath, I'd do it.'

I said to him, 'You have a think about that for a few days and, if you have no doubts about it, there's a few of us that would appreciate some outside help.'

He told me he didn't need time, but I told him to think it over anyway, and also not to mention it to anyone. After a number of days, I approached him again and he was as keen as mustard. From then on, a new plan was in the making. I then told [convicted killer] Jason [Nixon] about the help from the outside. For the weeks prior to [the volunteer] being released, he was briefed over and over again in the role he was to play.

I still had my doubts about him pulling it off, even to the night it went down. He soon managed to get hold of an M14 7.62mm rifle and six spare magazines, an SKS 7.62mm rifle and four spare magazines and a .22 automatic pistol and a silencer and ammunition. He was to get two pairs of large side cutters or small boltcutters to throw over the fence (two pairs each, just in case the first go in throwing them over failed); and at least two cars, the second car to be parked some distance from the jail. The plan was he would come to the fence at a specified time and flash his torch. If for some reason we couldn't go from our end, a piece of burning paper would be dropped out of mine or Jason's cell window. On seeing this, he was to clear out. If it was all go, he'd get a flash with a lighter ... But, as I've found on many occasions, things rarely go to plan.

On 17 September 1997, Brendan Luke Berichon, 19, walked out of Sir David Longland Correctional Centre after serving his sentence for armed robbery. Herald Sun crime reporter Paul Anderson later profiled Berichon in his book *Dirty Dozen – 12 True Crime Stories That Shocked Australia*. Abbott and the teenager who became known as his apprentice had much in common. 'Brendan Sjuka was born in Newcastle on 30 December 1977. After his natural parents separated, he and his two-year-old sister Linda were moved by their mother Julie to her hometown of Townsville. Julie remarried in 1982 and young Brendan was given his stepfather's name, Berichon ... But things started turning bad for the youngster when the family moved to the Brisbane suburb of Sunnybank in 1988.

'It was at Sunnybank State School where troublesome peers led the impressionable teenager astray, introducing him to marijuana, among other things. By Year 9, it became obvious that he was heading for trouble and he was expelled for violence. Welfare authorities deemed that the 15-year-old needed guidance. On the advice of Children's Services, Berichon was sent to the Boystown home for troubled youths near Beaudesert, about 50km southwest of Brisbane.

'He lived there for about two years, where interest in BMX bikes and boxing bloomed. His fellow inmates voted him mayor of Boystown and he earned the nicknames BB and Bags. "He really enjoyed it there after the initial upheaval," his mum told the *Courier Mail*.

'It was upon his release that he began a series of court appearances that would inevitably lead him to meet Brenden Abbott. By the end of January 1994, Berichon had been charged with crimes including burglary, car offences, breaking into homes and carrying weapons. While on probation, he started sheet metal work and was developing a positive attitude. But it all soon fell apart. When he witnessed the stabbing death of a friend at a party, he lost his way again. ...

'While still on probation, Brendan continued to commit crimes, graduating to a service station hold-up. In early 1996, he was convicted for armed robbery and sentenced to two and a half years' jail with a six-month minimum. He was released on home detention. But trouble brewed between him and his sister and, after breaching the home detention order, he was sent to Sir David Longland jail to finish his sentence. It was there that he would meet his criminal idol.'

It wasn't until 1 or 2 November that Brenden Abbott found out fellow 4B resident convicted killer Oliver Alincic regularly phoned Berichon to place bets on the horses. That meant Abbott could speak directly to Berichon, even though he wasn't on his approved list of callers. Alincic was brought in on the escape plan and, on 2

November, he rang Berichon again. Part of the conversation went like this:

> ALINCIC: 'I'll pass you on to an old mate.'
> ABBOTT: 'Hello, hello, hello.'
> BERICHON: 'How you going, mate?'
> ABBOTT: 'Hey listen, whenever you see that fuckin' Lyn, mate, tell her to get her arse in. Fuckin' ... visit wouldn't fuckin' ... go astray, you know?'
> BERICHON: 'Hey?'
> ABBOTT: 'When you see Lyn, tell her to get her arse in one day and visit.'
> BERICHON: 'Yeah, uh, Michelle's coming up on Thursday. [Michelle was code for Monday, 3 November 1997.]'
> ABBOTT: 'Oh, is she?'
> BERICHON: 'Michelle.'
> ABBOTT: 'All right. Oh yeah. Yeah, fuckin' oath, I'll see her. Make sure she's wearing something appropriate so she can give me a flash. [Don't forget to signal].'
> BERICHON: 'Yeah, yeah.'

But things did not go to plan. A fuming Abbott called Berichon the next day:

> BERICHON: 'Hello?'
> ABBOTT: 'How ya going?'
> BERICHON: 'How ya going, mate?'
> ABBOTT: 'All right.'
> BERICHON: 'I'm glad you rang ... fucking, uh, you know how I said fucking Michelle was coming up?'
> ABBOTT: 'Yeah.'
> BERICHON: 'She fucking had car trouble, man. She can't come up.'
> ABBOTT: 'Ah, right.'
> BERICHON: 'But, ah, fucking ... fucking Toni said she was coming up. [Toni was code for that night.]'
> ABBOTT: 'Ah, did she?'
> BERICHON: 'I was fucking spewing.'
> ABBOTT: 'Oh. Were ya? ... You reckon ... you reckon I would've been fuckin' spewing if she didn't rock up?'

BERICHON: *'Shit, mate.'*
ABBOTT: *'Ah right, that'll be fine. Not a problem.'*
BERICHON: *'It's a bit of fucking shit, mate, you know what I mean?'*
ABBOTT: *'All right, ah, that's no drama.'*

Abbott said later that relying on an inexperienced 19-year-old to get it right was one thing, but keeping the escape plan from the authorities was worse.

Initially, there were to be only three of us to escape – Jason, myself and one other. Once out, the three of us would pull off a few jobs and then go our separate ways. As for the outside help, he got paid off a nice figure and no one was to be the wiser to who he was. Diamond wire was required to cut the bars at either AGCC or SDL. Hacksaws were useless. The bars have a high carbon content in them that makes them hard as fuck to cut with hacksaws, as well as noisy. With diamond wire, the harder the steel, the better it seems to cut it. A brace was needed for the diamond wire. A handle off a drawer did that job. It was removed from a drawer from the kitchen. The screws that held the handle to the drawer were threaded on the whole length. Cutting both to a short length allowed them to be screwed into the handle to their heads.

(I already had the diamond wire required to cut the bars. I was allowed to have a stereo sent to AGCC, but I didn't get to have it in my cell. I was transferred to SDL a week or so after it arrived at AGCC. No security check was done on it at either centre. Even so, the chances of finding it were slim.)

Cutting the bar was a long and slow process that took me over three nights, but in actual time to cut the bar almost right through, about two and a half hours. Before cutting the bar, I had to dismantle the hinge connected to the bar and the louvered window. I'd acquired the allen key needed to do this some months earlier for the initial escape plan, which also included us cutting our way out of our cells. Once the hinge was undone from the window, it would be slid along the bar and the cut made where the hinge normally sat. When back in place, it would hide the cut in the bar.

I made my cut through the bar and left about 2mm of the bar to cut. On the night of the escape, just a good hit would snap the section still intact.

It was during one night while cutting the bar that the bloke in the cell next to me heard me working. This bloke was [convicted killer] Andrew [Jeffrey], one of the eventual escapees. As most confide with friends, he did so about me cutting my bar. Unknown to Andrew, his friend was also my friend. He wasn't sure if he should've told me about Andrew's discovery, but knew the consequences of jail talk eventually getting to the screws and gave me the mail. After a talk to Jason, it was decided to bring Andrew in on the escape. He was doing life and, when the offer was put to him, he didn't hesitate for a moment. He was in. He was drilled not to mention it to a soul.

After I'd done my bar, the cutting equipment went into Jason's cell. The diamond wire ended up breaking in half while he was doing his, obviously by putting too much pressure on it. Of course, he blamed the tool. We now had another problem – there was just the one diamond wire. How the fuck were we to get some more? One idea was to get it thrown on to the oval, another was to push it into a flip flop on a contact visit. The diamond wire is very fine, about 2mm thick. Pushing it into a flip flop would've been easy to do, but first it had to be bought and it wasn't the easiest thing to find in Brisbane. While that search continued, just by chance, I overheard a bloke talking about the non-contact visits area. He was only allowed non-contact visits due to a positive drug test. He mentioned how someone had used a lighter in an attempt to burn a hole through the perspex screen [separating prisoners from visitors]. He reckoned the hole was almost through. We could get the diamond wire in and by a way the screws would least expect. The non-contacts area had no camera and wasn't under constant watch.

We had another tool handy that was to be used for the initial escape plan – an 8mm drill bit with an iron bar welded on the top so you could drill by hand. They tried it out on one of the perspex louvers in the unit and it worked a dream. Next problem was how to get it to the visiting area. It was eventually smuggled over by someone who stuck it up his arse [inside a pen casing] and, later, someone used it to drill a hole through the perspex that divided the inmate and the visitor.

After a search for diamond wire was exhausted in Brisbane, a call had to be made to another state to get it. But, even then, there were delays. Then a person doing the shopping in Brisbane came up with carbide rods. They are sold at many hardware stores and are cheap. The girl who brought them in smuggled them in up her pouch and threaded them through the hole in the perspex. From the visits area, they were brought back in a pair of flip flops. All went well.

The carbide rods were about 4 to 5mm in diameter and cut the bars OK, but made far more noise than the diamond wire. Jason cut his bar first and then the gear went into Andrew's cell. It was around this time that [convicted rapist] Peter Sterling was brought in on it and Ollie [Alincic]. Ollie moved into the cell with Jason, and Peter went into Andrew's cell. There would've been another if I was allowed to have someone in a cell with me. But management would never allow me to be 'two out' for security reasons.

Next was the getting over the razor wire that surrounded B block. It was a jump of four feet to clear the razor wire. An idea someone had was to use the plastic chairs we had in the cells. Getting a number of them stacked up gave us the launching pad to get over the wire. But to get them outside with us [through the window] required us cutting the backs off.

After the bars were bent out the way, they could be managed through. Cutting the backs off was done by heating a knife on the kitchen cooktop's gas flame and then slowly melting through and across the back of the chair. It took forever. The backs that were cut off were stored in the large wheelie bin.

Before we all escaped, it was made clear to all that I would only team up with one of the others. The rest knew they had to go their own way. For the first few days, they could stay at the unit on the Gold Coast to change their identity and to lie low. From then on, they had to make do themselves. It was clear and simple.

Most of these tools we had came from prison workshops. The tin snips came from a toolbox of a contractor who'd come into the prison. These tin snips would play a vital role in the escape. Another part in the plan was to use duvet covers in making a rope. The material was a heavy drill-type fabric, heavier than bed sheet. It was thought that, once the bar was free, it would need the extra help in bending it back far enough to make room for a body to fit through. The makeshift windlass would be threaded around the bar, cut and then around the bars above the cell door and the two ends of the rope tied together. Then, by snapping off the support post from the bottom bed to the top bunk and using this to wind the sheet up, this would eventually pull the bar away. It soon turned out on the night that making up the windlass wasn't necessary. (Well, if there were two in the cell together, since it was possible to pull the bar back. Alone, it was a different story.)

On 3 November, around midnight, we were expecting to escape and the chairs with the backs cut off were divided up among the three cells and the ropes made were taken into the cell prior to being locked in for that night. Come midnight, no show, and, by 2am, I knew it wasn't on. I came to the conclusion that this bloke was never going to show all along. There were a couple of things didn't go to plan that he was to carry out after his release and then the no-show confirmed it. But I still hung on to some hope that maybe there was a good reason.

Contact was made the next day and, without explaining the details to me, it was obvious he had some drama. Giving some name [Toni], he indicated he'd be there that night. During that day, I was sweating on the screws finding the rope, chairs and the support bar on the bed that one of the others got ahead of himself and snapped off. After lock-up, the wait began. I was feeling the effects already of lack of sleep. The night before, I only managed an hour's sleep, if that. Then around midnight, there came the flash from his torch and then the response from us. Then I set up my windlass, removed the window hinge, snapped off the bed support and started to wind away. The bars in the cell either side of me gave way with enormous cracks that sounded like gunshots. I thought this alone would bring the screws. Next thing, there were four people outside my cell and my bar hadn't given way yet. The windlass was getting to the point where something had to give. I was straining in twisting the bed support around and, if I'd let go, it would've unwound like a spring. Then, all of a sudden, the rope snaps.

Ollie was sent back into his cell to get his rope. I wrapped it around the bars again and started winding again, until I got to the point of something giving way. The four outside were also pushing on the bar and, with an almighty bang, it gave way. I then grabbed the bar and pulled it around as the others pushed *the bar, then it broke off completely in my hand. Where the other support bar was welded to it, it broke off there. I slid my chairs out and put my head and arms through and they pulled me out.*

We stacked the chairs up next to the razor wire that surrounded B block and took turns in jumping over. When I got on top of the chairs, Ollie gave out a yell when his finger got crushed from my weight. Ollie was the last to jump over. Because there was no one to hold the chairs steady, he almost landed on the razor wire. When we got to the fence, the plan changed. One of them was already using the tin snips to cut the wire on the first barrier. This was a sensor fence made up of taut wire that surrounded the entire prison. This fence was about two and a half to three metres high and, as soon as this was cut, the alarms would've been ringing at the front gates security-monitoring area.

Three barriers bordered Sir David Longland Correctional Centre, including an inner-boundary wire strung about one and a half metres high. The second fence was the taut barbed-wire fence, about three metres high. The third barrier was a duraduct fence, about six metres high, built from weld mesh, fitted with an alarm and four rolls of razor wire at both the top and the base.

Then the bloke outside had the boltcutters ready to throw over the fences, but they were far larger and heavier than what was needed. We watched them sail towards us and then hit the drum atop the fence and land a metre or so in front of us, but on the other side of the fence. The next pair he tried to throw over were even larger. These didn't even make it over the outer fence and got caught up in the razor wire.

I was still waiting for the pistol to come over and I felt like we were sitting ducks under the floodlights. None of us realised he'd thrown the gun over before we made it to the fence and it was sitting just metres from us. Without the boltcutters, I thought we were fucked. Jason tells the young bloke to fuck off out of there, no point in him hanging around and getting caught as well. But he didn't want to leave us posted and grabbed the large boltcutters caught up in the first fence and started cutting it. Gutsy effort, I thought.

Meanwhile, the bloke cutting the sensor wire with the tin snips had cut a few strands and we were through that in no time. Then

*he started to cut into the fence that had the drum on top of it,
but no way was this going to be as easy; it played havoc with the
finger muscles.*

Earlier in the evening, the prison's daily ritual had run like clockwork.
Lockdown at 6.15pm, followed by a head count of blocks B, C and
K between 7.15pm and 7.30pm. The same again at 9pm, then at
9.30pm the various officers returned to their posts. They brought a
prisoner across from C block to cook the officers' evening meal in the
B block officers' mess. The next head count was due at 1am. The
regularity of the checks greatly benefited the escape planning.

Officers Helmut Fritz and Leigh Dixon were relieved from the
perimeter vehicle and came over for a meal with C- and K-block
officers. The alarm trilled in the main gate control room just before
12.30am, and three of its TV monitors automatically focused on zone
7. Acting control-room officer Derek Bax rushed to the screens and
saw inmates between the inner- and middle-perimeter fences. He
pressed the touch screen on another computer and brought up the
fence map. All three fences in zone 7 were red. Through the
microphones mounted around the perimeter, he could hear someone
struggling to cut through the fence wire. Bax grabbed for his
microphone and said, 'Crims on the oval or tennis court.'

This alerted the other ten SDL prison officers on duty that
something was seriously amiss. Bax was not a regular in the control-
room position and didn't instantly know the procedures. He tried the
local police station first, spending precious seconds establishing that
it was closed before dialling 000. The phone's placement meant he did
not have a clear view of the monitors, so, while he worked the phones
over the next half-hour, he couldn't keep anyone updated on events at
the perimeter.

An officer in K block rang 000 when he saw the escape was in
progress, but, as a prison inspectors' report later noted, 'The
emergency operator initially regarded his call as frivolous.'

Operations Senior Malcolm Harper, who took charge of the prison
at 7pm, was completing paperwork in the main-gate area, downstairs
from the control room, when the first alarm sounded. He rang Bax,
who informed him that five inmates were at the fence in zone 7.

Harper rushed to the control-room monitors to see it for himself.
He told Bax to ring police and everyone else on the contingency plan
contact list, not updated since 1993. Then came a chilling radio call

from the armoured Toyota Land Cruiser – it was disabled and taking heavy gunfire.

While the officers in B block waited for the C-block inmate to finish cleaning up after their dinner, the radio message came from the control room. Prison officers Leigh Dixon and Helmut Fritz responded immediately, running towards zone 7, on the perimeter on the prison's northwest side, about 220 metres behind and to the right of B block. In between zone 7 and B block were two tennis courts, one on a higher level. Fritz went towards the lower side of the tennis courts and Dixon went towards the upper side and then they saw the prisoners, standing almost casually beneath one of the fence lights. Fritz twice yelled, 'Get down on the ground.'

One of the group, possibly Jason Nixon, pointed menacingly at them and yelled, 'You cunts stay down, or you'll fucking go down.' As if to back up the statement, shots rang out in the darkness, but they came from outside the prison.

Abbott:

The bloke outside came close to the fence holding the M14 rifle. He was told to put a round over their heads and did so. The first round gave everyone a fright – we all took a slight dive. The screws decided to dive for cover completely. Who can blame them? Be an idiot to do otherwise. As the first round went off, Jason and myself were hit by something. I copped something in the arm and Jason in the leg. A day or more later, I picked a fragment of brass out from above my wrist area. Jason later also found what appeared to be a brass fragment in his leg. [Abbott suspects Berichon got soil or stone in the rifle's flash suppressor when he dropped it on the ground. The flash suppressor then blew apart, causing bullet fragments to hit the nearby Abbott and Nixon.]

Dixon and Fritz dropped to their stomachs, unarmed, without cover. They continued to monitor the prisoners over the next few minutes as they milled around the fence, becoming increasingly agitated. Fritz heard someone yell from outside the fence, 'I can't cut the wire. I can't cut the fuckin' wire.'

Officers Mark Irvin and Mark Fritz heard the call on the radio and raced around the perimeter towards zone 7 in the black Land Cruiser. They were much better equipped to handle the situation than the guards inside.

Moments later and we were still trying to get through the drum fence when finally the perimeter vehicle shows up. It was coming around from our left as we faced the fence and was some 20 metres from us when the bloke outside opened fire on the vehicle. After the first or second shot, it came to a sudden stop. The bloke using the rifle was manually reloading the rifle each time he fired it and I yelled out to him that he didn't have to keep reloading it, it did it by itself. Didn't have to tell him twice. He let go with a least half a dozen rounds and left a number of live rounds on the road.

The Land Cruiser contained a shotgun, rifle, two pistols and tear gas. But then gunfire hit the motor and they rolled to a halt. Peering down the road, they saw a muzzle flash about 75 metres away, near zone 7. Irvin contacted the control room on the radio as Fritz turned the vehicle's spotlight on a darkened figure in the area near the bright flash. As he did, bullets whistled past the Toyota and one came through the left windscreen. Fritz later told investigators, 'I could see what I thought was muzzle flash coming from just inside the tree line, northwest of zone 7 on the rise. I could distinctly remember seeing it coming from near a large tall ghost gum tree.'

Irvin ducked in the driver's seat while Fritz dived in the rear compartment to get the 9mm Marlin carbine. He looked out and saw the five inmates running across the road into the bush. After the last prisoner went through the fence, the figure outside followed them. Fritz told investigators, 'At this time, he was side-on to us and then he stopped, turned to face us, brought a firearm to his right shoulder, aimed the rifle in our direction and fired two or three shots straight at us. I saw at this time that this person was wearing a dark-coloured balaclava. After this, he ran off in the direction of the prisoners. Every time I would put my head up to see what was going on, the vehicle was fired upon by the person near the ghost gum tree.'

Both officers in the Toyota believed two gunmen, not one, were attacking them. Fritz felt a bullet whiz past his face. After the volleys of shots, the officers sat there in eerie silence, unable to communicate with the control room, or defend themselves through the Toyota's gun ports, which were east-west, while the vehicle faced north.

Fritz later told Brisbane's *Sunday Mail*, 'It was only luck that stopped us from losing several officers. These people meant business.'

The following day, the prison officer returned to work, only to be taunted by inmates, who dubbed him 'Target'.

Those working on cutting the fence called me over to have a go at it. I put the makeshift bag I made earlier that night from a windcheater (holding a '96–'97 diary and sunglasses) on the ground next to the fence and started having a go at it. Soon we had a hole big enough for the smallest of us to get through. The bloke outside grabs the boltcutters and continues to make it big enough for all of us. Then we had to make our way through the razor wire. Suddenly, I've got claret all over my right hand. I look at the palm and then back to see where it was coming from. Couldn't see the wound and didn't give it a second thought. The tin snips were useless in cutting the razor wire, as were the boltcutters. The best we could do is remove a clip that held some of the wire together and spread it apart, which gave some opening through. I was wearing a long-sleeve windcheater and track pants and remember pushing through the razor wire and feeling it catch on my clothes and ripping as I continued through.

Police records released under Freedom of Information laws show that the bundle containing Abbott's 1996 and 1997 diaries – which later mysteriously disappeared – his sunglasses and prison ID were found near the fence breach.

There was also an enlargement of Queensland's coat of arms on a piece of paper, which I had plans to use for something. And in my 1997 diary for that day, I drew a small 'happy face' and a small 'sad face'. Whatever the result from the escape, I'd be having one of these expressions.

After crossing the razor wire, Abbott was again a free man. But how long would it last this time?

The moment I was on the perimeter road, I felt vulnerable, a sitting target for the screws in the perimeter vehicle. I felt better once in the bush and heading in the direction of the dark figures moving some distance in front of me. Sterlo was near me at this point and we were both having problems keeping upright while running through the scrub. I ran across some corrugated iron that made a hell of a racket.

By the time I got to the car, the others were already in it and as I got to the rear door and went to open it, they drove off. Then someone in the back yells, 'Hang on, he's not in yet,' and the car stops. I got in and next we're on the road that goes past the prison.

Detective Sergeant Paul Mason and Constable Ian Wells of Oxley police responded immediately to a radio message about the escape. They saw the Falcon driving towards them and switched on the high beam, lighting up the crowd of brown tracksuits inside the car. The officers threw their car into a U-turn and the chase began. The Falcon turned left on to Ipswich Motorway access road and then a person appeared at the driver's side rear-passenger window with a rifle pressed to his shoulder. The police prudently dropped back and got busy on the radio.

Jason pointed the M14 at them and tried to fire it, but nothing happened. He passed it back to me to see what was wrong with it. As I later found out, none of them had any experience with this type of firearm, or firearms in general. The magazine was empty and I asked the driver where the spare mags were, and he said they were on the floor somewhere in the back. Sitting four across the back seat was a tight squeeze and searching for the magazines proved difficult. I was handed a magazine for the SKS (semi-automatic high-powered rifle) and explained the one I needed was a square type. One was found and handed to me, but the fucker was empty.

Then I got a full magazine, reloaded the M14 and sat myself outside the car through the door. The patrol car was sitting back some distance and I gave a burst of gunfire way, way above their car as a warning that they'd best fuck off. They got the message and faded away in the distance. Their statements would claim they saw sparks on the road in front of them and heard shit fly up and hit the car. Yeah, fuckin' sure it did.

The Falcon was about 200 metres short of Boundary Road when the shots were fired over the officers' car and forced it to drop back out of sight.

After the cops disappeared, the driver was told to turn down the first road we came upon and, after a few more turns, we had no idea where we were. I told him to find a block of flats so we can pull in and park, because we couldn't keep driving around the area, which would soon be swarming with cops. I was then told there wasn't a second car and there wasn't enough fuel in the car we were in to get to the Gold Coast anyway.

Eventually, I convinced them to pull up somewhere and we parked beside a shed and killed the lights and engine. Someone opened a car door and then a dog at a nearby house started going apeshit. Then everyone wanted to get moving again and away we went. I didn't like the move, but I was outnumbered.

City Security Services owner Paul Flanagan was patrolling the Acacia Ridge area when the call came across his scanner on a police channel. He turned his car around and headed for Wacol, and en route began following the Falcon, which had just shaken off the police car. He lost sight of it briefly and then came across it parked in the middle of Forest Lake Boulevard, Forest Lake.

Abbott:

We thought it was cops. We turned left and just around the corner I told the driver to stop. The others played up, so I told them, 'We can't outrun them, so I'll put a stop to them.' The car stopped, I got out with the M14 and the car chasing us pulled up at the corner. I let go with a number of shots – again, well over the top of the vehicle. The car was put in reverse and quickly disappeared down the street. I got back into the car and we headed down a few more streets and parked at a vacant block next to some houses being built.

We all cleared out of the car. Jason, Ollie and Andrew headed off one way, Sterlo, the young bloke and myself went in the opposite direction carrying the M14. We were out of the car for only a few seconds when a cop car appeared in the street. Some bloke was out in the front yard of his house across the road and next thing a helicopter was hovering above us. We got as far away as possible, ducking for cover when vehicles headed up the street we were on. Eventually, we ended up in a bush area no more than a kilometre from where we dumped the car, and that area was getting grid searched by a helicopter.

At one point, we were all submerged in a pond and the spotlight from the helicopter went directly on us, but didn't make us. It cruised by and we're out of the water and trying to make as much ground away from the car as possible. The chopper went over us at least six times and missed us. We all huddled together when we could see and hear it coming towards us. If it was using the heat-seeking device, I'm none the wiser. If so, the only reason I can think of as to why it didn't pick us up was due to being drenched from the pond. I honestly thought we were fucked.

Before long, the scrub we were in came to the back of houses and the helicopter was still checking the area nearby for what seemed like hours before all started to quieten down and dawn was soon upon us. One of the others made a suggestion that we bail up people in a house. I wasn't going to take part in such a stunt; I would take my chances where we were. If it meant sitting another night out here, so be it. I might terrorise people during bank jobs, but be fucked if I was going to terrorise a family in their home. I might be a cunt, but there's a limit to how much of a cunt I'll be. The bush we were in wasn't that thick with vegetation, but we found some cover and sat out many hours of the following day.

After risking their lives and losing custody of three killers, a rapist and a bank robber, the SDL prison officers faced one more indignity that day, highlighted on the *Courier Mail's* front page days after the escape.

While Abbott and the others sat it out in the scrub, police were bagging evidence in his old cell at SDL's unit 4B. Detective Sergeant Eric Giesemann reported, 'An inspection of cell 14 revealed an application for transfer in the name of Jason Nixon, which was approved and signed by B. Abbott. An inspection of cell 12 revealed an application for transfer for Brendan Abbott, which was approved and signed by Jason Nixon.'

That afternoon, Berichon went to the nearby Mount Ommaney shopping centre in Brisbane's southwestern suburbs, with a shopping list: tracksuits, to replace their prison browns, sunglasses, chocolate and drinks. When he returned, he told them the area was still crawling with police and, within minutes, a helicopter was buzzing directly above them again.

The door on its left side was open and it was flying so low that it was possible to make out the face of the person behind the pilots.

It flew directly above us, but we weren't spotted. After a few cruises over and near us, it moved on. We decided it was time to move on, too. We came out of the bush and walked up the street. A couple of women with kids were in the driveway of a house, one obviously about to get into her car and leave and the other one was seeing her off. They watched us walk out of the bush and kept their eyes on us all the way up the street. They would've been thinking, No, surely not. That wouldn't be them, would it?

I wrapped the M14 with garbage bags and hid it in the long grass with the intention of retrieving it some time later. It was later revealed on the news that it was found. I thought the cops fucked up on that because it was obvious it had been hidden. They could have staked it out and waited for us to come back for it. Halfway up the street, some bloke was working on his XD Ford station wagon on the nature strip. Without warning, Peter headed off to the front door of his house and we followed. Another bloke was inside and met us at the door. Peter asked if we could use his phone and the bloke had no problems with that. We invited ourselves in and sat in the lounge with this bloke. The cab was called and the destination I gave was Logan City shopping centre, but I intended getting the cab to go somewhere else.

Peter asked this guy for a drink and, without waiting for a response, he went straight to the fridge. Then the penny dropped – the bloke was on to who we were. His heart was thumping that hard you could see his shirt shaking and he had difficulty controlling his breathing. The bloke who was working on his car out front came inside, none the wiser as to who the guests were. He grabbed something and headed back out to the car. I tried to get a conversation going with the other bloke to try to settle him down a bit, to make him feel he wasn't in any danger. None of us told him who we were, but something gave it away. The poor bastard would have felt like the taxi was taking forever.

It pulled in the driveway within ten minutes and we left the bloke to change his jocks. He was on his phone as soon as we were out the driveway. I told the driver, 'Forget Logan City, mate, the city will do.'

We drove past Arthur Gorrie and the driver told us about the prison breakout the night before. I asked him, 'Is this the place?' indicating towards AGCC.

He said, 'No, a prison further over.'

We eventually got on to a freeway and not far out of the city, we spotted another helicopter flying parallel to the freeway, heading in the same direction as us. Surely it's not on to us, I thought. As we pulled up in the city, we got out of the cab and saw the helicopter then hovering directly above us. Not good, I thought.

Police relied on the taxi's global-positioning system to track it, but missed their chance to move in. It stopped at the corner of Albert and Elizabeth streets in the city centre, and the trio slipped into the late-afternoon city crowds. The Roma Street transit centre was shut down after reported sightings at 5.30pm, causing peak-hour chaos. The hunt widened to South Bank, across the river, after a report three men were seen trying to conceal firearms as they crossed Victoria Bridge. Armed police scoured the Queensland Performing Arts Centre and floodlit the area, believing they had the escapees trapped. Diners in nearby restaurants were locked in. The net closed. But the sightings were all false; luck had somehow stayed on the escapees' side. And, while they regrouped, the city of Brisbane locked its doors and shuddered. Anything could happen now.

After getting out of the taxi, Abbott and his fellow escapees walked around a corner and jumped into another one at a rank, ordering the driver to head for the Gold Coast.

After some distance along the freeway, the computer screen in front of the driver beeps and a message comes across. I couldn't make it out, but something soon changed in the driver's demeanour. Peter asked the driver if he was married and had kids. I think he said no to both. Not long after, he switched off the computer screen and there was very little conversation during the trip down to the Coast. At the Coast he dropped us off at a drive-through on the Gold Coast Highway in Broadbeach. I gave the driver $100 and away he went.

One of them booked into a motel, then went across the road to buy food at a Hungry Jack's store. 'Deja vu for me,' Abbott joked later, referring to when he and Aaron Reynolds had gone to a Hungry Jack's in Perth hours after escaping from Fremantle Prison.

The young bloke went over to get the takeaway and brought it back to the room. I had injuries from the razor wire and it was the first opportunity to attend to them. The worst was to my right hand, a deep cut to the soft area opposite the thumb. By then, the bleeding had stopped. The couple of nicks on the legs weren't an issue. I came through pretty good considering the state of a couple of others I later caught up with. After the feed and the shower, I felt it was time to move on. I wanted to head south towards Coolangatta. Walking was the best choice, but along the beach where we wouldn't stand out. By now, every person in the state would be seeing our pictures on TV. The young bloke was still the unknown.

We walked as far as Burleigh Heads. By now it was late in the night and the effect of sleep deprivation was taking its toll on me. In the past 72 hours, I had only had three hours' sleep. We decided to catch the bus to Coolangatta, and stay at a 24-hour motel I knew. I'd catch the bus at one stop and Peter and the young bloke would walk up to the next stop and get on. But there was a misunderstanding and I thought Peter was going to make a phone call at the phone box next to the toilets at Burleigh Heads beach. Then he'd let me know before they started walking. I went and sat in the bus shelter and lay back on the seat. I thought I had dozed off for a few minutes, but I must've been out for an hour or more and be fucked if I could find them when I woke. I managed to find out the time and realised I must have slept longer than I thought.

I'd already made arrangements with the young bloke just in case we split up, so I wasn't too concerned; midday at the Tugun post office if we split before noon, if not, at noon on the days that followed. Similar arrangements were made with Jason, on a certain day at the Kirra Surf Club at the car park of Pizza Hut. I was wondering if they'd both still remember. I eventually made my way to Coolangatta and found that the 24-hour motel was no longer open 24 hours. There was no sign of Peter and the young bloke. By then, all I was interested in was getting some sleep. There was an upturned lifesavers' boat on Coolangatta beach. It had drizzled most of the night and was still at it. I crawled under the boat and lay there, dwelling on the hectic past 24 hours or more; I'd had a lot of luck on my side. I went out like a light.

Chapter Sixteen

6 November – 28 December 1997

On front pages and TV news bulletins across Australia, five cold belligerent faces stared out at the world, as if daring it to come after them. Brenden Abbott's sister Diane got as big a surprise as anyone else.

The cops came to my house the day after the breakout. I was at a friend's house and I saw on the news that these people had escaped from jail. I looked at my girlfriend and said, 'Oh my God, that's my brother.'

[She said,] 'Yeah right, I'm sure your brother is that bloody good he could do that.'

I said, 'I'm telling you, it's him.'

She wouldn't believe me. She was raided two days later. They searched the house.

The cops came around [my home] that next night [6 November]. I was in the driveway ready to leave and these two coppers turned up. I walked over and she said to me, 'I don't know if you know why we're here ... I suppose we just need to ask that, if you hear from your brother, will you tell us?'

And I said, 'No. I have very strong morals and values when it comes to my family.'

That was the last time they approached me. But they watched my house 24 hours a day. Bastards.

Hundreds of police prowled Brisbane's streets. Both police and residents were understandably a little jittery because of the unknown armed accomplice adding to the tension – although it was less than a week before police had a clear idea the mystery man was Berichon, after they reviewed certain telephone conversations. Abbott, however, was at the top of the list, and stayed there: three were killers, but the media and the Queensland authorities immediately focused on him as the 'mastermind'. Years later, Abbott still bristles at being saddled with the notoriety.

I'm still solely to blame for the SDL escape in 1997 in the eyes of the government, prison authorities, the prisoners themselves and, of course, the majority of the public. The story I planned the escape solely ... crap. I selected those who escaped with me ... crap. The person responsible for shooting at guards etc on the night was doing it for me ... crap.

I played a part in the planning, yes, but taking along others to help the chances for me to get away, not so. The rubbish that it was all a well-planned escape: cutting bars on a cell window, running to the fence to cut a hole through it – yeah, that took some figuring out. Just months prior to the escape, they stopped the ritual of doing bar taps on every cell window. Did they think we'd miss them not doing that any more?

Exhausted, Abbott lay undisturbed beneath the upturned lifesavers' boat, and was woken by the sun around 6am. With some sleep under his belt, his head was clearer and he felt ready to move on. He walked down the beach until he saw customers emerging from a newsagents. He wandered in, head down, and grabbed the papers. His face was all over the front page, but the bloke at the till didn't look twice.

Abbott walked back down the street towards Rainbow Bay, glancing back casually to make sure the newsagent hadn't stuck his head out for a second look at his last customer. Satisfied, he sat down at the beach and first scanned the *Courier Mail* front-page lead, written by Sean Parnell and staff reporters: 'Brisbane was a city under siege last night as five prison escapees, three of them convicted murderers, remained on the run. Police appealed to residents to lock themselves in their homes, travel only in pairs and keep a check on their relatives and friends. Three of the fugitives were believed to be on foot in Brisbane's inner southside after a daring taxi ride from their daytime hideout.'

The *Australian*'s Leisa Scott, Megan Saunders and Fiona Kennedy reported, 'Five of Australia's most dangerous criminals were on the run last night after a jailbreak in which snipers from the outside fired high-powered rifles at guards while the prisoners cut their way to freedom with boltcutters and diamond-encrusted wire. Police fear the escapees, including three murderers, will try to shoot their way out if cornered, prompting warnings for parents to pick up their children from school and for residents in southern Queensland to secure their homes and cars... Police and Corrective Services spokespeople believe the mastermind of the break-out was armed robber Brendon James Abbott, 35, known as the Postcard Bandit.'

Abbott needed an update. There was nothing in the papers about anyone being caught, but the news was already hours old, so he could not be sure the other escapees were still at large. He walked to some phone boxes and called the supposed '24-hour' motel that had been closed the previous night. He told the receptionist the time Berichon and Sterling would have booked in, but she said the motel had been closed at that time. Abbott could only hope Berichon would remember the default plan: to meet him at the Tugun post office at noon if all else failed.

He returned to the beach for an hour, waiting for the nearby Tweed Heads shopping centre to open. Police had recovered the receipt from Berichon's visit to the Mount Ommaney Big W and the description of the clothes he bought was made public; Abbott now needed a wardrobe change. As he was about to walk through the centre's main entrance, a hand closed firmly over his shoulder.

I spun around, thinking the worst, and, fuck me, it was Sterlo, of all people. He and the young bloke were sitting in or near the Dolphin Hotel and had watched me walking down the street. The young bloke was still back where Peter left him and, as we were walking to where he was supposed to be waiting, we ran into him halfway there. I got the impression he thought he'd been left posted.

Berichon and Sterling explained to Abbott what had happened the night before at Burleigh Heads. Sterling had made his call and they'd continued on to the next bus stop, not realising Abbott expected them to come back first. They came across a motel at Kirra, just off the Pacific Highway, and booked in, assuming that it was the 24-hour place Abbott had referred to. The emergency rendezvous was also doomed – Berichon admitted that he thought the Tugun post office rendezvous was set for 6pm, not noon; in any case, the Tugun post office that Abbott remembered no longer existed. So much for plan B saving the day – it was only dumb luck that brought the three together again.

They decided to go to the motel that Abbott originally intended to book into the previous night; Berichon was sent to reception to sort it out. He joined them at the elevator and, on the way up, told them that there might still be a guy in the room cleaning the carpets.

When they arrived, the door was open and they could see the cleaner inside. But the man was engrossed and hadn't seen them, so Abbott grabbed Sterling and signalled to return to the elevator. They returned to the ground floor, where Abbott told Berichon that he should go back to the room and wait for the cleaner to finish, then meet them at the shopping centre where Abbott had bought the papers earlier. It also had a bar with a snooker room where Abbott used to enjoy a quiet one. But Sterling couldn't understand the need for cloak and dagger. Why not just go straight to the motel room?

> I told him, 'Our heads are all over the papers and on the TV. What do you think he [the carpet cleaner] does during smoko and lunch? It's bad enough fearing someone will spot us in public, but having someone knowing where we're staying would be even worse.'

Inside the bar, Abbott bought two stubbies of VB, casually scanning the area to make sure they weren't attracting interest. He walked back through to the snooker room, where Sterling was perched on a stool at one of the high round tables; Abbott put down the beers and picked up his newspaper again. Digesting the details of the escape, he noticed a discrepancy.

> I realised Peter was in jail for rape. I raised that with him, saying, 'You told me you were in jail for armed robbery, but the paper says you're doing time for rape.' I guessed he was ashamed of his conviction.
>
> He snapped back with: 'I fucking told you I was in for rape and I'm not good for it.'

Sterling poured the beer down his throat as though it were his last and then immediately reached for Abbott's. 'Buy your fucking own if you want more,' Abbott chided him.

'I couldn't help thinking that this prick had the nature of a Bali monkey,' he said later of Sterling.

Berichon returned soon after with the news that the cleaner had left. The trio went shopping again, buying more new clothes, hair dye, skin-tone make-up, toiletries and shampoo. Sterling also bought six more stubbies. When they returned to the unit, the transformations began.

I chose the balding-guy look and Peter gave himself a hairstyle that left the sides and the back of his head shaved. No changes were made to the young bloke's appearance.

Sterling, meanwhile, worked his way through most of the stubbies and was becoming increasingly morose at his prospects. Abbott was meeting Nixon at the Pizza Hut car park that day, and Sterling wanted in.

'You knew the story before we fucked off,' Abbott told him. 'I'm only teaming up with Jason.'

But Sterling was angry and insistent. Abbott tried to placate him, telling him that, if Nixon didn't show, he'd reconsider.

'So don't go then,' Sterling pleaded.

'Fuck off, I'm not going to do that.'

Sterling stormed off to the lounge to watch TV, yelling a parting shot: 'You know he'll show up, you cunt.'

Around noon, Sterling lay on the bed and appeared to have dozed off, the beer taking its toll. Abbott and Berichon left for the Nixon rendezvous at 12.30pm, intending to return later, since all their gear was still in the unit.

Two of Nixon's friends met Abbott and Berichon at the car park and drove them to a high-rise unit at Burleigh Heads. Abbott insisted on the usual precautions, and they each went to the unit separately. 'When I walked through the door to be greeted by Jason, he had a look on his face as if to say, 'Who the fuck are you?' He liked my disguise and reckoned it had him fooled.'

They talked about the escape and its aftermath and, more importantly, what they would do next. Abbott was reluctant to trust third parties and, even though Nixon vouched for his mate, that wouldn't necessarily stop him picking up a police tail. Nevertheless, he agreed that he and Berichon would return to the unit and be picked up by one of Nixon's mates the next morning. They would then stay with Nixon, Jeffrey and Alincic at the Burleigh Heads high rise, where they could all prepare to split up. But, when they returned to their unit, Sterling was gone – and so were all their belongings.

> *I wasn't going to hang around. We booked a room somewhere else that night and I had the young bloke use a different name to the one used at the last place. Meanwhile, Peter's desires got the better of him and he made his way to a Tweed Heads brothel. He spent some time with a girl and spilled his guts about his identity. She shot her mouth off to friends at work, then joined Peter in a local hotel for drinks and later invited him home with her. Someone who was aware of Peter being with her called the cops and he was arrested the next morning.*

Peter Sterling's double-barrelled stupidity, in confiding in the working girl and then staying with her, meant he was the first of the escapees to be returned to custody, in handcuffs and leg irons – and with a very bad haircut – on 7 November. He was grilled for several hours at Broadbeach police station and, the same day, the unit where the trio had stayed was raided. But the cupboard was bare.

Meanwhile, Nixon's friend picked up Abbott and Berichon from a prearranged point the next morning and they returned to the Burleigh Heads unit. When the news of Sterling's arrest hit the media, Berichon was agitated; some of the clothing Sterling had taken had Berichon's name written inside the waistband. His chances of remaining an anonymous figure behind a muzzle flash were looking increasingly slim.

They spent another two days at that unit, in which time, Abbott says, both Alincic and Jeffrey also tried to convince him to team up with them, but got the same answer as Sterling. Everyone knew the deal before we went.

The rent on the unit had been paid in cash, but Abbott shook his head when eventually told that it was booked using a name from stolen ID, and that an imprint of a stolen credit card was given as security. Nixon tried to convince him that all was OK, but the cautious Abbott was having none of it. He was out of there, right then, whether the others wanted to or not. Of course they did – they all knew it was only luck and Abbott's skills as a fugitive that had got them this far. Another unit was soon found near Coolangatta and, after several trips, the move was complete. But the time had come for Alincic to go his own way and it was clear he had no plans. Nixon said to him, 'If you didn't have anything planned, what did you fuck off for?'

Alincic shrugged. 'Beats being in jail,' he said.

The others nodded. They knew what he meant. A couple of days later they booked another unit, this time for two weeks.

All our gear was moved in and each of us drifted in one at a time over the next half-hour. The place was in a high rise and we intended to lie low here and wait for the heat to die down. After a few weeks, I would make a trip and recover some funds and other tools of the trade. Then I would go to work with Jason, pay off the young bloke and then we would all go our own ways. But it didn't work out that way. The young bloke was soon in the spotlight and he was in the same boat as all of us. A few boxes of blond hair dye then went through his hair. That didn't quite do the trick, but peroxide did.

Oliver Alincic somehow made it across the border into New South Wales and, on 11 November, his rogue French blood got the better of him. The *Courier Mail*'s Ben Dorries reported on his recapture on 13 November: 'A Nimbin man befriended by Oliver Alincic turned the tables on the convicted killer after the escapee allegedly demanded a sexual favour from the man's 17-year-old girlfriend. Alincic ... was arrested in possession of a .32-calibre pistol outside a service station in the northern New South Wales town at 5pm on Tuesday.'

Police announced publicly on 12 November that they wanted to speak to Brendan Berichon about the events of 4 November and his mother Julie made a tearful plea, as Sean Parnell reported in the *Courier Mail* on 13 November, 'A teenager who idolises criminal mastermind Brendan Abbott was suspected of being the gunman who helped Abbott and four other dangerous prisoners escape, police said yesterday. The boy's distraught family yesterday pleaded for him to come home, and police said they held fears for his safety.'

Berichon cringed at seeing his mum in tears on the six o'clock news, but Abbott reassured him. 'As long as we're invisible, we're safe,' he told him. 'And we'll stick together.' The kid had a lot to learn, but he had balls. The fact was, he'd put his life on the line on the night of 4 November; that rated highly in Abbott's outlaw moral code.

After several days went by, I decided I'd head off earlier than planned. But, when the time came, I got cold feet after a gut feeling to give it more time. We had enough cash to get us through, but Jason and I decided to go and look at a branch of the Commonwealth Bank that I was familiar with in Palm Beach. I was only intending to have a look at it when we left the unit that day.

Leaving the unit was done the same way as going in, with 10- to 15-minute intervals. Jason headed off first and walked along the beach and I followed. We stopped at a place at Tugun called The Breakers on the beachfront. It was behind the Tugun hotel next to the beach. I had a few drinks and meals here between '89 and '95, a quiet place with tables outside that overlook the beach. We decided to have a break and a couple of drinks. We looked like tourists, Jason with his hair dyed black, the straw hat and sunglasses and I was looking the part, too. Jason ducked inside to buy some drinks. Other than the couple of staff inside, we were the only people there. I removed my cap so the staff could see me as the balding guy. What started as a few bourbons ended up being four or five. Jason more or less needed pulling away from there and then went to the bottle shop nearby and grabbed four UDLs for the rest of the walk.

We got to a river mouth not far up and, since the tide was out, we walked across through the shallow water. By the time we got to Palm Beach, we were both a bit charged up. We had a quick look at a few things and I said we'd come back again in a few nights to carry out an idea I had for getting into the joint. I noticed that adjacent to the walkway between the bank and another building that the bank's windows were large sliding doors that weren't in use. Obviously a feature installed before the joint became a bank. I figured I could unlock them and, prior to opening, when staff arrived, we could simply slide the windows back and get the drop on them. Being on the walkway, we had plenty of cover. But Jason wasn't interested in coming back; he wanted to rob it now. I thought he was only kidding at first, but no matter what I said, he had his mind set on doing it there and then. He said, if I wasn't going to help him, he was going to go for it himself. In hindsight, I should've just let him. I can't believe that I ended up robbing the fucking place.

We had a handgun on us at the time and that was it. A few minutes later, we headed to a cab rank a few streets away, then

we went to the Elanora shopping centre and stole a Commodore.
Jason bought a tomahawk from a hardware shop and then we're
in the bank. I jumped the counter like some desperado needing
cash for my drug habit.

At 3.30pm on 13 November 1997, Abbott and Nixon entered the
Commonwealth Bank at Palm Beach on the Gold Coast Highway. The
desperado bolted for the customer-enquiry counter and launched
himself, making sure he was safely in the main chamber before the
security screens activated. Nixon, meanwhile, brandished the tomahawk
to back up the statement: 'Hit the floor and no one gets hurt.'

A woman walked to the front door of the bank, saw everyone on
the floor and ran next door to ring the police.

Nixon yelled to Abbott, 'We've been spotted, come on, big fella,
hurry up.'

Abbott, meanwhile, ordered all the staff to the floor and walked
briskly over to one of the female tellers, who later told police, 'I heard
a male voice … that said, "I'm not going to hurt anybody, we just
want the money." The next thing I remember is a plastic shopping bag
being shoved in my face and the male saying to me, "Put the money
in the bag, here, you, honey! Be fast, and all of it."'

Abbott:

We gained $12,000 at the most [media reports put the figure at
$17,210]. Fucking couldn't believe I resorted to robbing a bank
this way again. To top it off, I left a print on a glass screen.
Michael Jackson, I ain't. I didn't even have one glove on – a
complete fuckwit. We drove off and it didn't appear that anyone
saw the car and I wanted to dump it not too far away – but far
enough from the area just past the river we walked across earlier,
then walk along the beach back to where we stayed. Jason didn't
like that idea, he preferred we drive most of the way back. I
drove further than I originally wanted and not anywhere near
where Jason wanted to. We got out and proceeded on foot. From
that time on, I realised this bloke was a bad choice as a partner
in crime. He had a spontaneous nature and a 'couldn't give a
fuck' attitude to go with it. In jail, he may have had it under
control, but, outside in the big, wide world, he had so much to
learn; I realised it could be a problem.

The next day, he decided to rob a chemist. I wanted nothing to do with it and took no part in it whatsoever, other than spending the evening before and that morning trying to talk him and his mate out of it. Even his close friend approached me and asked me to try to talk him out of it. Nothing anyone could say was going to change his mind. That morning, I bought a scanner from the Tandy store in Tweed Heads and headed back to the unit. If he was going to come undone for it, I wanted to hear about it and decide my next move from there.

Nixon and his friend used a gun and a screwdriver to hold up a Broadbeach pharmacy on Gold Coast Highway, stealing hundreds of dollars' worth of drugs, including morphine. 'They got away OK and back to the unit. The sight I saw next [drug use] had me shaking my head in disbelief and deciding, "I'll be on my way in the next few days."'

The dumped Commodore from the bank robbery, and the pharmacy robbery, intensified the police focus on the Queensland–NSW border area. And the media was letting them know it.

Jason and myself were on the high-rise unit's balcony when we spotted what looked like jacks on foot with a clipboard in hand. They walked into the ground floor of the apartments, but there wasn't a site manager's office, and they soon left. I left the unit and made my way down the fire stairs to see if they were who we thought they were. It was night when this was going on and I left wearing glasses and without a hat on and the pistol in my waistband. I soon spotted them again walking into other holiday units and what looked like their car down the street. A quick glance inside confirmed it was a jacks' car.

I got back to the unit and told Jason they were jacks, all right. Would they come back or do we hope they don't take it any further? Not good detectives if they didn't. They just need to call the agency's number, which they'd no doubt written down. The following day, they would check bookings from a certain date onwards. It's a long shot, but that's how they solve cases. I told Jason I was out of there that instant. We needed to split up again and meet up in a week. We arranged to meet up at the same place as before at a set time. The young bloke joined up with me, while Jason, his friend and Andrew went together somewhere. That was the last I was to see of them for a while.

With a single suitcase between them, Abbott and Berichon headed towards the beach, back to the Kirra motel that Berichon and Sterling had first stayed in. Abbott settled into some scrub near the beach – where he had a view of the motel's car park and reception – and then sent Berichon over the road to book a room. Berichon emerged from reception with the manager a short time later and they walked across to a room. The manager appeared to have trouble with the key and they returned to the office, apparently to get the right one. The door was closing behind them when a carload of men in a late-model sedan pulled into the car park. 'The moment I saw it, I thought it was a jacks' car. The two in the front got out and made their way to reception. I was thinking, If they're cops, I know someone who'll shit himself.'

Abbott was right. When the two detectives walked in, Berichon was speechless with nerves. One of the officers glanced over to him and said, 'G'day.' He managed to nod in return, convinced that, in a few seconds, they would make the connection between the mug shots they were holding and the nervous, gangly blond kid. When they began their conversation with the manager, Berichon turned and walked out, the room key forgotten. Abbott watched him emerge from the office and walk down the passageway past the rooms, quickly disappearing behind the motel; their suitcase was left sitting outside the front of the room where the manager had first taken him. Five minutes later, the detectives – whom Abbott was now beginning to doubt were police – left the office and drove off.

With no sign of Berichon, Abbott decided to retrieve their suitcase. As he reached it, the manager emerged from the office and hurried over. Berichon had told him that he was travelling with his uncle, and the manager assumed it was him. He told Abbott he'd been busy talking to the police and Berichon had taken off without waiting for the key. Abbott reassured him that the young bloke had probably gone to the beach to look for him, because he'd wandered over for a look while the room was booked. The manager gave no hint of suspicion and gave Abbott the key, explaining the arrangements for breakfast. Abbott went to the room with the suitcase and left the door open.

The young bloke soon rocked up, looking as though he's seen a ghost and with his shoes soaking wet. He started going on about the cops and I said, 'Yeah, I know they were here, the bloke just told me.'

He had ended up landing in some water at the back of the

*motel and that's why his shoes were wet. The experience really
put the wind up him and he took some time to settle down.*

The next day, Abbott and Berichon caught a bus to Coolangatta and
booked a sleeper on the XPT express train from Murwillumbah that
night. After leaving their suitcase at the transit centre, they headed to
the cinemas at a shopping centre to keep out of sight for the day. That
evening, they caught the coach to Murwillumbah, where Berichon
boarded the train with the suitcase and then Abbott made a last-
minute dash to the platform to avoid scrutiny from other passengers.
Later, Berichon visited the buffet car for snacks and drinks and then
the fugitives settled in for the journey.

*We eventually crashed out. The sleep that night would've been the
deepest and best sleep I'd had for months and it was needed. The
stress level dropped considerably after the train was on its way; I
was finally putting some distance between myself and Queensland.*

Arriving refreshed in Sydney the next morning, the fugitives
immediately booked a sleeper on the train to Melbourne that night.
They checked their bag at a holding centre and then headed to the
cinemas in George Street to pass the day. Movie theatres would be a
favourite refuge of the pair throughout that summer, although, in a
year dominated by *Titanic* and *Spice World: The Movie*, their choice
was limited. The pair emerged briefly into the daylight and then
headed to another darkened room near the train station, where a
hungry Abbott and nervous Berichon took in the action at a strip club.

*We took turns disappearing into a room with one of the friendly
girls who walked around asking if you needed another drink or
'whatever'. I grabbed a 'whatever' after seeing the first strip. It
took the young bloke a few drinks first – this type of scene was
new to him.*

They arrived in Melbourne the next morning, freshening up with a
shower at Spencer Street station, where Abbott also spruced up his
balding-man disguise, shaving his head and applying skin-tone make-up.
After they put their bag in a locker and walked to the city, the first task
was to buy warmer clothes for Berichon. His wardrobe was more suited
to Queensland and, even though it was summer, Melbourne's weather

was brisk that morning. Shopping complete, they booked into a city hotel, returned to the station to pick up the bag, and then Berichon remained in the hotel room while Abbott began his fugitive's scavenger hunt. Years of planning for the future while previously on the run meant he had cash and key tools of his trade hidden across Australia.

First I called into a florist and bought a bunch of flowers and made my way to a Melbourne cemetery and paid a visit to a plot of a person who'd been looking after a sum for me for a number of years. It wasn't a great deal, but it was intended for emergencies. I headed back to the motel and showed the young bloke we were right for cash for at least a few months and gave him a few grand for himself. Some of it was paper notes and I told him not to pass more than one at a time. We went about getting rid of those first over the next few weeks.

Abbott had no intention of returning to Queensland for his scheduled rendezvous with Jason Nixon at the Kirra Pizza Hut. He planned to send Berichon up there on a day trip to meet Nixon and deliver an ultimatum – leave Queensland now or forget about teaming up.

On 19 November, several days after splitting from Abbott, Nixon and a woman booked into the luxury Belaire Motel at Caloundra on the Sunshine Coast. The hotel owners described the pair as seeming 'as if they weren't on this planet'. They ordered a cab the next morning and conveniently supplied their destination as the Netanya Beachfront Resort at Noosa. After a cleaner found a vinyl gun case under their bed – and staff joked that the male guest could be one of the escapees – the Belaire owners called Netanya staff to compare notes, just in case. After discovering that the couple supplied different ID at each place, the Netanya staff rang police.

The information led Sunshine Coast detectives Gary Kruger and Paul Zohn to visit the resort on what they believed to be a drug enquiry.

They knocked on the couple's door, but did not immediately recognise Nixon. A search of the apartment turned up a large amount of cash and hypodermic syringes and Senior Constable Kruger advised 'John Pedersen' he would be required to attend the police station. Nixon agreed, but said he needed to get a pair of socks from the other room. Kruger later told the *Courier Mail*'s Justine Nolan,

'He went to a sports bag on the bed and unzipped the bag and pulled out the shotgun. He spun around and said, "You're dead," and I grabbed it and pushed it up into the ceiling and that's when the gun went off.'

Sergeant Zohn, who was keeping an eye on the woman in the next room, heard the gunfire and raced to his quick-thinking partner's side. He recalls,

> As I've gone in there, the gun's pointing at my stomach and I reached down and moved the gun away. It was touching me. Gary was hanging on to the firearm and I was just doing whatever I could do to subdue Nixon. We were struggling with him. He's a solid little bugger, close to six foot.

The officers, who by this time had recognised Nixon, managed to disarm him and pin him to the ground until back-up arrived. Both later received Commendations for Brave Conduct. Nixon, on the other hand, got a total of 20 years' extra jail for his 15 days of mayhem. Such is the usual fate of jail escapees.

In Melbourne, Abbott soon heard about Nixon's arrest. It happened the evening before he was supposed to meet him in Kirra. It meant Berichon no longer had to go to Queensland to see Nixon.

> We headed back to Sydney some days later by train again and booked into a backpackers' hostel in Sydney city. By now, I'd done away with the balding-guy look and was completely bald. While in Sydney, I went to work on making numerous IDs in the room. The young bloke had a learner's permit that I worked from. I knew I wasn't able to get perfect-looking licences, but they were good enough to show as ID for booking into motels. From past experience, I felt photo ID was a necessity. Having ID to drive was a plan for the future, but we would need a home base to achieve this, not a motel room.
>
> We made a few trips to the library in the city to use the photocopiers and make enlargements of the young bloke's permit. Eventually I had a template to the scale I needed. Some paint, laminates and machine, Polaroid camera, packets of rub-on letters, slave flashes and a 35mm camera were some of the other items I bought to help produce IDs in different names for the young bloke and myself. They would serve their purpose well.

It was while in Sydney on this occasion that we found out about Andrew's arrest in Melbourne. I was surprised he had actually made it there.

Andrew Jeffrey's behaviour at the Royal Hotel in Footscray, in Melbourne's western suburbs, on 30 November, made the other three recaptured escapees look intellectually gifted. The knucklehead not only boasted to patrons that he was one of the escapees, he also picked a fight outside when they didn't believe him. A passing off-duty police officer tackled him and Jeffrey was duly extradited back to Queensland. The inglorious manner in which the four fugitives were recaptured confirmed to the authorities, media and public what they suspected all along. 'THE GANG WITH ONE BRAIN', one headline called them. 'FOUR DOWN, JUST ABBOTT TO GO', said the *West Australian*.

On 2 December, the Australian Bankers Association announced, at the request of police, a $100,000 reward for information leading to the arrest of Brenden James Abbott.

It was while in Sydney this time that I paid a visit to a brothel. It was the young bloke's first visit, although he had visited the strip club earlier. We made numerous trips to a place called Tiffanys in Albion Street, Surry Hills, on the fringes of the city. He came back from one visit there telling me about a girl he'd seen by the name of Coco. The way he was going on about her I couldn't help myself and had to see what all the fuss was about. Though she was all right, we certainly had different tastes. Coco was an Asian girl and the young bloke seemed to prefer the girls from that part of the world.

While in Sydney, we bought ourselves a suit each for the businessman look when checking into city hotels and flights around the country. Then we made our way back to Melbourne. I made a quick trip to Adelaide and collected my 9mm pistol that I had in safekeeping there and returned to Melbourne. In early December, we made a trip flying business class to another capital city where I had some business to attend to.

On the morning of 19 December, police swarmed over Melbourne Airport and two aircraft after a reported Abbott sighting. Passengers cowered, fearing a shootout, but it was a case of mistaken identity.

That day, on the other side of the country in Perth, Abbott prepared for the day's business. Dressed in a navy-blue suit, he applied a grey moustache and wig to complete the businessman disguise. At 8.50am, he strode calmly up to a female staff member about to enter the north suburban Mirrabooka branch of the Commonwealth Bank on Yirrigan Drive and directed her inside at gunpoint.

He threatened to 'blow the heads off' staff if they did not co-operate, and then targeted the treasury after ordering staff against a wall. He sent them into the toilet and left with a lot of money. $450,000 HEIST: WAS IT ABBOTT? The *West Australian* asked the next day, although police later said the haul was closer to $300,000.

A grey wig, ammunition, black bags and a tie were found by chance in a bin at the rear of a Belmont hardware store the next afternoon. That led to an irritating and lengthy national search to find a blood sample from Abbott for comparison. Months later, when West Australian police finally extracted a sample from Queensland authorities, the test results came up positive: the sweat on the wig was Brenden Abbott's.

The day after the robbery, Queensland Prisons Minister Russell Cooper announced a $50,000 government reward for Abbott's recapture. Cooper was under siege over the SDL breakout, resisting calls for his resignation over an escape that brought national attention to the deficiencies of the Queensland prison system. An election was looming.

Not long after our arrival [in Perth] I managed to turn up some more firearms, one being another 9mm that I gave to the young bloke to keep. It was identical to the one I had, except his was made of stainless steel, and the magazines were interchangeable. We bought a couple of vehicles, one being a late-1980s Land Cruiser. It was eventually put in storage in Alice Springs just prior to Christmas Day, along with two swags, a revolver, an SKS rifle and about three jerry cans of fuel. I wanted this in safekeeping for a number of reasons.

Would the WA police make a connection with it being bought by me? If so, they'll soon release the details of it in the coming weeks. If not, I'll renew the rego under one of the names of the driver's licences I hoped to have in the coming weeks. The rego was to expire in May 1998, so I still had plenty of time. Currently, it was in the name of one of the false licences I had made back in Sydney. Since ID was not required to transfer the vehicle into another name, it wasn't a concern and didn't require a licence number on the transfer form. Vehicle transfers were less of an issue there than in some states.

The drive to Alice Springs was a risk I had to take. Most of it was done through the Outback that brought us into Uluru via the west. From there, it was up to Alice and I wasn't prepared to risk it any further. From there, we caught the Ghan [train] from Alice Springs to Adelaide. On arriving in Adelaide, we booked two sleepers to Melbourne that night. There was a write-up about us in The Advertiser in Adelaide.

The 27 December report, 'Chasing the Running Man', written by the *Courier Mail*'s Paula Doneman and Sean Parnell, was a feature article that traced the anatomy of the SDL escape and the subsequent hunt. While there were many theories, it seemed clear that aside from the Mirrabooka job, no one had the least idea of where the pair was.

As usual, we passed most of the hours of the day in the cinemas. We were now watching some movies for the second time. I steered clear of Adelaide brothels after that close call with the law several years earlier. They may've been legalised by then, but I never bothered looking into it.

We arrived in Melbourne the following morning and, after using the shower facilities at Spencer Street station, the young bloke dressed in a suit and checked into a hotel in the CBD. That night, I made a trip to a place called The Harem and obtained services that helped relieve some of the stress I'd been under for the last few weeks. The young bloke paid a visit to the same place at a different time and was beginning to enjoy the lifestyle of the rich and infamous, as he called it.

By now, I was aware that he was cautious not to attract attention and make no contact with his family or friends. He did, however, send some money to someone, as I did myself. If it was intercepted, or if the recipient notified police, they would only have had an indication of the city it was sent from. I made one phone call to a person who was quite likely under close watch. I did this from a phone box in Melbourne city in the first week of January 1998. After that, I didn't contact anyone else I thought was of interest to the police in their investigations to track me down, as was the case with the young bloke. Later, I found out that police believed I may have been in Melbourne in early 1998 and I guess that was a result of either of the above.

One thing that did concern me was the young bloke's liking for heroin. I don't suggest he was addicted to it and was using it every day; every so often, he'd score in the city. He couldn't believe how easy it was to get in Melbourne. He wasn't even looking for the rubbish the first time he'd scored it. He was in a city video-game den when he was approached and asked if he wanted to buy the crap. From then on, it was never difficult for him to get if he wanted it. Unfortunately, this would lead to major dramas down the track.

Chapter Seventeen

January–April 1998

The success of the Perth 'business trip' allowed Abbott to move on to the next step in his plan to re-establish life as a professional fugitive – a new home base. After settling on Melbourne – a city with which he was familiar, but where he was not actively being hunted – he set about finding a house or unit that would suit their needs. He avoided estate agents – 'those fuckers want to know too much about you' – and eventually found a service that allowed potential renters to deal directly with owners.

I wasn't keen on anything in the suburbs unless it was among factories or had the right surroundings. The average suburban street was out of the question, because most are full of 'Dorrie Evans' [nosy gossiping character from 1970s soap opera Number 96] and 'Deputy Dog' characters [civic-minded citizens who report suspicious activities to police].

It only took a few minutes of wandering around the fashionable inner suburb of Carlton for Abbott to decide that a terrace cottage on Nicholson Street fitted the bill.

After discovering the rear laneway and rear roller door at the back of the place, as well as it being on a major road that had constant noise from cars and trams, I felt it would be perfect as a safe house. We could come and go without attracting the neighbours, unlike the normal suburban house. Every fucker wants to check you out when you come and go in quiet streets. The next hurdle was convincing the owners to let us have it. I never dealt with her personally, but had spoken to her on the phone and figured she was only young. She wanted to rent it out for 12 months minimum, but I spun the yarn that I'd just moved down from Queensland (wasn't lying there) and hadn't found a job yet (more truth). I asked if she would she be prepared to let me have it for six months and, if I found work, I'd extend. If not, I'd be heading back to Queensland. She wasn't interested in that offer until I told her I'd pay the six months' rent and bond in advance. That soon changed her tune and she came back with 'I'll have to discuss it with my boyfriend first.'

Next morning, she rings the motel we're staying at; I knew she would. From then on, I left it with the young bloke to deal with her. He made arrangements to inspect the place with her later that morning. I told him to take his time in looking around, and not just say yes to it straight away. I made him wear his suit and tie and spectacles. He came back to the motel an hour or so later and said the place would be ideal; she let him have it for six months. In the next day or so, money changed hands and the keys were handed over to him.

In mid-January 1998, Berichon paid $4,000 cash as bond and rent in advance for four months on a two-bedroom Victorian terrace cottage at 41 Nicholson Street, Carlton. Neighbours recalled later that the tenants always used the rear-lane access to the cottage. They were quiet, unobtrusive and polite.

The first thing to do was get curtains for the kitchen and dining-room windows. Directly in front of them was the fence dividing us and the neighbour. If he popped his head over the fence, he could see us inside quite easily. Other than that, it was ideal for the next six months. We now had some breathing space. There were still some more hurdles to get over yet, such as getting the gas and electricity on. By this time, I was aware that these utilities would require a driver's licence or another form of ID. I had to come up with something else. If worse came to worst, we'd just go without for a while.

I decided to use the name and licence number of someone being checked out by the police. Listening to the scanner, I would hear checks done on people much of the time. The details they'd air included all I needed when speaking on the phone to get the utilities on. The only problem was: did that person already have the gas and electricity on in his name? I got the details of a few people and, using the White Pages, discovered one bloke was still living with his parents, going by the address on his licence. Since there were no listings in the book for him and he was a cleanskin, I decided he would do.

The ploy worked and the utilities were connected without complications. Both fugitives now also had a mobile phone each and a good stock of Vodaphone start-up packs. Abbott imposed strict rules on their use of the phones, mindful of how a single call from Georgia Smith had led to his downfall in 1995. The phones were only used for calls to each other or to summon taxis, which were always instructed to stop at least several streets from their new Carlton home. A third mobile phone was kept in the cottage and was used as the contact number for their landlord.

The new tenants' first task was to furnish the cottage. Abbott kept the budget tight – no telling when they would have to flee at an instant's notice – but splurged on a $1,000 television for the lounge and a TV aerial connection for the loft, which was his bedroom. They also bought a PlayStation, plenty of games and a VCR for the many long hours they would be spending at home. Next came the purchase of two bicycles for $700 each. Abbott added saddlebags to his to carry groceries until vehicles and good-quality driver's licences could be organised.

Settling in Melbourne also gave Abbott the chance to attend to his dental health, booking in to see a Melbourne dentist for attention to a front tooth which had become discoloured. But, instead of walking out with one crown, as he expected, the dentist insisted he needed five. Berichon, meanwhile, visited a cosmetic surgeon about a scar on his neck, but using heroin as a painkiller after the surgery proved a big mistake – the soluble stitches tore while he was asleep and he woke with a gaping hole in his neck, forcing him to return to the doctor for more; rather than getting rid of the scar, he made it worse.

The other big news in Brendan Berichon's life was his new girlfriend. He met Michelle in a brothel on Swanston Street in the city shortly before they moved into the Carlton cottage, and was soon seeing her outside her working hours. He was smitten and was soon spending a fortune on motel rooms so he could spend nights with her. Michelle told them she was aged 23 and from Laos, but Abbott soon picked her as a Thai, and about ten years older than she claimed. He was not shocked at such dishonesty.

It seemed Michelle had as much to hide as we did. She didn't speak or understand much English. After some weeks, I told the young bloke I had no objections if he brought her home one night. I had a gut feeling she was an illegal immigrant, and, the morning after the first night she stayed, I went into his room while they were still in bed to discuss the day's agenda. I told him I was going to see my friend at Immigration. On hearing that word, I'm sure she shit his bed. It really had her tuning in to see if she could make anything of the conversation. Spotting this, I looked at her and slowly said, 'I'm going to see Immigration.'

All she could muster was: 'I not care.'

I left the room and could hear the young bloke talking and laughing, trying to settle her down and tell her I was joking. From then on, I had no problem with her staying at the cottage.

Within a week, she was staying every night. He was as happy as a pig in shit and I guessed she was his first real girlfriend. If she was still on the game, it would have been during the days, but I think she was doing out calls only. The young bloke said she'd given it away, but I wasn't about to tell him what I thought.

At times, I envied him, seeing how she pampered him. She knew where her bread and butter was. She may even have felt a connection with him. As time went by, I thought that he may have fallen for her and when the time came to leave the country – let alone sort out other business that was in the pipeline – he may decide otherwise. If that was the case, I'd worry about it when the time came.

I longed for the company of a woman, but, from past dealings, I knew better. I would get to that once I got overseas to live my days out. In the meantime, I'd use the services of brothels to fulfil my sexual desires. A relationship while I was a fugitive in this country just wasn't on.

In Abbott's absence, the wheels of Queensland justice continued to turn. On 2 February 1998, a court imposed on him a forfeiture order and pecuniary penalty of $1,240,487 – the balance of the unrecovered money from the Gold Coast robberies of which he was convicted.

The final phase of his plan to revert to a covert life was also its most risky – or, at least, no less risky than returning to his adopted home town to rob a bank while he was the nation's most wanted man. In the mid-1990s, he'd been able to steal driver's licence data cards and laminates simply by leaning over the counter in offices of the Queensland Transport Department. He believed that everything he needed to manufacture a genuine licence with a 'cleanskin' identity could still be obtained from inside a Transport Department office, or the bins outside it. With that in mind, Abbott began planning a trip back to the Gold Coast.

On 5 March, the fugitives caught a sleeper train to Sydney from Melbourne, arriving the following morning. Berichon booked a hotel room near the station and then called Michelle, who said she wanted to join him on the Gold Coast and also meet up with a girlfriend who lived there, a Thai national. Berichon and Michelle flew to the Gold Coast that day and met up, booking a room at a Coolangatta high-rise for four nights. On arrival, Berichon called Abbott to advise that all was 'bagsza' (rhyming slang for 'sweet'). On 7 March, Berichon bought a Holden Camira station wagon for $3,200 in a private sale at Coolangatta. Abbott, meanwhile, caught the train from Sydney to Murwillumbah on the same day.

An hour from Murwillumbah, Abbott called Berichon and told him to meet him at the station. Berichon took the bag from him and returned to the high-rise in a taxi, while Abbott took a separate taxi to the Dolphin Hotel in Tweed Heads.

> My bag contained our tools of the trade, including the young bloke's pistol. He was pleased to have that again when I arrived. I was a little dicey about carrying guns on planes, regardless of whether it was in the baggage hold.

After paying the driver, he walked through the hotel's back car park and towards the main road through Coolangatta. After passing the state border, he glanced into a restaurant he was walking past and saw a female prison officer he remembered from Arthur Gorrie in 1995–96. The woman didn't spot Abbott, who hurried to the building next door – the high-rise building where Berichon was staying. He explained the situation to Berichon and then stationed himself on the unit's balcony until he saw the prison officer emerge with a man and a woman and leave in a late-model Ford sedan. 'I was wondering after that encounter if returning to Queensland was such a good idea after all and said to the young bloke, "Maybe the Northern Territory would've been a better choice."'

Abbott was annoyed that Berichon had forked out $3,200 for a rundown Camira station wagon. He tried to explain the art of haggling to him – without success. Berichon's lack of bargaining skills would cost them more money when they returned to Melbourne.

Berichon told Abbott that he had been seen by someone he knew that day, and they recognised him in spite of his dyed hair. 'As a result of that, he put another dye through his hair. Michelle made it clear she didn't like the blond hair colour and I started to wonder if the story where he ran into that chap was a blowie.'

Early that evening, the fugitives left Michelle at the unit and drove to the Transport Department offices at Burleigh West, but their wheelie bins were next to the building rather than out of sight at the back and Abbott thought passers-by would be able to see anyone rifling through them. The next stop was the Transport Department offices at Bundal. At the front was a telephone box, which provided a good excuse to stop, but this office was in an industrial area and they couldn't hang around for long at that time of night without arousing suspicion. Berichon pretended to make a call while Abbott examined an industrial bin next to the office building. There were rubbish bags inside, but he would need a torch to see the contents – and that would soon have the CrimeStoppers switchboard lighting up. Abbott returned to the phone box and told Berichon, 'Fuck it, we'll check it out tomorrow during the day.'

> We headed back to the unit for the night. If necessary, I was going to contact the local council to find out the rubbish-collection day for Burleigh West. Hopefully, as is usually the case, the bins would be beside the road during the night. It would've been easier to pull up beside the wheelie bins and throw the bags in the car.
>
> Next morning, Sunday, 8 March, I bought the Sunday paper

and soon discovered that maybe the young bloke's yarn yesterday wasn't bullshit. There was a write-up about him and even a photo of him. No mention about being spotted by someone who knew him, but they wouldn't believe that [based on what was written in the story]. It could've been a coincidence, too.

In the 8 March report, Brisbane's *Sunday Mail* ran the headline 'Cashed-up Abbott on Indon isle'. The story stated, 'Police believe prison escapee Brendon Abbott has left Australia and may be hiding on the tourist island of Lombok. The mother of the 20-year-old Brisbane man believed to be travelling with Abbott said yesterday police had told her Abbott had fled the country. Sources have told the *Sunday Mail* that police intelligence reports have placed Abbott in Lombok after travelling via Bali ... Julie Berichon, of the southern-Brisbane suburb of Salisbury, discounted a claim that Abbott and her son were in a homosexual relationship. "He's been over four months with Abbott. He's given away our family for him, his freedom for him and his whole life for this man. I just can't understand why he chose Abbott over our family."'

After reading the paper on Sunday morning, they returned to the Bundal Transport Office again; Berichon returned to the phone box while Abbott made a beeline for the bin. He reached in and started tearing bags open and immediately spotted Polaroid negatives from the licence photos.

Spotting those got me so excited I considered having a toss. I quickly made my way to the car and passing the phone box, I told the young bloke 'bagsza'. We hopped in the car and I decided we'd go back that night for them. I needed to buy a torch so the young bloke could jump in the bin and grab the negatives.

Their next stop was the Southport Transport Centre, the largest of its kind on the Gold Coast and surrounded by a cyclone fence. Abbott scanned the area and spotted the industrial bins – and also an adjacent vacant block with scrub on it that would give him enough cover to cut the fence and enter the compound. But, depending on how things went at Bundal that night, it might not be necessary. They spent the rest of the day at the unit, although Berichon and Michelle were relaxed enough to go to the beach for a few hours. Berichon raided the Bundal bin that night, and they returned to the unit to examine 20 to 30 negatives. Abbott decided that not enough of them matched their age groups, so later that night they headed to the Southport complex again.

The young bloke quickly hopped out of the car and I drove off, heading east on the Nerang–Southport Road, then parked near some houses in the area. He called me on the two-way radio and told me 'bagsza'. I gave him instructions to just sit in the bushes after he'd got the bags and, as I'm just about to pull up, I'll give him a call. As I pulled up, he came out with two green garbage bags, opened the back door and tossed them over in the back, got in and I drove off.

Berichon told him there were still more bags in the bin, so Abbott stopped at some shops at Southport to check to see if they would need to go back for more. They were in luck – there were handfuls of negatives in the bags. The next stop was a phone box to ring Michelle, who had been visiting her friend for the afternoon. But Berichon couldn't make head or tail of the address her friend was trying to tell him. He shook his head, mystified, and handed the phone to Abbott. He soon worked out what she was trying to say and, before handing the phone back to Berichon, told her, 'OK, thank you. We see you soon and we bring Immigration.'

When they arrived at the address, Michelle jumped into the back seat and slapped Abbott across the back of the head in mock punishment. She was soon complaining about the stink of rubbish in the back seat but had to tolerate it until they arrived at the high-rise again. Abbott parked in the street behind the building, near the fire escape. They walked around to the front entrance and, while Michelle returned to the room, Abbott and Berichon made their way to the fire escape from another floor and then went down the stairs to the ground-floor rear exit. Berichon held the door open and Abbott quickly took the bags up to their room.

I took them into the bathroom and sorted the negatives from the rubbish. There were also a few bonuses. Some actual photographs that had flaws, one complete, and a couple torn in half, but, with glue or tape, they could be stuck back together. They were perfect to use as a guide for making the licences. I still had the young bloke's learner's permit but it was laminated. After sorting them out, I went through the dates of birth and, surprisingly, we ended up with about half a dozen each that would suit us. I thought this would suffice. Months later, we could get more; there were plenty of Transport Department offices in Queensland and the NT. Having an actual licence was the priority for now. With that, we could cover far more ground without the fear of being pulled over and having nothing to show police other than a couple of 9mm pistols.

So far, so good. I was feeling good about it, but the young bloke didn't really understand the importance of our score so far. I considered our find as valuable as gold. Next was getting the actual laminates used by the Transport Department. I didn't expect this to be as easy, but it would save me a lot of fucking around making my own. I even considered doing that, but, come Tuesday morning, we were back at the Burleigh West Transport Office.

The office interior was the same as Abbott remembered from the last time he visited, in early 1995. There were security cameras but he wasn't concerned by them. The area where the licences were put together was next to the enquiries counter, which was not always attended. But security appeared to have been stepped up and there was no sign of any data cards or laminates. After a quick scan of the area, Abbott went back outside and explained the set-up to Berichon, then went back inside and joined the enquiries queue. Berichon sauntered in soon after and Abbott indicated the area where he believed the laminates might be stored.

Berichon didn't hesitate, jumped the counter with a small backpack in his hand and squatted behind the counter out of sight as he began rifling through drawers. Abbott scanned the staff for a reaction. Amazingly, none of them had seen Berichon. But an elderly woman near Abbott did, and she nudged her husband, who wasn't interested. Berichon soon found what he was looking for and stuffed an entire tray of laminates into his backpack, slipped it on his back and jumped the counter again.

He caught the old girl looking at him and he smiled at her and then disappeared through the door. I couldn't believe it – no one spotted him going in or out, other than the old girl. I stuck around for about 15 to 30 seconds before making an exit myself, but not before old Mrs Deputy caught the attention of a staff member and started to explain what she had witnessed. Her husband looked embarrassed by the fact she was giving the mail. I casually walked out, no one the wiser I was in on it.

Abbott returned to the Camira and drove off to a pre-arranged rendezvous point at a nearby shopping centre. He called up Berichon on the two-way and within a couple of minutes, they were on their way back to the high-rise.

I couldn't wait to get there to see what he scored. When I saw the quantity and type of laminates, I was impressed. And I was more than impressed with his courage and effort. The laminates he grabbed were for heavy-vehicle licences, learners' permits, standard open licences and even some 18-plus ID laminates.

The mission was complete. Michelle was sent to Coolangatta Airport that afternoon to return to Melbourne, and the fugitives booked a sleeper on the express train to Sydney. After a careful search of the unit to ensure nothing was left behind, they drove to the coach pick-up area at Tweed Heads. Berichon took the bags and caught the coach to Murwillumbah, while Abbott drove the Camira to the Dolphin Hotel car park and left the keys in it. He then caught a taxi to Murwillumbah, telling the driver he was on his way to say goodbye to a friend. For a third time, the fugitives crossed the Queensland–NSW border undetected.

After arriving in Sydney the next morning, they put their bags in the luggage holding area and went to book a sleeper to Melbourne that night. But sleepers were booked out for two nights, so Abbott reluctantly accepted two seats. They passed the day the usual way – watching a couple of movies – and had lunch at a restaurant. Abbott also had something else in mind.

Before the train left that evening, Abbott and Berichon stopped at the terminal's newsagents to buy some reading material. Standing at the counter, Berichon nudged Abbott and showed him the *Who* magazine he was about to buy – there was a pointer on the front page to a story on Abbott and photos of him inside.

I was starting to feel a little uncomfortable. I'd be sitting on a train with people walking past to the buffet car and toilets for the next ten hours or more. The young bloke assured me I looked nothing like the photo in the magazine, but that did nothing to ease my concerns. We departed Sydney and, some time later, I made a trip to the buffet car. You wouldn't read about it, the Who magazine was on sale in there and the bloke serving was actually reading the magazine. My disguise obviously worked, though, because I got off at Spencer Street station without being greeted by police. After that trip, the young bloke swore he'd never take a sit-up trip on an inter-city train again. He had turned into a snob in a matter of months.

They caught separate taxis to Carlton and met several streets from the cottage. Abbott approached cautiously and checked his 'security tape' on the doors; their home was undisturbed.

It was then I finally felt I could wind down. It was a relief to be back in what was my safe domain. Since leaving for Queensland, I'd been highly strung the whole time. It drained me and I felt like I needed a holiday.

The trip went better than expected and it was time to go to work on the next project. It required buying all the equipment I'd used in the past when making ID. This time, though, I had computer skills and that would save me so much time and effort. I bought a laptop and printer and the Microsoft Works program that I was familiar with from SDL, doing computer courses and working as the librarian.

After a few days, I had just about everything I needed. In just over a week, I had the template complete and then it just required photographing the different disguises the young bloke and myself would use. He had two or three different looks, as did I. He had different-coloured hair, the last being peroxide blond again. With me, I had a full head of hair, the balding look and the completely bald look. The photos went to different places to be developed and enlarged to five by ten. These days, a decent digital camera and better printer would've saved us the hassle. It was just a matter of sticking the enlarged photo on to the template and taking a photo, then cutting the developed Polaroid photo to licence size and laminating it. For the next licence, it was simply a matter of changing the details on the template to another name and all the particulars, including our handwritten signatures in that name, then photograph and laminate again.

Berichon had serious doubts about whether Abbott could make licences identical to the real thing, but he changed his tune as soon as he saw the first one. They were so good that, later, Queensland police initially suspected that someone in the Transport Department had supplied them to Abbott.

Australia's most wanted men now had plenty of cash, reliable false identities and disguises, weapons, a home base and the confidence to travel. And the authorities had no inkling of their location or their plans. What could possibly go wrong?

Chapter Eighteen

April–May 1998

In *Postcard From Carlton*, published in *The Age* later in 1998, feature writer Gary Tippet wrote, 'At Russell Street, just up from Bourke Street, Berichon watched and waited, checking out the heroin deals. After a while, he sidled up to one user, a 17-year-old street kid, and made a business proposal. You score the smack, he said, and I'll pay and share it with you. The kid thought that sounded like a good deal. Mark, as he knew Berichon, was not much of a user – he would shoot up a little hit then throw up – but a relationship soon developed.'

Abbott:

He met up with some street kid who he'd get to buy the gear for him. Prior to him buying the crap that way, he used to deal directly with a young Asian girl he met in video-game dens. Apparently, he would approach her and then follow her through city arcades or laneways before she'd do the transaction. He told me she'd take the money off him and, in front of him, put her hands down her pants and dig a cap out of her pouch. The caps were wrapped up in balloon material.

Many times I told him that I wasn't happy with the fact he was buying the shit in that manner, due to my fears that, if the cops had her under surveillance, he could get busted. His only response to that was: 'It won't happen, I'm careful.' I was a little pissed off by that and I warned him, if he brought any heat due to that crap, I'd be on my way.

On 4 April, Berichon went to Oakleigh, in Melbourne's southeast, and bought a silver Ford Fairmont Ghia station wagon, which was advertised in the *Trading Post*. On 14 April, he bought a 1983 blue Toyota Land Cruiser in Bendigo, telling the owner he caught the train from Melbourne. Stacks of crisp $50 notes were used in both sales. Too many stacks, according to Abbott.

The Ford needed some work before passing a safety certificate. He paid far too much for the Land Cruiser wagon and it required thousands to be spent on it to get it up to scratch – but it passed the inspection anyway. The young bloke had no mechanical skills whatsoever, so I couldn't expect him to spot what would be obvious to me. He was only 20 and still had a lot to learn. I didn't want to buy the vehicles for fear of being identified, either then or later down the track. The Land Cruiser was to get the most attention. It ran on LPG and the bottle was behind the back seat. I planned to disconnect that and pull the bottle out, because a V8 diesel engine was going in, along with a long-range fuel tank. Both cars were to be fitted with two-way radios. We had some plans in the works that required us travelling some distance and then lying low in the scrub for a period. I also planned to buy a heavy-duty camper trailer.

On 18 April 1998, the *Good Weekend* – the flagship magazine of Fairfax papers *The Age* and *Sydney Morning Herald* – ran a cover story with a picture of Abbott, aged 13, standing proudly in front of a red car with black stripes; it posed the question: 'How did this boy grow up to be Australia's most wanted man?'

Frank Robson's article, titled 'The Making of an Anti-Hero', was based mainly on an interview with Abbott's sisters, Diane and Janet. The in-depth piece was the first time anyone from the family had spoken at length to the media. Janet, in particular, said plenty about her father, mother and siblings.

As Abbott pored over the story in the Carlton cottage that weekend, he boiled with rage. His sister's portrayal of the Abbott family's early years was nothing like the way he remembered his childhood. The following year, in a rare letter to his father, Abbott wrote:

'[While in Melbourne] I read an article in the local paper (I think it was The Age) regarding myself, my childhood and even yourself had a mention. To say the least, I was appalled by what was written and totally disgusted with Janet and Diane [Diane later clarified her role in the story with her brother] for what they said and for even taking part in such an interview. Over the years, there were many stories written about me, but this was the first where family history was made public that I knew of. What was the most concerning were the untruths describing yourself and the way you used to discipline me. No doubt these type of comments, regardless of how untrue they are, would have been distressing to you. If it means anything to you, I just want to make it clear I've never had any disrespect or grudges towards you. As you and I both know, you never treated me as described in that article.'

So Brenden Abbott was in a dark mood on Monday, 20 April 1998, after his weekend of brooding about what he'd read. The world could say what it wanted about him; he didn't care. But he couldn't abide members of his family publicly throwing dirt at others. He headed out for the day, intent on scavenging parts for the Land Cruiser from wreckers' yards. Berichon, meanwhile, had instructions to drop off the Ford to have its windows tinted and also to call the landlady to arrange a time for the cottage to be inspected. Berichon's final task was to track down his mate in the city and score.

An hour or so after we left the house, he contacted me on my mobile and informed me he'd phoned her and the inspection would be the next day. He also told me he couldn't find his mate and would soon be heading back home. Not long after, I received another phone call to say he'd found his mate and they were in a cab heading out to a suburb of Melbourne, Box Hill. I told him that he shouldn't be going out there with him, just send him out. He replied with: 'We're already in the cab, I'll be all right.' I told him I wasn't happy with it and left it at that.

An unmarked police car passing the Box Hill Central shopping centre swung towards four men loitering in front of a laundrette, which was a known drug hangout. Berichon and his mate slipped away, but, instead of leaving the area, they kept looking. He was determined to score and it seemed his habit was not as casual as it once was. The persistence paid off and they eventually scored half a gram.

The police hadn't left the area, though. A few streets from where they first crossed paths, Sergeant Scott Roberts and Senior Constable Peter Baltas sighted the pair again. As the national manhunt for Abbott and Berichon continued, the media had dubbed the gangly kid 'Abbott's apprentice'. Now these policemen would put the apprentice's knowledge and skills to the test. Confronted by the officers, Berichon produced a fake Queensland driver's licence, but was unable to control the adrenalin pulsing through his body. Baltas looked closely at the shaky kid. He told him to empty his pockets and take off the bumbag. Berichon put the bag on the ground in front of him, his mind and heart racing.

Abbott would have known exactly what to do. But, as he bent down, Berichon only saw one course of action in which he could walk away from this. He unzipped the bag, revealing two spare magazines and rolls of $50 notes, and then – believing that the cop could see the ammunition – reached for the prized 9mm semi-automatic pistol Abbott gave him as a birthday gift. Baltas had time to ask, 'Is that a replica?' before Berichon flicked off the safety and changed all their lives forever. Baltas, standing only a metre away, took hits in the leg and the thigh.

In his book *Dirty Dozen*, Paul Anderson quotes Baltas: 'He let a few go at me, then he turned to the right, because Scott was at the back of the car checking the other bloke. He shot at Scott. One [round] went through the boot of the car as he worked his way up. Another went through a piece of paper Scott was holding and through his bicep. Berichon's mate pissed off to the west. Berichon went east through a house. Scott pulled out his gun and let off four. I pulled mine and pointed it in Berichon's direction, but he wasn't visible to me, so I didn't fire. One of his shots, the one that went through my love handle, actually hit my trigger guard, so I'm not sure if the gun would have fired anyway.'

Berichon later told police, 'I was fired upon as I ran away. I heard bullets – two bullets, I think – go past my head. I felt the wind of the bullets going past my head.'

Inside the bumbag – which Berichon dropped when he began shooting – were 32 rounds of ammunition in the two magazines, $3,696 in cash, a mobile phone, an address book, house keys and a wallet containing, among other things, a fake Queensland driver's licence.

Berichon ran fast and hard, blinded with adrenalin. *Escape. Get back to Abbott.* He focused on the two thoughts and then stuck a gun in a woman's face, ordering her to drive him to Carlton. Berichon leaped from the car in Nicholson Street, near a block of high-rise commission units.

Abbott was furious. He'd told Berichon last time this sort of shit was just not on. An hour after Berichon's call on his way to Box Hill, Abbott tried him again and the phone rang out. He tried again half an hour later and the same thing happened. He continued his parts hunt and was in a wrecker's office when the call finally came. 'As soon as I heard his voice, I knew there was a problem. He told me to remove my SIM card and to get home ASAP. That alone told me there was big dramas and not to make enquiries on the phone.'

Abbott was only a few minutes from home. He pulled up a few streets away when he saw the police helicopter circling overhead, briefly considering if going home was such a wise move.

A short time later, he opened the rear roller door to find Berichon crouched under the opened wheelie-bin lid, providing cover from the helicopter.

He rushed towards me, telling me to open the door to the cottage. Then he told me he shot two cops. He tried to explain what happened and I indicated to be quiet and nodded inside. When we got inside, he told me he'd just shot two cops and thought he may've killed one of them. Then I asked for his gun and smelled it to find it had just recently been fired. I dropped the magazine out and found it contained one round and there was one in the spout of the pistol. He then told me about some woman he bailed up and got her to drop him off near Carlton – that explained the helicopter. Then came the news I didn't need to hear – he'd dropped his wallet and bumbag at the scene.

Berichon later said, 'He was quite calm about it and said we had better go … leave the house, because the helicopter was flying around the Carlton area.'

Abbott's mind raced. He knew the landlady's phone numbers were in the bumbag, along with a new identity Berichon had used to buy the Land Cruiser. That wiped the cottage and the 4WD. But the Ford's owner hadn't worried about the paperwork and left it for them to sort out, so that was still one vehicle they could safely use; they would need to pick it up from the tinting place. They packed quickly. Abbott had enough clothes to fill an overnight bag and a suitcase, but Berichon – despite Abbott's advice – had a roomful of clothes, runners and CDs which had to be left behind. Abbott also grabbed the laptop and all the licence-making gear, leaving only the printer.

He brought the Land Cruiser to the adjacent street, loaded it up and they left. Five minutes down the road, Abbott turned around – he'd left something behind. Berichon pleaded with him to keep going, convinced that the police would be all over the cottage any minute. Abbott reassured him that it would take them time to work through the evidence and make the right connections; it was still safe. He parked around the corner and then walked in through the front door, straight to the open fireplace in the kitchen/dining area. He reached in and plucked $2,000 from a steel ledge in the chimney, then returned quickly to the Cruiser.

A short time later, Abbott paid for the tinting job and drove off in the Falcon, after swapping vehicles with Berichon, who then followed Abbott to the Melbourne Airport car park. All their gear was transferred to the Ford station wagon and they were away, fugitives again, heading for Dandenong, east of Melbourne.

I'd recently caught up with one of my past business partners and had something in the making with him. I had to advise him of the sudden change of plans. By the time I got to his house, it was nightfall. His wife answered the door and invited me in without hesitation. I had interrupted their dinner and walked in to find my mate feeding his baby son. I gave him the nod that I needed to talk and we headed for the lounge. As soon as I mentioned the shooting, he said he first thought that it may've been me involved. When he heard it was the young bloke – who he'd never met – he gave me a piece of advice that I knew was right: part company with him. I told [the associate] I couldn't do that because I owed him – I wouldn't be out if it wasn't for him. I also told him that he had no idea how to avoid the cops as yet and, if these pricks in Victoria got him, there'd be a good chance they'd kill him. It was then that I found out that the cops were OK and their injuries weren't life threatening.

Abbott and his unnamed associate arranged to postpone their plans until around Christmas. They shook hands and parted, the associate wishing Abbott well.

I walked a few blocks back to the car and decided to head for Adelaide that night. After crossing to the western side of Melbourne, we filled up the car and drove west. After I drove across the South Australian border, I felt a little better. I had thought there was the possibility of a roadblock. The young bloke had a few hours there where he didn't say a word. I think the situation finally hit home and he thought he'd never see Michelle again. He swore he'd never touch the heroin again and apologised to me for not listening and getting us in this situation. I thought he was concerned that I may leave him posted. The thought honestly hadn't crossed my mind at the time, getting us clear of the drama that was about to unfold was my concern. Within the next day or two, I knew our names and photos would be over the news across the nation.

Abbott knew they needed to move quickly. The more distance they put between themselves and Melbourne, the better. Around 4am, he decided to stop just past Murray Bridge, 78 kilometres from Adelaide, to rest for a couple of hours. They could have continued to Adelaide, but Abbott didn't want to drive into the city's deserted streets – safer to wait until peak hour built up so they had some cover. He pulled into a parking/lookout area and lay down on the back seat, while Berichon reclined his seat, and they both tried to doze off. Less than 30 minutes later, a car's headlights swept into the parking area and then settled on the Ford. 'Then it became obvious it was a cop car, a sedan. The young bloke shits and yells, "Cops!" and grabs his pistol from out of the glove box. I told him to "put that fucking thing away".'

Abbott climbed out the rear-passenger door and the police car pulled up next to him. The lone male officer said G'day to Abbott and then asked him why he had parked there. Abbott explained he was tired from driving and was catching up on sleep. Satisfied, the officer continued on his way, blissfully unaware that he had almost become the third police officer in less than 24 hours to face the wrong end of Brendan Berichon's pistol.

Abbott waited a few minutes and then decided to press on – there'd be no more sleep after that surprise interlude. The next stop was a service station in the Adelaide Hills at Eagle on the Hill. Abbott bought a drink and *The Advertiser*, which carried the latest story about the manhunt: 'Police last night converged on a block of flats in suburban Melbourne where they suspected a man who shot two police officers was holed up in a laundry. The laundry was locked and had fresh blood on the outside door handle. But there was no trace of the man.'

The news was hours old, but at least Abbott now knew the police had a slow start to their pursuit. Because, once the cottage was found and their involvement was established, their faces would be all over the papers and TV again.

Abbott then drove through the city to Largs Bay, near Port Adelaide, to consider his next move, even driving around the area looking at holiday units, but he rejected the idea. (Coincidentally, Adelaide detectives believe one of Abbott's closest associates lived in Semaphore, adjacent to Largs Bay, but the link was never confirmed.) The next stop was a truck stop near Gepps Cross, where they had breakfast – although a tense and nauseated Berichon couldn't keep his meal down. While ploughing through his bacon and eggs, Abbott reached a decision – they would head to Alice Springs to pick up the Land Cruiser that was in storage there. Then they would return to Adelaide to buy a camper trailer and go bush for at least a month.

It was here that I made another decision that I would later realise was bad judgement. If we had a woman with us, she could help in being a cover with booking into motel rooms for the next few days before we're ready to head bush after getting what we need. The police would be looking for two blokes travelling together. A woman booking the rooms would save us putting our faces on show, or even one of us wearing spectacles and being with her, a couple. But, I thought, has the young bloke been keeping to the rules with the phone calls etc?

Abbott grilled Berichon: Was there anything in the bumbag, wallet or address book that could connect Michelle to them? Berichon said there wasn't. Abbott persisted. 'They'll be kicking her door in today looking for us,' he told him.

Berichon was firm: 'There's no way they'd be able to link her to me.' But had he ever called her on his phone? 'No.'

I asked him if he was certain about that and he seemed adamant he hadn't left any links to her. Then I hit him with the idea about bringing her over to join us. He asked if I was sure about wanting to do that. I outlined my plan and stressed that, if he was certain he left no links in what he dropped at the shooting or at the house, all would be fine. If it was otherwise, they'd be on to her in no time. He guaranteed the cops would make no connection. I then decided we'd get her over to Adelaide with us. He got on the phone to her and then again later on to find out the time she'd be arriving. His appetite soon returned and he managed to keep his food down.

But the fugitives had forgotten one vital detail – Berichon had a picture of Michelle in his wallet. Abbott had even seen it, but neither of them remembered it. As a result, two white men and an Asian woman were about to become flashing beacons on the police radar. Across the nation, police would tail up to 150 young men travelling with Asian women over the next few days.

After a close examination of the contents of Berichon's bumbag, the cottage was raided on Tuesday, 21 April – the day after the shooting – by the special-response squad. It still contained enough evidence to point straight in the direction of Abbott and Berichon – their fingerprints, for a start – and, on Wednesday, police announced publicly that the pair had been at the cottage and also that Berichon was the suspected Box Hill gunman. The headlines changed from 'POLICE HUNT GUNMAN' and 'OFFICERS SHOT IN THE STREET' to 'BOX HILL GUNMAN FLEES WITH POSTCARD BANDIT'; 'ABBOTT'S APPRENTICE MORE WANTED THAN HIS MASTER' and 'BANDIT PAIR'S COVER BLOWN'.

The much-travelled and streetwise Detective Senior Sergeant Brian Rix told the Melbourne media: 'These two are Australia's most wanted men. We believe at this stage Abbott and Berichon are together. We believe they are at least armed with the 9mm pistol and more likely with revolvers as well.'

Abbott and Berichon picked up Michelle from Adelaide Airport that night. They stayed in a hotel and then rose early the next morning to set out for Alice Springs. A police officer parked on the side of the highway, on the outskirts of Port Augusta, made Abbott nervous, but they passed unchallenged. They stopped for lunch in the town and, later that afternoon, booked a room for the night further down the highway. They arrived in Alice Springs on Thursday, 23 April, and Berichon and Michelle booked two rooms at the same motel where

Abbott had stayed with Reynolds and Ayuda in 1989. 'I went and checked the Land Cruiser out that was in storage and to retrieve the rego papers, because I knew it wasn't far off expiring. Then I tried to start it up, but the battery was fucked. I went and bought a new battery and fitted it and it fired up in no time.'

Driving around the town the following day looking for a phone box, Abbott pricked up his ears at a radio news report that said police had a new lead in the hunt for the fugitives.

> *I've leaned over to turn the radio up and I remember saying sarcastically to myself, 'Oh yeah, I'd like to hear this', thinking they've got nothing. Next thing, they read out the rego of the car I'm in. I shat. How the fuck did they get on to this car? The mention of it having tinted windows was the giveaway. Did the young bloke have a card given to him after dropping it off? Or was it through the mobiles either one of us had used in booking it in? Whatever, it was the least of my worries. I had to get rid of the car sooner than planned.*

He drove to the storage shed – keeping one eye on the rear-view mirror – and then swapped the Ford for the Cruiser. On his return to the motel, he told Berichon about the loss of the Ford. Berichon had been in to town to buy two tickets to Perth, where he was going to re-register the Cruiser in one of the false identities that had not been compromised. Michelle was to accompany him and, after they returned, they would head down to Adelaide. 'Then that night, the news showed a photo of Michelle. I couldn't fucking believe it. What else could go wrong? They put no name to the face; I felt they didn't have any idea of who she was yet. The photo they showed was from his wallet. I remembered seeing it myself in his wallet some time ago, but forgot about it until that night on the news.'

The photo made Berichon more nervous than he already was; he no longer wanted to fly to Perth the next day. Abbott was rapidly running out of patience.

> *I had told him, 'Either you both go or one of you go. It has to be done.' It was pretty stressful. The young bloke had kept me in the dark about certain things and the police were getting more and more information. But the following morning, I told him to scrub the trip to Perth. The new plan was Darwin and then to*

Broome. Both places had high populations of Asians, tourists as well as locals. Michelle wouldn't be out of place in either town. They caught the coach to Darwin that night and I followed as far as possible before I had to pull over and sleep on the side of the road in a swag [sleeping bag].

The next day I arrived at Katherine. I had told the young bloke to book a room at the Travelodge on his arrival in Darwin. I tried to phone him at Katherine, but couldn't get in touch. Obviously he'd forgotten to turn the phone on – or worse had happened.

(The mobile we had was the one I used in Melbourne – I had put a new SIM card in it. But, in recent years, I think. even after changing a SIM card, the authorities can still trace the phone itself by its own electronic fingerprint, IMEI, or International Mobile Equipment Identity, regardless if you change the SIM card. Never stop learning!)

Abbott stuck to the plan and eventually got hold of Berichon on the phone in Darwin. Abbott arrived in the city and the trio stayed together in a room at the Travelodge on The Esplanade. The next day, 27 April, Berichon and Michelle flew to Broome to re-register the Land Cruiser. The couple booked into room 1 at the Roebuck Bay Hotel on Monday, 27 April, paying $330 cash for three nights. The Do Not Disturb sign went up and staff only saw them to pass fresh towels through a half-open door.

The lack of mobile-phone coverage again hampered Abbott's efforts to contact Berichon, but the younger fugitive called Abbott at the Travelodge when he realised the problem.

Abbott: 'I told him I was checking out of the Travelodge on Tuesday morning and would sleep in the swag out of town during the night. He wasn't able to fly back to Darwin on the same day he transferred the registration because of a lack of flights.'

Amid all the drama of the Box Hill shooting, the fugitives' narrow escape and the intensified nationwide police hunt, the *Courier Mail*'s Paula Doneman had a story that topped all other angles. 'ABBOTT SUSPECTED OF COOPER KILL PLOT' appeared on the front page of 27 April: 'The plan: The escape of five prisoners, including Brendon Abbott, last November was the first step in a plan by a major drug syndicate to launch armed attacks on Queensland jails to free the country's top armed robbers and assassinate Prisons Minister Russell Cooper.

'The criminals: Australia's most wanted man, Brendon Abbott, and Frank Post, ranked as Australia's number-two armed robber, were the main targets to be freed in a series of jailbreaks …

'A top-secret Queensland police operation involving up to 60 of the state's elite crimefighters uncovered the plot in February. The plot was outlined by prison sources to the *Courier Mail* two months ago and confirmed by police yesterday.'

When he heard it, Abbott could hardly believe it.

What crap. Fucking politicians will pull any trick to save their arses at any election. With the Labor Party running full steam with the escape from SDL, Cooper and the other parasites in the party pulled a beauty out of their bag of dirty tricks. When I became aware of the story, I told Berichon that even those who get around with their heads up their arses will see through that one. It was in Darwin I'd become aware of this bullshit yarn. I couldn't help but think that they were justifying putting me off when – or if – they caught up with me. Wasn't a nice thought. But months later, it was revealed that it was the typical political bullshit the masses got fed every day and tend to swallow.

Russell Cooper was supposedly the target of the 'assassination plot' because of the security clampdown at Sir David Longland in the wake of the November escape. The previous December, the *Herald Sun* quoted a 'jail source' in Brisbane who said Abbott was now despised by other inmates: 'He promised the world and he wiped everyone. Everyone he left behind in that unit has had to pay the piper.'

The rest of the media treated the story as if it stank to high heaven. On 2 May, in a piece headed 'ASSASSINATION PLOT'S ODD RING', the *Australian*'s seasoned crime writer Mark Whittaker reported, 'A Queensland police spokesman said, "a very firm decision had been made to make no further comment … maybe too much has been said already." Queensland Opposition spokesman Tom Barton accused Mr Cooper of "setting up a scapegoat to cover his inability to manage the prison system if there were problems between now and the election".'

Months later, Queensland police would reluctantly admit the blindingly obvious: that all the claims were 'bullshit'. Berichon re-registered the 4WD in Broome on Tuesday, 28 April, without any hitches. Berichon and Michelle were booked to fly back to Darwin the following morning, but Berichon suddenly got cold feet. 'The morning after he transferred the vehicle, I was watching the *Today* show. (I had a small portable TV in the Land Cruiser.) Michelle's name was revealed. I expected that was coming. No good regretting she was with us – did that back in Alice Springs.'

Abbott rang Berichon, who was also aware of the news and 'spinning like a top'. He didn't like Abbott's suggestion that they continue with the plan and return to Darwin, but reluctantly complied. On Berichon and Michelle's tense flight to Darwin, an adjacent passenger was reading a newspaper with their faces plastered all over it. But Berichon looked nothing like the shaven-headed sullen teenager in his mug shot and they arrived without incident.

Abbott says, 'I picked him up out the front of the airport. I was wearing a white, long-haired wig a lot of times up in Darwin, with baseball cap on top and sunglasses. He nicknamed me Poiter, from that comedy show with Eric Bana.'

Abbott told Berichon to book a unit at Luma Luma Apartments, a high-rise complex in the Darwin CBD, where he and Michelle would be staying for a few days, and where Abbott had earlier got to know one of the local working girls – 'a Chinese piece, pretty one at that'.

He and Michelle booked into the room and we stayed in there for a few nights together. In the next few days, I found a camper trailer that was for sale. First, though, I wanted the owner to get some details of it right with regards to the rego papers. I didn't want to be pulled over and, because of the discrepancies, it could have been enough to have the law look into it further. The owner sorted the problem out for us. I also bought a car fridge-freezer and had to get a fuse connection fitted. Also had a new muffler installed on the Cruiser. The day we bought the trailer, I got the young bloke to book a room for me at the Top End Hotel. The trailer was delivered there by a tow truck – I needed to remove the tow ball off the Land Cruiser because the trailer hitch was different. I wasn't able to remove the ball and it required a gas axe to get it off the following day.

On Friday, 1 May, Berichon booked a room for Abbott at the Top End Hotel in Mitchell Street, Darwin, at 4.40pm. Unknown to the fugitives, Northern Territory police were mobilising a massive search operation for them. And Abbott believes it was the actions of

Michelle in Broome a few days earlier that led to the police net closing on Darwin – a city with a distinct lack of alternative road exits.

> *[Michelle] rang her girlfriend on the Gold Coast ... My under-standing is that, after the photograph of Michelle was televised, a day or so later, someone's come forward and identified her. Maybe through that or an informant they became aware of her friend on the Gold Coast. They visited her friend and she advised them about receiving the call from Michelle a few days earlier. The police then had all the phone carriers search their customer records (an easy task) to see if any customers' accounts listed Michelle's friend's phone number. It's most likely that Telecom's check listed a call made from the Roebuck Bay Hotel around the time she said she got the call from Michelle. The WA police were informed and visited the Roebuck Bay, only to find they'd already checked out. A check on the phone account for that room would show a cab being called prior to booking out. Enquiries with the cab company would reveal they were taken to the airport. Only one flight was leaving at that time and it was going to Darwin. That's why they focused on Darwin.*

Commander Gary Manison, of the Northern Territory police, has a very different version of how his officers were brought into the case:

> *Abbott was unfortunate, to say the very least. Some interesting things happened and his luck ran out. There was [another] phone call picked up, allegedly from the Gulf [of Carpentaria] country in Queensland. This guy [a senior detective] from WA made a mistake. They analysed the call and said it was Abbott's voice. I wouldn't have started the operation otherwise. The whole operation was predicated on this. So I made the decision to put roadblocks up in that area. But Abbott was in WA at the time [Abbott denies this]. And then he came into town [Darwin].*

(Abbott is dubious: 'I don't believe this at all. I believe they just don't want to reveal their tactics with regard to the phones.')
Abbott:

> *At the motel, I'd just finished some minor work on the car before the trip. I was supposed to go to Alice Springs. I was going to*

pick the young bloke up at the airport there. [Michelle] was flying out of Darwin the next day, and he was making her think he was flying out in the morning, when actually there wasn't a flight until after hers left. She was going to Brisbane or the Gold Coast and the flight to Alice Springs was after hers. He was to leave her in the morning and stay in the room I had at the Top End Hotel. That afternoon, Berichon was to catch his flight to Alice Springs. After Michelle arrived on the Gold Coast, the police would have eventually caught up with her. I was sure she'd give us up about our last movements. That would've led police on a wild goose chase. When I picked Berichon up from the airport at Alice Springs, we were to head off towards Ayers Rock and set up a campsite behind a hill somewhere out that way. I had planned to remain there a month or so. If we needed supplies, we would have made a trip to the supermarket at the township at Ayers Rock. That was basically the plan.

While I was working under the car, a bloke was standing next to the Cruiser, some 20 feet away, and was staring up at the top floor of the Top End. I thought it was odd because he stood there for five minutes. (I later recognised him as a jack. He was waiting to see if there was anyone else in the room I was staying in.) I then went to the laundromat to get some washing done. After I put the load in, I went into the café at the end of the shops (Harriet Place) and had a snack.

I then used a phone box around the corner from the shops. Because there were no phone books to find the Luma Luma number, I rang the operator. As I often did, I scratched the number into my wallet. I then phoned the young bloke and let him know of my intentions – I was leaving once I'd finished washing my clothes. As I was on the phone, I spotted an older-model Japanese sedan parked in the corner to my right. There was one person sitting in the car and thought it was odd him sitting there like that. He then drove off after a few moments and, when I hung up the phone, I walked over to where he was parked and squatted to the height at which he would have been sitting. From the position where he was parked, it was possible to see the back of the Cruiser where I parked it. By now, I knew there was something odd going on, but hoped it was just another of those paranoid moments I'd experienced many times over the years.

I went to the laundromat again and then to the supermarket to buy some cereal, milk, sugar and orange juice for my trip and put them in the fridge in the car. I went to the laundromat again and saw a Land Cruiser and then another and then all these fuckers with bulletproof vests and knew I was fucked. I heard a lot of screaming and knew I'd best hit the deck. My bumbag, containing my P9 9mm pistol, was removed. My wrists were zip tied together instead of with cuffs. After I was restrained, they asked who I was and I identified myself by my real name – pointless to do otherwise – and I told them, 'I guess you blokes will get a pat on the back for this one.'

One of three men who witnessed the events in Harriet Place – from the balcony of a budget hotel near the laundromat – said the scene looked like something from an American cop show. He told the *NT News*, 'It was just like it is on the TV. First, this four-wheel drive comes screaming around this corner and then another comes around this corner, and these coppers jump out with their massive guns and start screaming at this man to get down on the ground. He got on his knees and they pushed him down. He looked stunned. After he stood up, we recognised him. He was that Postcard Bandit bloke – he was a bit fatter –and we thought: Unreal.'

Abbott:

One of the TRG [territory response group] blokes was having difficulty in unloading my P9 and asked me how to pull the slide back. I told him he had to take the safety off first. I was placed in a wagon and taken to Darwin police station. I was greeted by some high-ranking detective and a question he had to ask was the whereabouts of the young bloke. No pardon was on offer for the answer to that question so I wasn't able to help him. After the formalities and my objection to my prints being taken, I was placed in a cell.

Commander Manison: 'His first question when he got here [police headquarters] was "Could we get his washing from the dryer in the laundromat?"'

Property seized from Brenden James Abbott, 5.40pm, Harriet Place, Darwin, 2 May 1998:

1985 Toyota Land Cruiser 1ABZ 435 and contents
$23,432 in cash, mostly new $50 bills
Brown trailer NT TA429. Four jerry cans, two 9-litre gas bottles, spare tyre, fitted gas stove, green cover. Cutlery, crockery, cooking utensils and pots and pans, a shower, tents, torch, batteries, sunglasses, mobile phone, vehicle lubricants and fluids, an axe, toilet paper, food and water supplies, a fridge, wood ladder, tent pegs and rope, ground sheet and a tent tarpaulin.

Abbott says, 'The wigs and revolver and two-ways are not listed. The WA jacks took them for evidence, i.e. the [Mirrabooka] robbery in WA.'

Three wigs – long blond, long brunette and short black – were in his backpack on the front seat. The laptop computer with software used for producing fake driver's licences; theatrical make-up; cannabis; a two-way radio and scanner, tuned to police frequencies, both fitted to the vehicle; a 9mm Browning pistol; 420 rounds of SKS rifle ammunition; two boxes of 9mm ammunition; and a .45 pistol. A guitar case – the right size for the automatic weapon found in the Ford wagon – was also found in the Alice Springs storage shed.

That night, Julie Berichon paced the hall of her Brisbane home, bracing herself for the news her son was dead. She told the *Courier Mail*,

Things are going through my mind now … what if they shoot him, how are we going to face him? He'll be dead. I will have to tell my mum and my daughter, and how am I going to face it? It's horrendous.

On Monday, 4 May 1998, the *Courier Mail* reported on how the police net closed: 'The operation began when police from Queensland's Operation Korn – launched after Abbott's 5 November breakout from Sir David Longland Prison – alerted NT police he was seen near the [Queensland] border at Avon Downs on Saturday morning [the sighting was a mistake]. Roadblocks were immediately placed on all roads leading in and out of the Territory. But police believe he slipped in before the checkpoints were set up. Hours later, the breakthrough came as Berichon was identified from photographs by Top End Hotel staff who had seen him book a ground-floor room. The police put surveillance on the unit hoping to catch Berichon returning.

'Instead, at 4.40pm on Saturday, Abbott appeared at the hotel. Holding off until Abbott was in a position where he could be arrested with the least danger to the public, police watched him disappear into the small unit and come out again. They followed him as he drove a few blocks to a small shopping centre on Harriet Place, where he put clothes into a dryer at a laundromat, went to a supermarket and bought a pizza. It was his last act as a free man.'

In his first call to lawyer Chris Nyst on the Gold Coast, a bemused Abbott rejected the breakout and assassination-plot claims and added, 'They had me in solitary for 18 months last time. I just hope that they don't go over the top this time. On Monday, I was taken from the prison back to the police station where I was interviewed by Queensland detectives. They were seeking info on the young bloke's whereabouts, but, as was the case on Saturday, they didn't offer me a full pardon for my crimes so I wasn't able to help them out.'

Detective Sergeant Tim Brinums and Detective Sergeant Charles Barham, from the Queensland major crime squad, interviewed Abbott at Darwin police headquarters on 4 May.

BRINUMS: *'Are you going to talk to us at all about any of your involvement in the escape from Sir David Longland or ...'*
ABBOTT: *[inaudible.]*
BRINUMS: *'OK, that was on 5 November but a few things happened since then.'*
ABBOTT: *'Like what?'*
BRINUMS: *'Well there's been a couple of armed hold-ups down the Gold Coast. One at the Commonwealth Bank at Palm Beach and there's also been the Westpac Bank down the Gold Coast shortly after the escape and there's also a chemist shop. Do you wish to tell us anything about those armed robberies?'*
ABBOTT: *'Chemist shop? Westpac Bank? You're kidding me.'*
BRINUMS: *'No, I'm not Brenden. [Laughter.] No, I'm not, in actual fact.'*
BARHAM: *'Here's the facts here.'*
BRINUMS: *'Your fingerprint has been found at one of the banks down the Gold Coast.'*
ABBOTT: *'Oh well, I do believe I've got [inaudible] in the Commonwealth Bank. It's alleged I have a fingerprint of mine in the Commonwealth Bank but ... not the Westpac and a chemist. You blokes know better than to ask me about fuckin' chemists.'*

He remained unco-operative when asked about Berichon and Michelle, not realising he had already given police everything they needed to catch them.

Abbott says,

I used to buy kangaroo-skin wallets ... I didn't like having a pen and paper and taking notes, so I used to rub a lot of the details into the wallet, but it didn't scratch it permanently. You get a bit of saliva, wipe it over and just rub it with the keys. Five minutes before I got pinched in Darwin, that's when I finished calling [Berichon] at the hotel where he was staying, to let him know that I was only about half an hour away from finishing my laundry and then I was heading down south.

That plan unravelled as soon as Abbott walked out the Darwin laundry's door. And the phone number on his wallet now also sealed Berichon's fate. Northern Territory acting Assistant Commissioner (Crime) Tom Baker later said, 'An intelligence officer noticed that something was scratched on the back of a brown leather wallet seized after Abbott's arrest. It was difficult to read and he put it under a "poly light", which varies the shade of light, in the fingerprint bureau and it came up as the number for the Luma Luma Holiday Apartments.'

Within minutes, crosshairs and telephoto lenses focused on the apartment. Police established that a man calling himself Jason Parker booked into room 608 on 29 April, and was travelling with an Asian woman. A negotiator established phone contact and, in a ten-minute phone conversation, Berichon recalls, 'I told him that I was armed with one pistol, the 9mm pistol. I told him that I had one magazine loaded and I told him that I would come quietly and would not attempt to shoot at police or anything like that.'

A short time later, Berichon and his girlfriend were in custody and on their way to police headquarters. The hurricane of fear and violence that this pimply, naive 20-year-old unleashed on the nation six months earlier had finally run its course. It seemed a miracle that no one had died in the jailbreak and subsequent crime spree.

Victoria extradited Berichon within days to face the two attempted-murder charges over the Box Hill shooting and he was later jailed for 13 years, with a nine-year minimum. He spent years fighting to be returned to Queensland to face the attempted murder charges over the shots fired at guards during the escape. But when he became eligible for parole in Victoria in 2007, the situation reversed and, at the time of writing, Berichon had just lost a Queensland extradition application. He had married Rhiannon Krakouer, the sister of AFL footballer Andrew Krakouer, in a prison wedding in December 2006.

Berichon's bond with Abbott – described during his long court battles as an 'evil spell' – survived the inglorious end to their wayward adventure, and the two stayed in contact by letter. Berichon initially agreed to co-operate with this book, but, after receiving a list of questions in 2004, wrote, 'I do not wish to be part of the book … I am a different person now and that chapter in my life is finished.'

In the *Sydney Morning Herald* on 5 May 1998, Frank Robson reported, 'Bank robber Brendan Abbott chatted to his sister by phone from Darwin's Berrimah Prison yesterday. Typically, according to Diane Abbott, Australia's most wanted man began by cracking a joke. "He said, 'Come and see me, sis, and I'll tell you where all the money's buried.' Then he said, 'Just joking, just joking' and we laughed. It was the first time I'd talked to him in seven months." …

'During the six-minute conversation, Abbot told her he was being held in a sweltering two-metre by one-metre maximum-security cell. "He said it was as hot as blazes, but he sounded in good spirits. You never can tell with Brendan, though – the worse things get, the more he makes jokes."'

Diane Abbott knows her brother better than most. He writes,

> *'The harshest treatment I received came after I was arrested in Darwin. At that time, to top it off, I caught the flu. The nights in Darwin's prison were fantastic. A cell without windows and very little ventilation. More or less a small dungeon with a small window on the door. It was a steam room. I needed to pour water over myself during one of the nights and day to keep my body temperature down. All they gave me was a foam mattress. No pillow, no sheets. The mattress was 100 years old, black with dirt and without a cover. It smelled great. Yeah, I knew I'd kicked goals in Darwin. Come court day for the extradition hearing, I guess they didn't want me delaying the transfer. It worked.*
>
> *'The media circus was unbelievable at the court entrance and, during the trip back to the Darwin prison, I was being stalked. The NT TRG escorted the vehicle I was in and tried to stop any*

cameramen from getting a shot of me from the back of the vehicle. On one occasion, they miscalculated and actually ran into the vehicle, knocking me over.'

While Berichon's return to Melbourne was low-key, on a commercial flight accompanied by two detectives, Abbott got the first-class treatment on a jet chartered by the Queensland Government. Queensland Corrective Services Minister Russell Cooper claimed victory:

I'm pleased this criminal has been caught and I think a lot of people throughout Queensland and Australia will be sleeping a lot easier. We will not be listening to any of the do-gooders who are obviously enamoured with him and were the ones who made the security situation in Queensland jails very difficult beforehand. He had them conned and he won't be allowed to do it again.

Blaming the escape on unnamed do-gooders – rather than substandard prison-security measures and procedures – and also promising to send Abbott to maximum security 'forever' were attempts to make political mileage from a damaging series of events for the National Party Government. Abbott's recapture also ended one of the Queensland Labor Party's pre-election advertising strategies, in which it distributed 150,000 stickers posing the question: 'Where is Brendon Abbott?' From this point on, the answer was available 24 hours a day, via a phone call to the Woodford control room.

Abbott says,

On arrival to the MSU, I was followed by a screw with a video camera. The footage of me supposedly sitting on my bed, putting my head on my hands, after being placed into the cell, I don't recall happening. I believe the first thing I would've done was make my bed. As I said, I was feeling great with having the flu. The whole ordeal was a drain.

Several Queensland Government MPs are known to have requested and viewed the video footage of the morose Abbott's arrival and congratulated themselves on a job well done. But their smiles vanished when a minority Peter Beattie Government was elected on 13 June 1998. The One Nation party and the stunning rise of Pauline Hanson decided the election, after many Queenslanders warmed to her brand of fear and loathing. But the major parties used fear, too – fear of crime and of Brenden Abbott, a symbolic bogeyman. None of the Government's assurances on law and order mattered, as long as Opposition Leader Peter Beattie could keep enquiring about his whereabouts.

When he was caught, Abbott became a trophy in a cabinet, to be pointed at whenever the Opposition made noises about law and order. Abbott took some small satisfaction when the keys to the cabinet changed hands, but what he didn't know was that the new government would wholeheartedly embrace the previous government's attitude. He says, 'Although I was doing hard time at Woodford when the election was held, it brightened up my day seeing that Cooper and his cronies were no longer in power. But it hasn't stopped me being a political football.'

Chokey in Fremantle and years of maximum-security isolation at Arthur Gorrie and Sir David Longland didn't change his ways. Now the Queensland Department of Corrective Services – spurred by the embarrassment and consequences of the escape – would give it another shot. And, this time, Brenden Abbott's life of isolation promised to be harder than ever before.

Chapter Nineteen

1998–2002

Brenden Abbott's face was pinched with exhaustion and red-nosed with the flu when he arrived at Woodford Correctional Centre, 80 kilometres north of Brisbane, late on Wednesday, 6 May 1998. The extradition from Darwin was a day earlier than planned 'for security and convenience'.

> *The day after I faced court, I was flown back to Queensland on the police jet. On arrival in Brisbane, I was transferred to a helicopter and flown to the helipad on the river and driven to the magistrates court. After fronting the beak, I was driven back to the helipad and flown to Woodford Prison, where the helicopter landed out front of the prison. I was put in a dual cab 4WD and driven to the front gate, where the media could get their shots of the monster. I was then taken to maximum security and shown my new abode.*

In the Brisbane Magistrates Court, Abbott was remanded for a committal hearing in June over the escape charges and then put on parade outside Woodford. He reappeared in the same court on 15 June, when he indicated he would plead guilty to escaping but not to the four counts of 'preventing arrest by attempting to fire a projectile' – otherwise known as attempted murder. Outside court, the standard Abbott security operation involved dozens of officers.

The armed-robbery charge over the Gold Coast bank robbery with

Jason Nixon was remanded until later in the year. When he appeared again on 28 June, Abbott pleaded guilty to escaping and the four amended charges of serious assault to prevent arrest. Outside court, lawyer Chris Nyst said Abbott was prepared to 'cop what's coming to him' and was thinking about taking up study in prison. There'd be precious little else to do.

> *In the first three months at Woodford, I wasn't allowed any association with another inmate. When it was, it was with people they chose and the two they did select are people I'd prefer to avoid. I got out of my cell for two hours a day. This time period of exercise was all I could get, despite what they said in court documents claiming I could get up to five hours or more. In the first 12 months, they had 19 to 20 inmates within that MSU. It held 20. There were seven exercise yards and inmates were only allowed to associate with one other during that time.*

Abbott says these circumstances meant he often only got one hour a day of exercise in a yard covered with wire mesh and stinking of urine because of the lack of toilets.

> *When the numbers dropped in the MSU, the exercise hours increased. It also increased the number of times I was moved from cell to cell. It happened once that I was awoken at 10pm and moved to another cell. The rest of that week, I was moved every day to another cell. From then on, until I arrived at Arthur Gorrie, I was moved from cell to cell at least twice a week. I was the only inmate they did it to. This went on for almost two years. It was solely for the purpose of getting some response that would justify the continued stay in the MSU. There were many times their objective was almost gained – almost. Someone really seems to have it in for me.*

Abbott was sentenced to a further six years' prison over his role in the escape and also belatedly classified a serious violent offender when he appeared in the Brisbane District Court on 14 September 1998. This meant he had to serve at least 80 per cent of any sentence imposed. Senior Judge Gilbert Trafford-Walker described the breakout as 'showing a level of violence and planning that has not been seen in this state before'.

Ten days later, Jason Nixon was sentenced to an extra five years' jail over the 13 November Gold Coast bank robbery.

AAP's Suzanne Klotz reported, 'Judge Fred McGuire, also president of the Queensland Children's Court, commented that both men had started their criminal careers as juveniles – Nixon at four – and that the system had failed them. "Experience – bitter experience – has shown that many career criminals, such as Abbott and Nixon, started out as juvenile delinquents and, for one reason or another, the system – the social, police and judicial system – could not adequately deal with these offenders and it has developed into monumental offending over the years."'

Meanwhile, in Perth, after Glenn Abbott (aka Salmon) was sentenced to eight years' jail with no parole in August 1998, over the Lee Watson shooting, the *West Australian*'s David Reed reported, 'Glenn Norman Salmon was held under strict security for 14 months in Casuarina Prison's special-handling unit because of fears his brother, notorious bank robber Brendan Abbott, would help him break out, the Supreme Court has been told.'

In December 1998, unnamed 'Abbott supporters' told Sarah Harris, of the Brisbane *Sunday Mail*, that a United Nations convention governing treatment of prisoners was the basis of a Federal Court challenge to the way Corrective Services was treating him. They claimed authorities breached the treaty by continuing to hold him in isolation.

The same day, a spokesman for Queensland Prisons Minister Tom Barton dismissed the claims: 'We are concerned about the public safety, rather than the comforts of Brenden Abbott.'

Abbott missed a milestone in Perth that month. On 15 December, at the Raffles Hotel in Applecross, the Perth armed robbery squad gathered to soak up river views, war stories and gallons of beer. The squad's Christmas shows were legendary, but this one held special significance. Like many other similar CIB squads around the nation, it was to be disbanded to make way for a new brand of policing. 'Robbers Rocks The Raffles – The Last Hurrah' was a big night with an appropriate sense of history: this was the same hotel where Brenden Abbott had divided the proceeds of what was once Western Australia's biggest bank robbery, the Belmont job, in 1987.

In Abbott's tiny cell, there was plenty of time to think and reflect on the past. On 4 February 1999, he wrote a letter to his father, Brian, who lived in Melbourne, but would move to country Victoria with his second wife in June that year. The letter read, in part,

'It came to my attention that you came through Brisbane some years back while I was in custody. [Abbott's brother] David mentioned you were going to visit me while here. He said that, due to notice needed before you could visit, you couldn't stay in Brisbane that long. Maybe you were just as apprehensive as I was to visit you when I had the chance [while on the run in 1990] ... But, if ever in the future you're up this way, I'd be more than happy to see you. I've no grudges or disrespect towards you whatsoever. Whatever happened between you and my mother isn't unique, it's just a fact of life and I don't blame anyone but myself for my actions in life. Anyway, if you do decide ever to drop in, you do need to give this lot plenty of notice ... I've got the powers-that-be on edge and they are going to extreme lengths to see I don't miss the next head count.'

The letter, signed 'warmest regards, Brenden', led to the father and son re-establishing their relationship, and maintaining contact. Later, after Abbott took up painting, he sent several portraits of famous Australians to his father as gifts.

Abbott also had a new woman in his life. Paula Doneman reported in the *Courier Mail* on 9 March 1999, 'A woman who fell in love with Brendan Abbott, Queensland's most notorious prison escapee, has been banned from visiting him after she flashed her genitals at him. Prison sources said the woman began visiting Abbott at Woodford Jail's maximum security unit several months ago after reading about his exploits in the media. An officer overseeing the non-contact visit in the unit found the woman, who was not wearing underwear, with a leg out of her jeans – exposing herself to Abbott. The woman has been banned from visiting the jail and having any telephone contact with the armed robber for six months.'

But their bizarre relationship had only just begun. Later, in 2004, Tilly Needham – the daughter of a policeman, the ex-wife of a policeman, a mother of six, a 'nail technician' and an aspiring member of parliament – explained her association with Abbott on her website:

Almost seven years ago, a man entered my life. This man has shown and taught me compassion, caring, patience, trust and faith, plus much more. These qualities were already within me, though it was this man who brought down the walls that partially surrounded them, and allowed me to give freely. This man is Brenden Abbott, and he will receive my support and caring and caring and remain dear to me for the remainder of my days. In early 1999, I departed Brisbane (after an 'error in judgement' during a visit at a correctional facility).

Her website also carried contrasting pictures: A demure head shot of a political candidate with a polite smile, perfectly coiffured hair and classy gold chain; and a raunchy woman in boots, skin-tight jeans, white singlet, cowboy hat, perched casually on a tree stump. Abbott's attitude lacked Tilly's unrestrained passion. He called her his 'stalker', and more than once ordered her out of his life. But the phone calls, letters – and later, more visits – kept coming. It was, at least according to Tilly, 'the greatest love story never told'.

In April 1999, Abbott faced trial over the 1997 Commonwealth Bank robbery at Palm Beach on the Gold Coast. Although his face was plastered around the bank on wanted posters at the time, and some staff members were previous Abbott victims, no one identified the bourbon-fuelled bandit. But the prosecution said Abbott had left a fingerprint on the counter when he swung himself into the banking chamber. He was framed, Abbott's barrister, Dennis Lynch, told the court; the print was a fake. But the jury disagreed and found Abbott guilty on charges of bank robbery and car stealing after a ten-day trial, during which he also lost his appeal against his six-year sentence for the escape.

Courier Mail chief reporter Tony Koch followed Abbott's case and took aim at the bank robber and his fans and apologists in a vitriolic column titled 'Dumb Crims do not Aussie Heroes Make', on 15 May 1999. It read, in part, 'Abbott was no romantic, modern-day Ned Kelly, forced by the authorities to an outlaw's life. He was a bone-lazy coward, a bullying thief who brought about the mental and moral destruction of many he encountered so he could live a life of luxury. The newspaper and magazine articles on Abbott over the past decade contain adjectives such as clever, larrikin, genius, fearless, courageous, calculating and intelligent. What nonsense. He is the lowest of the low, a bludger in the true sense of the word ...

'He was a spiv, a social reject who hung out with broken-down whores and desperates who stayed around for only as long as it took for him to squander his money on them ...

'Abbott is now deservedly doing as he should; to use the prison vernacular, chewing corn. He was no postcard bandit – just your common, garden-variety dumb crim.'

Abbott later sent Koch a Christmas card. There was no reply. The true size of Abbott's corn stockpile only emerged at sentencing for the Gold Coast robbery on 29 June 1999.

AAP's Suzanne Klotz reported, 'Notorious criminal Brendon Abbott has been jailed for another seven years for an armed robbery while on the run, making him 71 years old before he will have completed all his outstanding prison sentences ... Abbott, who is now serving a total of 39 years, can't apply for parole until 2025, and still hasn't been sentenced for his escape from Fremantle Jail.'

It was bad news all round. The regular trips to court should have been a welcome distraction from 22 hours a day in his Woodford cell. But Abbott was moved to sarcasm by the 'fun' of court outings: 'They woke me at 3am and I was given breakfast and was in the escort vehicle by 4am. I really loved court days. The ritual of being put into a body belt and leg irons from that time until being returned late in the afternoon was enjoyable.'

On 8 October 1999, two courts dismissed his appeals against the robbery sentence and the serious violent offender declaration. The security surrounding him was relentless. Fed up with the constant cell changes – which also irked other prisoners affected by it – and angered by his inability to change the situation, Abbott went on a three-day hunger strike on Sunday, 28 October 1999.

Early in 2000, Abbott applied for an interstate prison transfer to Perth on compassionate grounds. Thelma Salmon – who had not seen her son since the brief visit at AGCC after his 1995 arrest – backed up the application with a letter of appeal to the WA Justice Ministry:

'Brenden will not be eligible for release until he is 71 years of age. Therefore I humbly request he be transferred to Western Australia. First and foremost, I am Brenden's mother and as such wish to be able to visit my son and give him emotional support through his lengthy sentence. Secondly, as I am in receipt of a disability pension, I am not in the financial position to travel to Queensland on a regular basis. Brenden does not have any family or friends residing in Brisbane. He is totally isolated from family and community contact. As he will not be released from prison during my lifetime, I wish to be able to offer some comfort.'

Brenden Abbott's application for transfer, on both legal and welfare grounds, was lodged on 1 October 1999. But the application – dragged out for a year – was denied on both grounds, and the isolation continued. A letter from the Corrective Services chief executive to Abbott on 28 April 2000 stated, in part,

> *'In considering whether to issue a new maximum security order (MSO) in accordance with section 43B of the Corrective Services Act, I acknowledge that your level of interaction with custodial and programme staff has been acceptable. Your continued participation in art classes has also been noted. These factors are, however, not necessarily sufficient to override concerns that you present a high risk of escape or attempt of escape.'*

Abbott wrote on 14 September 2000, of his continued optimism, 'I do believe my application [for transfer] will be successful and could be any time in the near future.'

He again turned to the courts, trying to force changes to the way Queensland Corrective Services treated him. Lawyer Chris Nyst filed a writ in the Brisbane Supreme Court on 19 October 2000, alleging that Corrective Services' treatment of Abbott was illegal. The details were spelled out in Abbott's affidavit, which read, in part,

> *'I recently completed an anger-management course in an attempt to control the rage I feel as a result of the constant [cell] movement, but it has not really helped me. I am now at the point where I am concerned that I will lose control and react angrily, even though I know that the guards involved in these moves are merely carrying out orders.'*

In a letter to his sister Diane, Abbott writes,

> *'The hours out of cell increased further when I filed for a Judicial Review in December 2000. This is around the time a certain screw's attitude was getting a little bit nasty at times. I guess they had to do more work, or the fact I'd mentioned how some of them were making remarks or facial gestures after they read my affidavit for that hearing. I made no mention of any names at all. Some, I guess, took it personally or felt that I was pulling a swifty with my current state of mind etc. The effects of solitary*

confinement on a long-term basis come in many forms. As you know, the court action brought very little for me. The constant cell changes didn't cease. An incident did eventually happen in which I reacted by placing tissue paper over the lens of the camera in my cell. It was in protest at having some of my property [his stereo] removed from my cell.'

On 25 October 2000 – six days after Nyst lodged the writ – Abbott was charged with interfering with a security device. He appeared in Caboolture Magistrates Court on 22 February 2001, with the requisite 20-odd police and prison officers in tow. The magistrate said he was satisfied Abbott's intent was to interfere with the security system. He sentenced him to six months' jail – oddly, to be served concurrently with his existing sentence – making the entire exercise a waste of time and taxpayers' money. An annoyed Abbott unsuccessfully appealed against the conviction in the District Court.

I was the first inmate ever charged for covering a cell camera in Queensland. These cameras have been within some cells as far back as 1992. In that time, there have been hundreds of incidents where inmates have covered the cameras. Some inmates have even used their own shit to wipe over the lens. Never charged. I do it and I'm before the courts. The charge they got me on – interfering with a security device. And with future MSOs, they are wringing as much out of that one as they can.

It seemed there was nothing he could do to change his situation, so Abbott often resorted to humour to hit back at the system:

Whenever I was taken out of my cell, I was strip-searched and, on returning, the process was repeated. It involved taking all items of clothing off and handing them to a screw. Arms stretched out in front of you, fingers out straight, turn hands over, palms up. Arms up above my head so they can look under your armpits, turn around and lift the soles of my feet. Then squat and cough, but depending on the screws, you were told to bend over and pull your arse cheeks apart. They also told you to pull your stone sac up and those with a foreskin had to peel it back. This part of the strip search was stopped after an incident. An inmate refused to do it and was then held down while a screw pulled the foreskin back. The Prisoners Legal Service in this state made a song and dance about it. The screw who did the pulling of the foreskin was awarded the nickname Skinner. He loved being called that.

One time there, I thought I was in trouble after addressing him as such. This prick is the size of a house and would knock you into next week if he landed one on you. He came to work one day with stitches on top of his forehead. Like most of these rock-eating screws who get around as tough guys in uniforms, he shaved his head. I made a comment to one of his offsiders, asking if the stitches were the result of him grabbing a bloke on the cock again. Well, he told him what I said, and it didn't go down too well. The fact a crim had his workmates laughing hurt his pride, I guess.

On 16 December 2000, Fairfax journalist Frank Robson followed up his 1998 *Good Weekend* story 'The Making of an Anti-Hero' with 'Cruel and Unusual – The Breaking of Brendan Abbott', which read, in part, 'Once quick-witted and healthy, the prisoner is now said to be pallid, dull-eyed and withdrawn, with long hair and a shaggy beard, "like Robinson Crusoe" … His extraordinary treatment has nothing to do with the sentence he received in court. It is an additional punishment – political revenge, if you like – for the acute embarrassment caused by his dramatic escape from another Brisbane prison in 1997. "Abbott was a high-profile escapee who made a fool of (authorities)," says lawyer Ian Dearden, president of the Queensland Council for Civil Liberties. "So the thinking was: 'Right, let's get this bastard!' … And if the Government's (solitary confinement) regime ends up sending such prisoners stark, raving psychotic, that just seems to be a risk the authorities are prepared to take."

'Early in November, I [Robson] called Queensland police headquarters to ask what became of its investigation into the assassination plot. "We were never able to find any substantial evidence to back it up," said spokesman Brian Swift, adding that Russell Cooper's police protection was ordered before the threat was discredited. But it turned out to be bullshit? Swift: "Yeah, it was bullshit. A bit of a spin, a bit of a stunt."

'"What they are doing to Abbott and others is a breach of every human rights guideline ever devised," says solicitor Karen Fletcher, co-ordinator of the Queensland Prisoners' Legal Service. Fletcher won a Supreme Court action against the Corrective Services department on behalf of nine inmates of the Woodford MSU early in 1999, when Justice Moynihan found that the men's indefinite solitary confinement regime was unlawful under the Corrective Services Act. Prisons Minister Tom Barton got around Justice Moynihan's ruling by rushing through an amendment to the Act. It means that, although maximum-security orders must now be reviewed half-yearly, they can be renewed ad nauseam by the department itself – still without any form of public accountability or independent scrutiny.'

A few days later, on 21 December, Justice Glen Williams ruled on Abbott's writ against his MSO:

> *Counsel for the applicant is correct when he says that the applicant's criminal history is something which occurred in the past and cannot be altered. The only change can be with respect to the applicant's behaviour. To date, the prison authorities have been prepared to acknowledge that his behaviour has been acceptable. A time must therefore arrive, if behaviour remains acceptable, when the past criminal history, including that of escape, will no longer be capable of reasonably dominating the decision-making process. But I cannot conclude that such a stage has so clearly been reached as to justify a finding that the making of the recent maximum-security orders was unlawful …*
>
> *However, it is a concern that the renewal of maximum-security orders in this case may become a rubber-stamp exercise. … If there is an appropriate review every six months, then it cannot be said that an indefinite period of segregation has been imposed upon the applicant.*

Reporting the proceedings on 23 December, the *Courier Mail* quoted Abbott's lawyer, Walter Sofronoff QC, telling the court,

> '*Abbott had been refused a computer or the chance to study for university qualifications, and was only allowed to talk with one other prisoner at a time for a maximum of two hours per day.*' *John Logan, QC, for the chief executive of the Department of Corrective Services, said there was nothing unlawful about the order regarding Abbott. Corrective Services Minister Tom Barton said the court decision had left him "very happy".*'

In April 2001, Diane Abbott became increasingly concerned about her brother and his mental and physical health. He was vague, repetitive in his speech and didn't sound like the Brenden she knew. She rang Woodford on 24 April to check on his welfare, only to be told, 'He's not here any more.' She rang her mother, who made the same calls and received the same answers. Only after she rang the Queensland Ombudsman's office did the truth begin to emerge.

At 3am that day, Woodford guards had woken Brenden Abbott and ordered him to dress. He was shackled and placed in one of the US Hummer vehicles, hurriedly purchased by the Queensland Government in the wake of the 1997 escape. (They were hopelessly unreliable and the $3 million fleet ended up as rusting wrecks just a couple of years later.) His new surroundings were depressingly familiar – the maximum-security unit at Arthur Gorrie Correctional Centre.

In the *Courier Mail* on 25 April 2001, Paula Doneman and Tony Keim reported in 'Cars Hit as Jail Convoy Passes': 'Two of Queensland's highest-risk prisoners inadvertently caused a three-car accident on the Ipswich Motorway yesterday as they were being transported under heavy guard. Postcard Bandit Brendan Abbott and an underworld crime figure were shackled during their transfer in a Hummer vehicle from Woodford maximum security unit in a convoy to two Wacol-based prisons. The accident occurred as traffic stopped to allow the maximum-security escort involving at least ten prison and police vehicles to turn off the highway about 6.15am yesterday.'

Diane Abbott – mother of five, university student and childcare worker – immediately began the expensive and complicated process of travelling from Cairns to Brisbane to confirm for herself that her brother was OK. She was eventually allowed four two-hour visits from 17 to 21 May. The thin man with the strained smile and long-absent curly mullet seemed more like the brother that she remembered, and less like the vague, confused and depressed voice she'd heard on the phone from Woodford. Over four visits, they spent hours talking about their childhood and family and Abbott assured Diane he was being treated more humanely. That made it no less difficult for her to part after the final visit, though.

The following month, Diane wrote,

I have spoken to Brenden and he appears to be OK. He has got his paints now and is in the process of doing some more portraits. It would be nice to see the set when he has finished. As yet, I haven't heard anything from Amnesty, I am still waiting for a call.

In March 1999, Abbott made an appeal through the media for the public to stop sending him 'fan mail'. The letters were from a mix of young men who admired his criminal exploits and women who wanted to bed him. But, when he arrived at Arthur Gorrie, he discovered dozens of other letters were never allowed through.

I did receive some fan mail and made the mistake in answering a few. After my arrest it helped receiving some mail and support. I found out the hard way it was best not to respond. When I arrived at Arthur Gorrie and collected some of my property, I first became aware of in excess of 40 letters that were never passed on to me. I was absolutely furious on discovering this. It was just fan mail and photos of some of the writers. Some good-looking girls, too, I must say. I never bothered writing back because most were sent near on three years before.

Despite his family's fears of further deterioration, Abbott slowly changed at Arthur Gorrie. The constant surveillance continued, but his general treatment improved and the hours outside his cell increased. Not surprisingly, his state of mind grew more positive.

In a letter to Diane Abbott in April 2002, he wrote,

'My conditions since being transferred to Arthur Gorrie have improved. I'm out of my cell most of the day, though there isn't much to do anyway other than go into the exercise yard. I'm able to cook up some meals if I wish by buying food on the canteen list. The constant surveillance continues – cameras in the cell and everywhere I go.

'The strip-search ordeal no longer takes place as it did at Woodford. I find the screws are professional at their job and don't chew rocks for breakfast. The joint is wired up, so one must be aware that someone is always listening in. My past experience with this place is even comments made in jest are written down.

'I've recently been approved permission to purchase a computer so as to take up studies. I've been requesting to buy a

PC for over three years and been getting the runaround. It seems the powers that be didn't want me learning in the IT field. So much for the purpose of being locked up so as one can correct their criminal ways. I want to learn computer programming, but with the hurdles I've experienced, it may be some time before I do. To help pass the time, I've discovered I've a talent as an artist. Watercolours is all they'll allow for now. Eventually, I'd like to move on to oils.'

But swapping his balaclava for a beret and an ambition to become a computer nerd were not nearly enough to convince authorities that Abbott was a new man, worthy of mainstream freedom and trust or deserving of an interstate transfer. Deep down, Abbott feared that this time there really was no way out – ever, no matter how hard he fought. That he was condemned to be forgotten, isolated for the rest of his life, paying for his sins in a claustrophobic maximum-security unit.

Chapter Twenty

2002–2005

Official Visitor Kevin McGhee knew Brenden Abbott well. He interviewed ten corrections staff to form opinions for a review of his maximum-security order; and when Abbott was previously in Arthur Gorrie, before the big escape, McGhee saw him monthly for more than a year. In his review, dated 12 January 2002, McGhee, a lawyer, gave the most thoroughly researched opinion yet of Brenden Abbott's past, present and future in Queensland prisons:

> 'I believe a mainstream Abbott will be targeted by criminals [so] his personal security must be guaranteed ... I believe Abbott accepts he must serve his sentence. It is the manner in which it is served which is of concern. Upon completion of all indicated interviews and files, the following facts emerged: ...
>
> '(C) Abbott's high-profile presence is not, I believe, of Abbott's making, but generated – as Acting Chief Judge McGuire suggested on 24 Sep 98 when sentencing Nixon – "by the Press". I believe it suited the media, encouraged by the police, to give Abbott an almost mythical Scarlet Pimpernel-type aura as the Postcard Bandit. This notoriety was enhanced by the group escape from SDL ... I have found Abbott to be much more phlegmatic than his assumed notoriety suggests. This unsolicited notoriety is inconsistent, I believe, with Abbott's nature, which is more unassuming and almost self-

effacing with respect to his criminal activities ... Abbott does not boast or brag about his exploits ...

'*(E) Sentencing principles suggest that, at some time during the next 25 years, he will leave an MSU. The question therefore not only becomes when Abbott will leave an MSU, but how. Because of his history, escape by Abbott is always a possibility. Whether it is a probability is speculative because of Abbott's high-profile notoriety and the greatly improved security since the 1997 escape. Opportunities such as those presenting to the SDL five, I believe, no longer should exist in Queensland, except due to staff negligence ...*

'*(J) ... Unlike others who have had an unfortunate upbringing, Abbott doesn't appear to blame his upbringing for his circumstances. He seems proud of the professionalism he brought to robbing banks and the fact he has never intentionally hurt anyone. When reminded of the staff traumatised, he expressed regret, merely acknowledging their presence while suggesting they faced no real physical threat from him; he gave me no answer for the group use of small arms in the SDL escape.*

'*(K) Allegations in paragraph G on page 5 of the Department's 30 April 2002 letter to Abbott that he was "the instigator of the escape" from SDL contradict, I believe, not only sentencing remarks by Justice de Jersey when he was sentencing Nixon for his part in that SDL group escape, but also the [prison inspectors'] report by Carl Mengler ...*

'*(O) AG Sentence Management Coordinator Mr M Kriesch ... felt it is time for Abbott now to "move on" through the system ... cynically, Mr Kriesch stated the sooner Abbott was back in mainstream the sooner he would be killed – either by criminals resentful of Abbott or when again attempting to escape, at which time Abbott could be expected to suffer from an increased security reaction allied with "improvement" on the means used to effect the group SDL escape ...*

'*(Q) ... in unprotected mainstream Abbott's existence can be expected to be lonely, except for ulterior motives affecting his personal safety ...*

'*(X) Irrespective of Abbott's future, the refusal for some six weeks now to give Abbott the computer for which he has paid is incomprehensible. The sooner Abbott gets his computer, the better.*'

Extract from Brenden Abbott letter to Diane Abbott, 14 April 2002:

'Well, it's coming up to the end of the current maximum-security order I'm under. I've no doubt that they'll continue with making another six-month order, as they have done for the last four years and regurgitating the same reasons for doing so. In the four years I've been under an MSO, I've seen some come and go, and a few return again and again and [be] released again back to mainstream. Some of those are placed in the MSU due to escaping custody or information received suggesting they planned to escape or because they've in the past murdered another inmate. Then there are those convicted of horrendous crimes against young children. One person (if you can call him that) who comes to mind is [convicted serial killer] Leonard Fraser. These types never set foot in the MSUs.'

Abbott realised that any hope of achieving his aim of leaving maximum security in Queensland and returning to Western Australia required rehabilitation of his public image. In October 2003, Chris Nyst told the ABC-TV documentary series *Australian Story*: 'There are some surprises about Brenden Abbott. Some years ago, he said to me that he was going to take up painting and I expected to see kind of a stickman, amateurish thing. But he sent me a painting of [stockbroker] Rene Rivkin, and it was just extraordinary. If his life had been different, then I think he might have achieved a lot.'

Others began to paint a different picture of Nyst's notorious client. On 12 July 2002, AAP reported, 'After years of robbing banks, notorious "postcard bandit" Brenden Abbott is holding up paint brushes to raise money for charity. The infamous escapee is painting famous faces, including Mike Tyson and Ned Kelly, to help fill the 18 hours a day he spends alone in his cell ... Abbott's painstaking watercolours take more than month to finish. Twelve paintings are expected to be ready within two months for an exhibition proposed for a gallery on the Gold Coast. The paintings, which feature Abbott's signature and thumbprint, will be sold to raise money for The Smith Family.'

Despite his supposedly high intelligence, Abbott says he did not participate in the National IQ Test, hosted on the Nine Network by Eddie McGuire and Catriona Rowntree in August 2002, explaining dryly that he 'couldn't work out the knobs on the TV'. He at least had a remote control and used it to watch hours of news and current affairs – his only regular link with the outside world.

> *I don't keep in touch with many people these days. Then again, it's pretty much how I've always been. Those I do keep up with are usually long-time friends. One or two I've met in the prison system, most I'd rather not have much to do with. I drop Berichon a line now and then, as he does with me. Some past girlfriends have been in touch.*

Jackie Lord – aka Rhonda Green, Jackie Flint and now Mrs Jackie Dines, a mother of two from her first marriage – was among them. She last spoke to Abbott before the SDL escape. She met and married Tony Dines in 1998, and they lived in Perth, running a successful promotional business. In mid-2002, she got back in contact with Abbott and they were soon writing and talking on the phone again. In August 2002, she said,

> *The first letter was about ten pages. He doesn't always write, but when he does he writes a long one. He said he was glad he was out of Woodford. In this letter he says, 'It's half past ten, I'd better go. These blokes watching me on the camera will wonder why I'm up so late. I'll probably get a piss test in the morning.'*
> *Diane said he was getting a bit shitty because they were making it hard for him. He says in the latest letter, 'Don't believe everything you read, they say 20 years, but I'll probably only do 10 to 15.' I thought, I'll let him keep his vision. I don't think they'll let him out in a big hurry. But I won't say anything to the contrary. He said he was looking forward to us going over there and visiting him.*
> *Tony's all right, but I think it's going to be hard for him. He said, 'Where does that leave me?'*
> *I said, 'Well, there's no drama. That's life, isn't it? I'm just doing it to help him out.'*

Jackie's renewed interest in Brenden grew. She and husband Tony sold their business and put their house on the market, having previously resolved to move to Queensland. Tony's misgivings over his wife's longstanding relationship with the nation's most notorious bank robber seemed to evaporate. He also talked regularly to Abbott on the phone and was keen to make the move to where his wife would be able to visit her first love on a regular basis. Tony also believed that God could save Brenden Abbott, just as He saved him and Jackie. Jackie later told *Australian Story*,

> *I hadn't seen Brenden for about 13 years. And so we had already decided at this time, my husband and I, that we were going to move to Brisbane – actually, to the Gold Coast. And, upon that drive over, we also discussed whether or not it'd be a good idea to go and visit Brenden in jail. I went there mainly because I thought ... well, curiosity. What's he like now? And is he the hardened criminal that they keep showing me on the TV, you know? Cos they always had pictures of him that made him look like a real devil ...*

Abbott wrote to her,

> '*I have given up asking why it is that I still feel the way I do about you after all these years and what I have been through. It has to be chemistry, simple as that ... I look forward to seeing you again. I haven't changed much, other than some grey hair and wrinkles around the eyes, as you would expect from a 40-year-old.*'

Late in October 2002, Diane Abbott took three of her children, Harley, 12, Storme, 10, and Crystal, 14, to introduce them to their uncle Brenden at Arthur Gorrie. She also took James, 11, to see his dad for the first time in four years. It was a big day for the Abbott family. With five of them in one room, perhaps the prison guards should have expected trouble.

Diane recalls,

> *Crystal has no concept of the prison system. [After we went in the room for the visit] she hides behind the door and the guards – three of them – have gone to get Brenden to bring him in. She jumps from behind the door and yells, 'Freeze! Put your hands in the air!'*
>
> *We cracked up, but the guards almost went into panic mode. One guy went bright red when he realised it was just a kid having fun. Brenden laughed. This poor guard, you could see how worried he was for a moment.*

> *It was a stressful visit, especially with Harley there. He was*
> *really full-on. Brenden brought out the cards for the kids to play.*
> *I told the kids, 'Just fucking shut up, all right?'*
> *And Brenden said, 'Don't speak to them like that.'*
> *[One of them said,] 'That's OK, Mum talks to us like that all*
> *the time.'   Brenden's only comment after the visit was 'Jesus*
> *Christ'. It was very stressful for him.*

Abbott presented his son with a new stereo, some music CDs and a
quilt, and he enjoyed the chance to finally spend some time with the
boy. A few weeks later, a dramatised, fictionalised version of the same
scene played out on a movie set in Sydney, when filming started on
the telemovie *Postcard Bandit*. The writer and producers faced the
same hurdles journalists always faced with Abbott's case. No one was
allowed to talk to him. So Abbott had no direct input on the movie
and says he felt embarrassed by the attention. When his sister told
him Tom Long was cast in the title role, Abbott snorted, 'Sounds like
a fuckin' porn star.'

On 7 February 2003, Jackie wrote, 'I had a visit with Brenden
today and found him to be very relaxed. He had just been on the
computer … We believe God can do miracles, Brenden doesn't believe
in it, but there is still a glimmer of hope in his eyes. He comes over
sometimes like there is no way they are going to change his living
arrangements, so he accepts the routine.'

Diane Abbott travelled from Cairns to visit her brother again early
in May 2003. Abbott was now getting up to four hours a day on his
computer, looked healthy and had put on weight. He signed a
statement in readiness for his latest application for an interstate
transfer and was feeling confident. But later that month, in phone
calls to his father, Abbott sounded depressed after learning of the
rejection of his latest transfer application – and the prison was under
lockdown because of new rumours of a breakout plot.

The inevitably controversial telemovie *The Postcard Bandit*
screened nationally on 1 June 2003. It drew mixed reactions. Two
days before the premiere, Abbott issued a media release, distancing
himself from the production:

> *'I don't want it to paint me as any sort of hero, because that*
> *would be far from the truth … I don't want anybody,*
> *particularly young people, thinking that my life has been*

glamorous, because it hasn't ... When I was recaptured after the Sir David Longland escape in 1997, a lot of misguided people seemed to think I was some sort of hero. At the time, I asked prison authorities for permission to make a public statement setting the record straight – but it was refused. Now that the minister has agreed, I want to state clearly that I regret the way my life has gone. I do not want to be glamorised in any shape, manner or form. If I could turn back the clock, and I'd had different opportunities as a kid, I'd love to have been a doctor, lawyer or a journalist, or anything other than a criminal who now spends his days in a prison cell.'

Scriptwriter Peter Gawler had explained in the film's publicity,

The Postcard Bandit *is BJ's story. It celebrates his spirit, his vitality, his ingenuity, his derring-do. But it doesn't seek to glorify the man. It's an honest, warts'n'all account of a unique, gifted Aussie bloke who took the wrong road and is now paying an appropriately heavy price.*

After it went to air, Abbott's film review was harsh:

That movie was terrible. It was a load of crap. They got the facts wrong. I was embarrassed to watch it. It painted me up as a right dickhead.

What I found most upsetting was the way they portrayed me as an out-and-out thug who beat up his brother, co-offenders and, most of all, the scene with that female bank teller. Yes, there was yelling and screaming for the first few seconds when working, but never like that. Once control was taken, I'd talk to them calmly without putting further trauma on to them. Now I'm to be haunted again with the release of the DVD. Probably be put on the video channel within the prison. Like most, the people in here believe it's true. I'm no angel, but facts would've been best suited when they claim 'based on a true story' ... I'm changing my name!

Several years later, the movie *was* played on the prison video channel, by which time Abbott's attitude to it had softened; he even managed a few laughs at his own expense.

There was no character portraying Jackie in the film, but, in the real world, her role in Abbott's life steadily increased, with weekly visits and regular phone calls. On 30 July 2003, she said Brenden was now calling 'eight or nine times a week' and she researched computer information on the internet for him while he recited instructions on the phone. Brenden wasn't painting any more, but was 'right into the computer'. She designed him his own 'shackles' logo for a shirt in case he faced court again for another scheduled compensation case by a traumatised bank officer.

Abbott: '[Calls to Jackie and Tony] were the only local calls I could make. I didn't know anyone else. There was no one else to talk to in the MSU at the time and I'd had no association with anyone for months.'

Late in August 2003, Abbott's mother Thelma Salmon dared to let herself hope she might get a chance to see her most wayward son. Her health had been poor. A mystery ailment was causing low blood pressure, resulting in fainting episodes, and a battery of medical tests shed no light on the problem. Then she received an official letter containing a statement she had waited a long time to read:

'It has been requested that a report be prepared for the Queensland Corrective Services pending the possible interstate transfer of your son Brenden. It will be necessary to discuss a range of issues, in particular the accommodation which you have offered to your grandson.'

The following month, Thelma had a seizure at home and passed out, breaking a leg in the fall. One of Diane's daughters, Nicole, came to stay and keep an eye on her grandmother. In spite of the stress of her illness, Diane said her mother sounded better than she had for years; but she was worried the authorities unfairly raised her mum's expectations.

It turned out Thelma's meeting with a corrections officer was only to ask if she could look after James. She told the corrections officer, 'Yes, when I'm better.' But the officer understood James was moving there permanently, not just visiting for school holidays if his father transferred. In September 2003, Diane said the Queensland Attorney-General had now considered her brother's latest application for an interstate prison transfer and Abbott was anxious, waiting on the answer.

On 8 October, a double murderer named Mark Day was bashed and stomped to death by Abbott's fellow escapee Jason Nixon in the Sir David Longland MSU. Then, on 10 October, serial rapist Troy Burley was bashed at Arthur Gorrie. In the *Courier Mail* on 14 October, Paula Doneman reported, 'State Prisons Minister Tony McGrady has put a Brisbane jail on notice and warned its private operators they may lose their contract after the company failed to report an assault on an inmate in a maximum-security unit.'

On 16 October, Diane Abbott said her brother's maximum security order had been renewed again. He sounded depressed by the monotony of the high-security regime and told her he was going to begin a hunger strike.

On 23 September 2003, Diane received a letter from Corrective Services Minister Tony McGrady, reassuring her that concerns about her brother's wellbeing were unfounded: 'Appropriate steps will be taken to ensure his safety at all times while he is under the supervision of the Department of Corrective Services. Should Mr Abbott have fears for his safety, he should raise these issues directly with supervisory staff.'

In a letter to his sister, Abbott wrote,

'It appears the minister hasn't done his homework. The recent murder of an inmate in the SDL MSU goes to show that the decision I made some 12 months or so ago in not associating with anyone in the MSU has merit after all. Most within the MSUs demonstrate an attitude of not giving a fuck. I distanced myself from the likes of these types as far back as 1998 while held at Woodford MSU. Unfortunately, due to my profile, I am housed with many who have a jail gangster mentality and the attitude of "if you're not with them, you're against them". Well, they consider I'm the latter. There's a demeanour similar to that of crocodiles. Because of that, they are predictable. I've been able to read the play of them and do my best to avoid any dramas. So don't go getting yourself overly concerned about my safety, Diane. Hopefully my transfer to WA will come through before my transfer to the mainstream in Queensland. If not, then I'll have to be on guard wherever I am placed.

'As you know, my regime is back to that of what I had in the

early days of the MSU. After the murder at SDL, the minister gave the directive that no inmates were to associate.'

On Friday, 10 October, Troy Burley was bashed at Arthur Gorrie, but prison officers did not report it.

Abbott writes,

'The reasons why aren't difficult to figure out. A parent of the inmate assaulted made a song and dance and contacted the media. The media contacted the prison in an attempt to verify the claims. On Sunday afternoon, the screws who were rostered on that Friday were ordered in to make a report. The minister got wind of the incident and was seen doing backflips in his office. The shit hit the fan, and, because the screws didn't report the incident, it made it look more like a cover-up attempt.

'Since then, ACM Management [managers of the privately run prison] has revoked all other privileges. So basically, because the screws fucked up, I pay the price. As you can imagine, I wasn't impressed whatsoever and, in protest, went on a hunger strike for two days. Started it on Thursday, after having my last meal on Wednesday, 15 October, at 4pm. On Friday afternoon, I was allowed some privileges (20 minutes on the computer) and I commenced eating again that day at 5pm. Maybe the hunger strike was not such a clever move. It seems silly that I would bring further misery on myself to show my discontent. Sometimes, I feel it's all you can do to bring to light the unjust actions of the powers that be. One thing I did notice over the two days of not eating – I never realised there were so many cooking shows on TV.'

The 23rd of October 2003 was just another day for Brenden Abbott, but also a statistical milestone – 2,000 consecutive days in maximum-security units, an unprecedented duration in modern Australian history that narrowly topped the five and a half years of freedom he had enjoyed in the early 1990s.

Jackie Dines's husband Tony, a deeply religious businessman, took most of Brenden Abbott's portraits off his hands as an 'investment'. Among the subjects were tennis ace Pat Rafter, Olympic champion Cathy Freeman, former Test cricket captain Steve Waugh, disgraced stockbroker Rene Rivkin and rugby league legend Allan Langer. Tony

Dines said Brenden Abbott now called to speak to him and Jackie almost daily, often when they were at work. 'He'll just listen to us on the speakerphone, while we're working,' Tony said. They also moved again, this time from the Gold Coast to Brisbane; consequently, their trips to prison see Brenden Abbott were much shorter. But Jackie and Tony's arrival caused serious tensions in Abbott's life. Early in 2004, he took action. 'I wrote to her and said that her demeanour was somewhat belligerent, not towards me, though. It was obvious to me that the new business they'd bought was causing dramas for them. I told her I would 'drop off' because she had mentioned that Tony wasn't comfortable with the calls. I told her that, when things got better, to surprise me with a visit or write.'

With no shortage of spare time, Abbott decided to embark on an ambitious art project – an entry in the Archibald Prize, Australia's most prestigious art award. But who did he know who was famous and also prepared to sit for hours behind 7cm-thick security glass in a maximum-security prison? Who better than author, screenwriter and criminal lawyer Chris Nyst? He sat for the portrait with a hand against his face, his posture reflecting boredom, his eyes distant. The portrait 'failed to capture my rugged good looks', he joked later. 'I've been framed a few times in my life but this is probably a better look than any of the others,' he told the *Courier Mail*'s Greg Stolz on 6 March 2004.

On 28 May 2004, in another story headed 'POSTCARD BANDIT GAINS BREAK FROM SOLITARY', Paula Doneman and Greg Stolz reported, 'Postcard Bandit and serial escapee Brendan Abbott could be on his way back into the mainstream jail population after almost six years in a maximum-security cell which was purpose-built for him. The convicted armed robber was moved into the detention unit at Brisbane's privately run Arthur Gorrie Remand and Reception Centre on Wednesday. After months of deliberation, Queensland prisons' Serious Offenders Committee agreed to the move. Abbott, however, will remain under constant surveillance ... A Queensland Corrective Services spokesman said, "The movement relates to the first step of the assessment to determine whether he is suitable or not for full or partial reintegration to mainstream prison population."'

Abbott:

After my release from the MSU on 26 May 2004, I was transferred to the Detention Unit. There were two Detention

Units then and one was not in operation at that time. I had a week within one DU and then management decided to open the other one, solely to house me. I was kept there until my transfer three months later.

During that three months, they stationed three officers there during the day, one of whom was a Correctional Manager. I was let out of my cell for most of the day between 7.30 and 5.30. In that time I carried out cleaning duties of all the vacant cells and stripped the floors of the old sealant and then resealed them. During these three months, I had access to my personal computer that was in an interview room in the DU. At all times while I was out of my cell, two screws had to be on the floor with me and one was stationed within the control room. In that three months, my only contact was with the screws or other prison staff.

So much for 'mainstream' prison. By early July 2004, according to Diane Abbott, her brother's spirits had 'lifted considerably' because he was adjusting to the new environment. She also said her other brother Glenn, now in the medium-security Albany Regional Prison, had a parole hearing that week. But the excitement in Diane's voice related to news that was more unexpected – the Queensland Attorney-General had approved Brenden Abbott's transfer to Western Australia.

On 7 July 2004, AAP's Tim Clarke reported from Perth, 'Western Australia has no interest in granting the wish of prison escapee Brenden Abbott – the so-called Postcard Bandit – to return to the state, WA Justice Minister Michelle Roberts said today. Authorities in Queensland, where Abbott is incarcerated, said they would clear the way for the infamous bank robber to return home to serve the rest of his sentence. But Ms Roberts said Abbott, who is one of WA's most notorious criminals, would not be assisted in his bid to get back to WA. "I think he is just trying to rort the system and I am not about to help him do so," she said.'

Abbott was unperturbed by Michelle Roberts's rejection. She had no say in it – the decision rested with Attorney-General Jim McGinty, who wrote to Abbott's lawyers weeks later and told them to disregard Roberts's decision because it was under review. Just as he kept chipping away at the Queensland system, Abbott was determined to do the same in WA. Meanwhile, his 'transition process' in Queensland continued.

In the *Courier Mail* in August 2004, Paula Doneman reported, 'Postcard Bandit Brendan Abbott has finally made it back into the mainstream prison population for the first time since his violent escape from a maximum-security facility in 1997. After almost six years of solitary confinement in maximum-security units since his recapture, Abbott was transferred to Australia's largest prison last week. The convicted armed robber and serial escapee is now a resident of N block in the high-security section of the 1,000-cell Woodford Correctional Centre, north of Brisbane.'

But the move wasn't quite that simple, says Abbott:

I was told to pack my property because I was being transferred to another centre. They wouldn't tell me where. The vehicle I was placed in had all its windows covered up – a standard practice when transporting me by road. I first thought I was going to the airport to be flown to a prison in the north of the state such as Townsville or Lotus Glen.

As time elapsed, I soon realised I wasn't heading to the airport. After what seemed like hours, I reached the destination – Woodford. My past experience at Woodford wasn't a pleasant one. In the six years I was within an MSU, I spent over two years at Woodford. They really gave me some therapy while I was there. It was obvious that someone in the DCS head office had an axe to grind. The SDL escape upset someone high up and continues to do so. I was singled out to take the brunt of their paybacks. But their tactics failed in getting the response and effectively giving them justification to hold me in MSUs. My experience within the Woodford MSU will remain with me for the rest of my life, as will the memory of those who made it so memorable.

Upon being processed on my arrival, I was interviewed by [an] Intel [officer], who asked if I had any problems with any inmates at Woodford or any concerns with my safety. I didn't want to go to any unit at Woodford. I asked to be placed in the DU on Section 38 [special-treatment order]. I had fears for my safety, all right – I have enemies in the system I don't even know. These could be friends of those in the MSUs who I refused to associate with. Or, as many screws have expressed to Official Visitors, those who wish to get a name for themselves within the prisons. Taking out the Postcard Bandit would slot them into the system's totem pole. The prison system is full of imbeciles with this mindset.

After I expressed these concerns and asked for placement in the DU on Section 38, a manager was contacted and came to the reception area to talk to me. That manager turned out to be the same manager who ran the MSU at Woodford while I was there. Yeah, I kicked. She briefly spoke to me and refused to place me on Section 38. Not long after, I was escorted to the medical centre and interviewed by medical staff and a prison psychologist, a standard practice for all newcomers to the prison.

The prison psychologist was the first manager who ran the Woodford MSU when I arrived there in 1998. I remember when I first found out back in 1998 that he was a psychologist. He left a few months after I arrived in the MSU in 1998 and this was the first I'd seen of him since. I expressed my concerns to him, as I had with Intel and the manager and reiterated that I wished to go on Section 38.

After brief discussion with someone out of my eye sight, he returned to me to tell me I was going to a unit in which he felt I should be OK. A unit that held 50 men. I hadn't been associating with anyone for the past one and a half years. This came all of a sudden, after six years and three months of what was a solitary existence. I was spinning like a top. When it came time for me to be escorted to a unit, I refused to walk and sat on the floor. I was handcuffed and placed in a wheelchair and wheeled up into the unit. All the prisoners within that unit were herded out into the main exercise yard prior and viewed through the windows as I was wheeled into the unit and lifted out of the wheelchair and placed on a bed and the cell door shut as they departed. The whole incident was videotaped by one of the screws.

It wasn't long after that a couple of inmates came up to the cell-door window to introduce themselves. Then a face I recognised from the time I was in the SDL DU in 96–97. He was a friend and it was good to see him. After a short chat and reassurance that it was all good in the unit, I contacted the screws on the intercom to be let out of my cell. I proceeded out into the main exercise yard, my heart racing, ready to defend myself if need be. The state I was in then was similar to experiences I'd been enduring for years. It hasn't been until just recently that it's been diagnosed as anxiety attacks. Even talking to people I don't consider a threat; and even times when I've had family members visit, I've suddenly had them. Sometimes, I've ended the visits to get away from them, to be back in my own space in a prison cell. Even on visits with my lawyers it's happened. It's a really fucked feeling, I've got to say. I never spoke to anyone about it until recently. Over the years it has become worse and more frequent. Even in my sleep, I have started to have them, suddenly waking up with my heart racing and then not being able to go back to sleep until the early hours of the morning. There have been times I had to walk around my cell at night in trying to settle down. There have been times I get bad shakes all over and have very hot showers as that seems to ease the attacks.

Ironically, bank-robbery victims often describe similar symptoms.

Diane Abbott was rightly concerned about her brother's welfare and arranged a trip to visit him weeks later, in September 2004. His return to a prison he considered to be a 'shit-hole' was not smooth. Constant cell shifts after Abbott's arrival caused tension in his 50-cell section. Diane says Woodford Prison staff were verbally aggressive to her and made it clear they resented having to do overtime to accommodate her special six-hour visit. Her brother's paranoia grew further after a series of lockdowns over fights and security issues and he believed prison management tried to link his return to mainstream with a tougher security regime for all inmates. Clearly, life outside maximum security was going to be a daily challenge for Brenden Abbott.

Epilogue

Over in Western Australia, Glenn Abbott's life was at last looking up. After the stabbing and consequent hard time in Casuarina Prison's special-handling unit, he was transferred to the medium-security Albany Regional Prison.

Diane Abbott says Glenn suffered severe migraines throughout his life, possibly linked to childhood head injuries. After the move to Albany, he had an operation on his ears and Diane says it put a stop to his migraines and changed his temperament. But his refusal to do an anger-management course blocked his eligibility for parole. His relationship with Kelly Fisher, the mother of his two children, had broken down. She was living in Albany and still brought his sons into prison to visit him and he doted on both.

On 20 July 2004, Glenn Norman Abbott rejoined society, moving in with a couple in Perth who agreed to sponsor his transition. Diane Abbott says, 'It won't be easy for him. He really has no idea how much the world's changed since he went away. And as Brenden says, "Coppers don't like people who shoot coppers."'

In March 2005, Thelma Salmon said,

Glenn's changed. He's got a lot more patience. He had his boys for three weeks over Christmas and plans to go down to Albany for Connor's birthday soon. He's so good with them. He always has been. But they're a bloody handful. He [Glenn] asked me, 'Was I that bad?' I told him he was worse and he didn't believe me. [She laughed.] It's payback time for all the trouble he gave me.

Back in Woodford, after his August 2004 move, the highly strung Brenden Abbott says,

After a few weeks, I started to settle into the unit. Most I didn't have much to do with. Many of them were what they classified as special-needs inmates. Due to Queensland mental-health facilities lacking funds in their budgets etc, the prison system is the only place some of those with mental disorders are placed. Met some real weirdoes. While at Woodford in the mainstream units, I was put on what's called a reintegration management plan. It is standard for inmates who come out of MSUs. But, in my case, they've made an exception. There were no changes to the ongoing plans. I was confined to the unit. At first, I wasn't even able to get a unit job. I wasn't allowed to attend any educational courses held in other areas of the prison. Wasn't allowed to attend the prison library nor was I allowed to go to church if I wanted to. Any movement outside the unit in which I either had to attend the medical centre or even going to the visits area, all other prisoner movement had to cease. The walkways were deserted other than the occasional screw. My visits were strictly non-contact unless it was with family. Even the contact visits with family were in a separate area than normal.

The special treatment I endured while at Woodford got up the nose of some of the officers and I had a few that let me know what they thought of me. The fuckwits took it out on me over the extra burden they had. I wasn't responsible for the regime I was under, nor were the managers of the centre. DCS head office was calling the shots of my management plans etc. As it turns out, there was a long-term plan in progress and they were seeing it wasn't going to be fucked up.

On 27 January 2005, Brenden Abbott wrote,

'My transfer application was knocked back by the WA Attorney-General. [One of the reasons given was Abbott refused to sign his latest management plan.] The state election coming up would no

doubt have played a part in his decision. It came as no surprise and it's far from over yet. Just another hurdle, as it was with Queensland's Attorney-General. When Queensland knocked it back, we filed for a Judicial Review. A few days prior to a directions hearing, he changed his tune and repealed his decision. Three months later, he consented to the transfer. We will be filing in a WA court this week against the WA's Attorney-General's decision. You'll see them changing their tunes in a few months, too.'

Ben is a friendly old mongrel, but nearly blind and deaf. His gait is more a hobble than a walk, but his tail manages a subdued wag when he wanders up to Thelma Salmon's back door for a pat.

When the author visited Abbott's mother in August 2003, old Ben was a shadow of the exuberant young mongrel Brenden dropped off at her modest Belmont home back in 1991. Abbott told his mum then he'd return and pick up Ben in six weeks. He probably thought she'd give him away when he didn't come back. But, as long as the old dog's aches and pains did not seem too much to bear, Thelma was determined to hang on to him. The words are unspoken, but painfully clear – she's not giving her boy's dog away again, the way she did when he was a boy.

Six months later, in February 2004, the robber's dog was on his last legs and Thelma reluctantly had him put down.

She, too, is in poor health with no solution or answers in sight. She weighs just over 50 kilograms and has suffered several more collapses. 'It just pisses me off,' she says at the time. 'I'm just about ready to give up.' But at the time of writing, she sounds better on the phone, is still living independently, seeing plenty of the paroled Glenn and hoping to soon see Brenden again at last.

On the other side of Australia in a Victorian country town, Brian Abbott was embracing a new passion for his family. Not the five children and former wife that he left behind decades before, but the descendants of his grandfather's grandfather, George Abbott, a Belfast protestant who arrived in Sydney in 1839.

Since retiring from truck driving, Brian had become an amateur genealogist. He reckoned his research had turned up evidence of links between the Abbott clan and the family of one Edward 'Ned' Kelly. Brenden and his siblings are seventh-generation Irish-Australians.

Brian Abbott rattles off towns and locations that lie at the heart of his family's history – and also the Kelly legend – including

Donnybrook, where George Abbott is buried, and where fellow Irish immigrant John Kelly, Ned's father, worked as a carpenter around 1849. And at one point, he says, the Abbotts and the Kellys lived on adjacent properties.

Brenden Abbott's father provides tantalising hints of the connections he suspects between the families – specifically, that the link relates to the Quinn clan, which included Ellen Kelly, nee Quinn, who was John Kelly's wife and Ned Kelly's mother. But Brian will not elaborate. Could Brenden Abbott, the Australian outlaw of the 1990s, be related to Ned Kelly, the best-known Australian outlaw of them all? It seems too perfect, but Brian Abbott sounds convinced.

After he was slung back into solitary on a maximum-security order in April 2006, a bitter and angry Brenden Abbott wrote to his lawyers, laying out his treatment since he was first released from maximum security two years before.

> 'What more can I say other than that there's no bottom to their barrel of dirty tricks. They are just filthy fucking parasitic puppets. This latest tactic [new MSO] by the powers that be has been on the cards for some time now.
>
> 'The [2004] release from the MSU was only brought on by the application to have that current MSO judicially reviewed. The matter was to be heard the following week. It was obvious DCS didn't want a precedent set. In hindsight, it would have been wise to continue with the Judicial Review, regardless of the fact that I was released from the MSU.
>
> 'After about eight months at Woodford, I had myself a couple of hospital trips. One evening while playing volleyball, I split my right index finger open. I had attempted to spike the ball at the net and a player on the opposing side had the same idea. His forearm came down on the tip of my finger and pushed it backwards. It split my finger to the bone. Yeah, it hurt.
>
> 'I was taken to the Maroochydore Hospital to have it dealt with, but it was hours before I left the prison. My SERT escort had to be arranged. There were SERT members throughout the hospital corridors dressed in complete body armour and balaclavas and carrying M16 assault rifles. Even in the treatment area, they positioned two SERT members with assault rifles. The hospital staff were spinning.

'It was only weeks after that trip that I was taken to Brisbane's Princess Alexandra Hospital to have my ongoing stomach complaint checked out. I'd been experiencing pains for about nine years or more that would come and go. A colonoscopy and endoscopy were performed and all was fine. Due to the complaint occurring in bouts, one diagnosis was that I had irritable bowel syndrome. But it appears that this complaint and the chest pains I would get were due to anxiety and panic attacks.

'The stomach and chest pains only exacerbated my psychological problems. At times I thought I had stomach or bowel cancer or serious heart problems. After having the tests done, it helped relieve my fears of having a serious life-threatening disease – well, in those parts of the body at least. I would then think I had cancer of the left lung or my pancreas or spleen.

'During the ten months I was at Woodford [August 2004–June 2005], anyone that the authorities saw I was getting along with and associating with, they'd move them out of the unit. They weren't going to let me associate with who I wanted. They had spies within the unit, as they do in most units throughout the prison system. With me, they weren't taking any chance whatsoever. In that nine months, the cell changes were a common occurrence also. Not the twice-weekly thing as when in the MSU there some four years prior, but every few weeks I was moved. Always cells on the bottom floor on the side where my cell window faced the control room that was manned 24 hours.'

In spite of this, Abbott's mind remained fixed on his future, first in a Perth prison, and then beyond. And yet he still attracted constant attention. Within months of arriving in Woodford's mainstream, he was sent back to solitary twice – once for being the alleged ringleader of a gambling ring linked to a TV game show. And when Abbott developed a friendship with another inmate and they played Scrabble regularly, the man was moved to another part of the prison.

On 5 June 2005, in 'Abbott Fights to Serve Time in WA', Jim Kelly of *The Sunday Times* reported, 'Notorious bank robber Brenden Abbott is taking legal action against Attorney-General Jim McGinty in a bid to serve his jail time in WA ... Queensland has approved the prisoner transfer, but the move is being blocked by Mr McGinty, who says Abbott's record of armed robbery and escaping from legal custody makes him a risk to the community ... "Having considered the material before me I was, and remain, of the opinion that the return of Mr Abbott to Western Australia is not in the best interests of the state," he said. Abbott's lawyers are demanding a more substantial explanation and expect to lodge a writ in the Supreme Court requiring Mr McGinty to disclose full details of the advice he received ... His [Abbott's] girlfriend, who wants to be known as Sally [Tilly], said Abbott was a changed man who just wanted to come home and do his time. The flamboyant bandit was anxious to have the outstanding arrest warrant and other pending charges dealt with, she said.'

On 17 June 2005, to Abbott's chagrin, Tilly Needham began publicly proclaiming her love for him, explaining to Greg McLean of the *NT News*, 'I've always shunned publicising my relationship with Brenden because it is ... sacred to us, but I want answers from Mr McGinty.'

But Jim McGinty vowed,

I'll be fighting this matter every inch of the way through the courts to make sure we are not forced to take Queensland's criminal. He poses a real threat, not only to prison authorities but to the community of WA ... The irony of him wanting now to be imprisoned in Western Australia has a touching point to it [but] I don't think the prison system or our society owes anything to Brenden Abbott.

Abbott had more moves ahead, though, but it was mostly in circles. In his letter to his lawyer, he continues,

'*It was just before unlock. I was still in my shower when my door opened and three screws were there. At first, I thought it was for a piss test, a practice they usually performed at that time of the day. Instead, I was handcuffed and taken to the DU, but was not told why. The screws had no idea why either.*

'*After about an hour, a photo was taken of me and I knew it was an escort on the cards but had no idea where to.*

'*Not long after, my DU cell door opened again and with the screws were a few SERT members in plain clothes. I was bodybelted with the usual two handcuffs and leg irons and placed into a vehicle parked next to the DU. I was then driven out to the front car park area of the prison and placed into a helicopter and flown to AGCC, where the helicopter landed on the oval within the prison.*

'*I would remain at AGCC for approximately six months in a mainstream unit [June 2005–November 2005]. The AGCC unit I was held in had numerous Asians, mainly Chinese and one Japanese. They cooked meals every evening and I got along well with them all and they were more than happy to let me join in on their cooking. In that time, I was again on reintegration management plans similar to Woodford's. The cell changes also continued.*

'*One morning [November 2005], I was asked by a screw to follow him to a room outside the unit. When I walked in, I was greeted by two screws who were carrying my standard garb for being escorted externally or when taken out of the MSU to visit the medical centre. At first, I thought I was being placed back in the MSU, but the sight of the plainclothes SERT jokers told me otherwise. I didn't think I'd be going to Woodford again, but I was wrong.*

'*Within 15–20 minutes, a helicopter was again landing on the prison oval and soon after I was again back in the Woodford reception unit being photographed and processed. Within the time I was at AGCC, I had been eating well. Too well, in fact. I'd put on at least 10kg and was feeling the extra weight. All those who knew me at Woodford commented on my sudden expansion.*

'*The nurse at the medical centre picked up that I wasn't looking well and insisted that I have my blood pressure checked. It was high. The extra weight and anxiety of the sudden move to Woodford was having an effect. My blood pressure was monitored for a week or more and slowly it returned to normal.*

'*Some of those I knew from my last stint in Woodford were in the unit I was placed in. And again, as last time, certain people were moved out when I started to associate with them.*

'*I slowly started an exercise regime with the intention of losing the excess weight and avoiding a repeat of high blood pressure. This was also the advice from the prison doctor.*

'*In March 2006, it was reported that the Queensland Government had passed new legislation which would basically stop inmates who were on an MSO and within an MSU from having it reviewed by Judicial Review.*

'Reading about this, I knew my days as a mainstream prisoner were numbered. The regime since being let out of the MSU has been unlike any of those who have also been released from the MSU. The Government and DCS have had me in their sights from the day I left the MSU (May 2004).

'On the exercise bike one afternoon [30 March 2006], I experienced chest pains. I ceased my workout and the pain quickly subsided, but I was still experiencing pressure on my chest area for hours after. I advised an officer earlier about my chest pain when on the bike. I had agreed with his comment that I was just getting old. I said nothing more until later on at lock away. The pressure on my chest was still there and I asked if I could get a nurse to just check me over.

'I was taken down to the medical centre and an ECG was done. The nurse gave me a tablet to put under my tongue and, shortly after, the pressure on my chest subsided completely. Another ECG was performed some time later and the reading was different to the first reading which the nurse had showed me.

'I was told that they would keep me in an observation cell within the medical centre overnight to keep an eye on me. I asked if I could go back to my cell in the unit and, if I had any problems, I'd contact the screws through my cell's intercom. They said I would be staying in a cell in the medical centre.

'About half an hour before, I was placed in an ambulance and I became aware of the fact that I'd be going to hospital. The prison nurse had been on the phone to the PA Hospital speaking to a doctor about my complaint. Due to the difference in my ECG readings, it was recommended I be taken to hospital.

'Arriving at the Princess Alexandra, it was swarming with SERT members in all their gear and with M16s. More ECGs were done, chest X-ray, blood taken and I was put on a drip to thin the blood. I was put into the secure unit at the hospital overnight and, during the early hours of the morning, more ECGs were done. The next day I was taken to another part of the hospital where a stress test was done on a treadmill. My heart and blood pressure were monitored. This test, and all others, showed my heart was in good shape. One doctor suggested it may have been a mild case of angina.

'In the interview I had with the psychiatrist, Dr Kingswell, some weeks later, he diagnosed the symptoms I had as similar to what people experience when having extreme panic attacks or anxiety attacks.

'Some have suggested that the whole thing was staged and an escape plan was in the making. I may have some abilities, but manipulating an ECG machine is above my capabilities. If I was able to get a crew together to snatch me from an escort to hospital, I wouldn't choose to do it that way. I'm well aware of the security that surrounds me while on an escort. People would die and, more than likely, I'd be the first to get it. It would be less risky to have the crew get me from my prison cell at night. There wouldn't be the highly trained SERT to deal with.

'The powers that be are quick to credit me with having some intelligence in justifying the way they deal with me. To suggest that I may have had a plan to escape on a hospital escort is saying I'm a complete fuckwit.

'After the stress test was done, a few hours later, I was transferred by road with a nine-car police escort. They didn't cover the windows up on that trip. I was taken back to AGCC. At first I thought I was going to the MSU, but I was put into a cell in the prison hospital for the weekend.

'On Monday afternoon, I was taken to the DU and placed on Section 38. Management's excuse for this was "the security and good order of the prison". The prison manager has the authority to impose a Section 38 for a period of no more than seven days. To extend it further, it has to be approved by DCS. An extra month was approved by DCS but, before that was up, I was transferred to the MSU.

'I was placed in the MSU on the afternoon of 28 April 2006, just under a month short of two years since being released from it in 2004.

'The following morning, the general manager, Jim Fisher, visited me in my MSU cell. He advised me that he was the one who made the application to have me put in the MSU. His reason for doing so – "information received". He refused to say what the information was, or from whom. (Jim Fisher was the superintendent of the Metropolitan Security Unit at Fremantle Prison. It was the MSU uniform that I copied for the Freo escape.)

'While on Section 38, prior to being transferred to the MSU, I was spoken to by someone who claimed he was an adviser *for DCS. His first name was Kevin. He asked that I be interviewed by Dr Kingswell because there was a concern about the medical complaints I'd been experiencing. I spoke to Dr Kingswell on 20 April 2006 [Abbott says his diagnosis was severe anxiety attacks].*

  'With the legislation just recently passed, I'm not sure if I'll get a statement of reasons re: MSO. I have been told that the new legislation will be introduced as of 1 July 2006.

  'As I stated earlier, DCS have planned this all along. They were never going to let me be. It's a fair comment that I'm a political prisoner. The treatment I've received from the state of Queensland since my arrest in 1995 has been unique. It's this treatment that is solely responsible for the psychological disorder I've been diagnosed with. It's the type of disorder that psychiatrists have warned DSC about by continuing to house and manage me the way they have.

  'Now they've put me back in the MSU on completely fabricated reasons. It's just absolute garbage and I am 100 per cent positive that they will never release the detail of the so-called information received.'

But Abbott got his statement of reasons just a few weeks after writing these words, and his theory proved correct: three requests for medical attention within 12 months were simply too suspicious, according to the authorities, and sufficient grounds for his return to the MSU.

  Concerned 'prison sources' were quick to advise the public of their worries. In 'ABBOTT ESCAPE PLOT FEAR', published on 3 May 2006, *Courier Mail* crime editor Paula Doneman wrote, 'Postcard Bandit Brendan Abbott is back in the state's most secure prison unit amid suspicions he has repeatedly feigned illness to hatch an escape plan from a Brisbane hospital. The serial escapee and convicted armed robber has had three visits to the prison's secure unit at the Princess Alexandra Hospital in the past year complaining of pains in his armpit, chest and heart.

  'Concerns from prison officials about Abbott's intentions prompted his removal on Friday night from Woodford Jail, where he has been a mainstream prisoner for the past 20 months.

  'Abbott has now been moved to the maximum-security unit at Brisbane's Arthur Gorrie Remand and Reception Centre. Prison sources told the *Courier Mail* that medical examinations found nothing to substantiate his claims of illness and they suspected Abbott was familiarising himself with security procedures in a plan to escape. "You never know with Abbott, the sky is always the limit. There is nothing concrete but these visits have certainly generated suspicion,'" a prison officer said.'

In spite of the constant setbacks, Abbott retained a rock-solid belief that, one day, he would again raise his middle finger on the right side of a prison gate. Early in 2005, he said,

> *I don't look at it as if I've got 20 years left. I look at it that I could be a free man in at least, 10 to 12 years. If I get transferred back to WA and get those matters dealt with – and I believe SA has an interest in me, so I'd go back there and get it all dealt with – then it all runs concurrent. So that's the light at the end of the tunnel. But the way the Attorneys-General are playing hardball, they're trying to make it so there's no light. But, because it's a matter of law, they're really bound to take me back.*

Abbott's access to his computer – a source of solace and distraction – was removed after his release from maximum security in 2004. He appealed to a court on the grounds that he was educating himself and had previously been allowed regular access to it, but, in March 2006, the Queensland Supreme Court ruled that access to a computer was a privilege, not a right.

It wasn't supposed to be this way. Thelma and her five kids were the family next door, living a dysfunctional late-20th-century suburban life familiar to most Australians and shared by many. Brenden Abbott should have outgrown his youthful anger and wild ways, and gone on to put a gifted mind to good use instead of becoming a criminal.

Instead, he wasted large parts of his life with only Fremantle's cockroaches and Queensland's cameras for company. And yet in the face of this treatment – unprecedented in modern Australian history – Abbott's defiance of authority, the powers that be, was unwavering; his determination to survive their treatment iron-clad. Law-enforcement agencies expended enormous amounts of time, money and energy pursuing him for traumatising bank staff and for stealing the banks' money. But Australian authorities in general – and politicians in particular – painted him as inherently violent and dangerous, even evil, used him as a scapegoat for the prison system's shortcomings and failures and 'rehabilitated' him in a manner more consistent with 19th-century Australia.

At the time of writing, July 2007, Abbott's life – and future – looked grim. He'd just learned of a surprise suspension of his current maximum security order and was about to moved from his special cell at Arthur Gorrie, although prison management, as usual, gave no clue to his destination.

Weeks earlier, Brendan Berichon had arrived in a different part of the prison to an equally bleak future. After becoming eligible for parole in Melbourne, he was extradited to Brisbane to finally face a string of serious charges over the 1997 SDL escape; his new bride would need to be patient. Brenden Abbott, the cheeky young bloke in the 'postcards' was a long-distant memory, replaced by a pale agoraphobic prone to severe panic attacks. Hated by the public, demonised by the media, reviled by so-called jail gangsters, taunted by the authorities' relentless mind games and in fear of his own life from 'imbecile' trophy hunters, Brenden Abbott had completed his journey from 'bad bastard' to self-confessed 'paranoid bastard'. Prisoner B41627 says,

What a fucking waste. Well, some of it. But it ain't over yet. I've got a plan – and this one's legit!